The Impact of Global Warming on Texas

HARC GLOBAL CHANGE STUDIES

The Houston Advanced Research Center (HARC) is an independent, nonprofit corporation established to promote closer links between the creators and users of scientific knowledge.

The Center for Global Studies (CGS) is the policy research division of HARC. Its mission is to increase awareness of the social and policy implications of science and technology, focusing on global environmental issues and sustainable development. Issues of concern include population growth, environmental quality, climate change, water management, alternative fuels policy, and U.S./Mexico environmental issues.

The Impact of Global Warming on Texas

A Report of the Task Force
on Climate Change in Texas

EDITED BY

GERALD R. NORTH,
JURGEN SCHMANDT,
AND JUDITH CLARKSON

 UNIVERSITY OF TEXAS PRESS
AUSTIN

First edition, 1995

Requests for permission to reproduce material from this work should
be sent to Permissions, University of Texas Press, Box 7819, Austin, TX
78713-7819.

∞The paper used in this publication meets the minimum requirements
of American National Standard for Information Sciences—Permanence of
Paper for Printed Library Materials, ANSI Z39.48-1984.

Also published in HARC's Global Change Studies: *The Regions and Global
Warming: Impacts and Response Strategies*, edited by J. Schmandt and
J. Clarkson (New York: Oxford University Press, 1992).

Library of Congress Cataloging-in-Publication Data

The Impact of global warming on Texas / edited by Gerald R. North,
 Jurgen Schmandt, and Judith Clarkson. — 1st ed.
     p.   cm.— (HARC global change studies)
 Includes bibliographical references and index.
   ISBN 0-292-75555-4 (alk. paper)
    1. Global warming—Environmental aspects—Texas.   2. Climatic
changes—Environmental aspects—Texas.   I. North, Gerald R.
II. Schmandt, Jurgen.   III. Clarkson, Judith.   IV. Series.
QC981.8.G56147 1995
363.73'87—dc20   94-15147

Contents

Preface

The Task Force on Climate Change in Texas was convened by the Houston Advanced Research Center, a consortium of Texas universities. Selection of task force members and review of the task force report was the responsibility of the Steering Committee, which oversees the activities of HARC's Center for Global Studies. Members were invited on the basis of their expertise and with the aim of assembling an interdisciplinary group from different institutions. The roster of members shows that industry is underrepresented. Despite a concerted effort, we were unable to persuade qualified experts from industry to serve. All members served without remuneration and in a personal capacity. Staff work was performed by the Center for Global Studies.

The group was assembled in 1991 and met three or four times a year, in plenary session or small groups. Various members of the Task Force were responsible for specific chapters of this volume. In some cases, associate members assisted with the preparation of the text. The work in Chapters 5–8 represents new research. Other chapters summarize available information and present a fresh, regional perspective on a global problem. The book identifies policy options, but leaves it to public debate to formulate detailed policy recommendations.

The work of the task force was supported by funds from the Ray C. Fish Foundation and the Wray Charitable Lead Annuity Trust, as well as a grant from the U.S. Environmental Protection Agency/Texas Water Commission. We thank them for their support.

This volume assembles the best available research on climate change and its potential impacts in Texas. It will be obvious to the reader that much remains to be studied. Even so, the Task Force on Climate Change in Texas is confident that enough is known to begin the task of considering climate change in developing policies for economic development, energy, water, land use, and pollution control.

| William Gordon, Chairman, Steering Committee | Gerald R. North, Chairman, Task Force | Jurgen Schmandt Director, Center for Global Studies |

Task Force on Impacts of Climate Change

Founding Members

Gerald R. North, Chairman	Department of Meteorology	Texas A&M University
Allen P. Beinke (resigned 12–91)	Executive Director	Texas Water Commission
William E. Evans	Texas Institute of Oceanography	Texas A&M University
John F. Griffiths	Department of Meteorology	Texas A&M University
Monty Jasper (resigned 10–91)	Environmental Sciences	Central Power & Light
C. Allan Jones	Blackland Research Center	Texas Agricultural Experiment Station
Tommy R. Knowles	Director of Planning	Texas Water Development Board
Ken Kramer	Lone Star Chapter	Sierra Club
Bruce McCarl	Department of Agricultural Economics	Texas A&M University
James Norwine	Department of Geography	Texas A&I University
Jane Packard	Department of Wildlife & Fisheries	Texas A&M University
Jurgen Schmandt	Center for Global Studies	Houston Advanced Research Center and University of Texas at Austin

Carol Tombari	Energy Management Center	Office of the Governor
Juan B. Valdes	Department of Civil Engineering	Texas A&M University
George Ward	Center for Research in Water Resources	University of Texas at Austin

Associate Members

George Bomar	Watershed Management Division	Texas Water Commission*
Lonnie Jones	Department of Agricultural Economics	Texas A&M University
William L. Longley	Environmental Section	Texas Water Development Board
Wolfgang Roeseler	Department of Urban and Regional Planning	Texas A&M University

Secretary

| Alan D. Jones (until 5–92) | Center for Global Studies | Houston Advanced Research Center |
| John D. Wilson | Center for Global Studies | Houston Advanced Research Center |

Editor

| Judith Clarkson | Consultant | Houston Advanced Research Center |

Member affiliations are shown for time of service and may not be current.

*Now Texas Natural Resources Conservation Commission.

The Impact of Global Warming on Texas

Introduction

Climate change has been studied and debated extensively at the national and international levels. It is known that the temperature of Earth's atmosphere is directly related to the atmospheric concentrations of greenhouse gases, notably CO_2. Released at the current rate, for example, the concentration of CO_2 in the atmosphere is likely to double some time in the next century, resulting in an increase in mean global temperature of $2-3°C$ $(3-5°F)$, according to various climate models. The Intergovernmental Panel on Climate Change concluded that at least a 60 percent reduction in CO_2 emissions was necessary to prevent a further buildup in the atmospheric concentration of greenhouse gases and to reduce the potential for global warming. These goals will be difficult to reach, because they will require large changes in the use of fossil fuels and, to get to the root causes of the problem, in levels of consumption and the rate of population growth.

Recognizing the need to reduce greenhouse gas emissions, our major trading partners, including Canada, Japan, Great Britain, Germany, and other members of the European Community, have announced plans to at least freeze emissions by the year 2005. The United States initially declined to be a party to any agreement that sets limits on CO_2 emissions. However, the Clinton administration has developed an action plan for stabilizing greenhouse gas emissions at 1990 levels by the year 2000. In addition, there is considerable support in Congress for increasing the fuel efficiency of motor vehicles, and significant environmental legislation has been passed, most notably the 1990 amendments to the Clean Air Act.

Nevertheless, while the last decade has seen a decreasing environmental role for the federal government, states are beginning to develop their own policies to reduce greenhouse gas emissions and address the consequences of global warming. The Task Force on Climate Change in Texas has chosen to consider this issue from a statewide perspective. Several states—California and Oregon in particular—have done this already, but this volume is probably the most comprehensive, state-level study of climate change to date. Several reasons prompted us to conduct this study and issue this volume.

While climate change is a global phenomenon (because greenhouse gas emissions from anywhere in the world have a global impact), the impacts will be felt locally, most likely in the form of higher temperatures, longer growing seasons, more frequent droughts and hurricanes, and loss of coastal land. Many studies have already suggested international and national policies to combat climate change and to adapt to likely changes. Yet national and international efforts must be complemented by action at the regional and local levels. Indeed, adaptation will largely be a task of state and local governments, though national-level policy guidance and financial assistance may be needed.

A second major incentive to write this book relates to size. Texas is larger than many nation-states and, therefore, may be forced to take on a more aggressive policy role than smaller states. In terms of greenhouse emissions, Texas is by far the largest contributor among American states, finding itself in the same league with the United Kingdom and Italy. International or national measures aimed at reducing emissions will have a large impact on the state's economy. It is important for Texas to assess this impact and participate in policy development with a clear view of the economic, as well as environmental, costs and benefits.

The third reason for conducting the study follows from the state's special vulnerability in at least two domains. The Gulf Coast, because of its gentle slope and existing problems with land subsidence, is at greater risk from sea-level rise than other coastal areas in North America. In addition, a large part of the state is semiarid, and higher temperatures will mean higher rates of evaporation and a greater demand for water. Should rainfall decrease, as suggested by some climate models, this will create an additional stress on water resources. The availability of an assured supply of water is critically important for future development in Texas. The need to reconcile its future development with the availability of water is a major policy challenge for the state. Success in this endeavor will mean that development will become more sustainable; failure will result in either a degradation of the natural resource base or damage to the economy.

Finally, many questions about the severity and timing of climate change cannot yet be answered with confidence. This study attempts to distinguish between matters that we now know with substantial certainty and other aspects of the issues where information is incomplete or missing. Water managers and coastal planners traditionally must look into the distant future when they consider new capital improvements. The impacts of climate change seem likely to materialize in a similar time frame, around the year 2020 and beyond. This volume provides a timely assessment of the possible impacts of climate change in Texas, so that managers and policymakers can begin to include this information in their long-range plans.

GERALD R. NORTH

1. Global Climate Change

The temperature of the planet is primarily determined by two opposing factors: the rate at which solar energy is absorbed by the system, and the rate at which energy is reradiated to space. On average, the heat energy that is reemitted to space balances that of incoming solar radiation, and an equilibrium is established. If one component of the system is perturbed, the system will adjust to a new equilibrium. For example, screening of sunlight by volcanic dust might cause the earth to cool. The resulting lower temperature leads to a lowering of outgoing radiation, which will restore the balance over time.

Restoring global climate to a new point of equilibrium following a perturbation is a lengthy process of unknown duration. Many factors affect the ability of the system to respond. One is the heat-retaining capacity of the oceans, which slow the adjustment process. Other components internal to the system amplify or diminish the thermal response of the system to a given perturbation, such as a volcanic dust screen. In order to understand these very complicated interactions, climatologists have developed computer models that attempt to reduce them to computer-solvable physical problems. However, climate modeling is not yet a precise science whose every prediction can be taken as an unequivocal call to action.

Defining Climate

Climate connotes something different for every individual. Many people have some idea that the climate has been changing, but they can only relate it to their own, often unreliable or unrepresentative, impressions. We must define climate quantitatively, so that hypotheses can be precisely formulated and tested. For the present purposes we may think of the "temperature" climate as an average of thermometer readings over some number of years, say 30, and over some spatial region, say the size of a few counties in Texas. The latter might be based upon the experience that 30-year averages typically change appreciably over distances of about that extent in this part of the world.

Examination of global climate data shows that fluctuations in surface temperature are strongly correlated over a span of about 1,000 miles. Hence, for many purposes, a disk with a 1,000-mile radius is a suitably-sized region for the definition of a statistical region. This means that there are fewer than 100 independent statistical regions on the planet. In assessing the global climate and how it might change in the future, we must poll these 100 regions and take their average. All members or regions will not agree with the global average when it comes to global climate change, any more than every voter would agree with the "average" voter in an election.

Although the nominal 30-year value has been taken as the agreed-upon averaging period, readings change on time scales of 50 and 100 years and longer, even though there is no change in the underlying factors that control the climate system. This is called natural variability, and it is always operating to confuse the investigator just when he is inclined to attribute a perceived change in average temperature to some external agent such as solar variation or a change in atmospheric composition. One reason for the natural variability of the climate is the long adjustment time of the oceans' heat storage and current systems. The time it takes for water to circulate from the deepest portions of the oceans back to the surface is estimated to be several hundred years. This means, for example, that a pool of extra cold water that is singled out and stored below by some freak mechanism might remain sequestered from the surface for a century or two before re-emerging and producing a local, cool climate change. This is typical of the mechanisms leading to natural variability.

The definition just presented is sufficient to begin formulating quantitative theories of the Earth's climate. Such theories have evolved over the last century, and they have started to become comprehensive and reliable with the advent of modern computers and global observing systems.

The Greenhouse Theory

The popularity or acceptance of the greenhouse theory by scientists has had its ups and downs over the last century, but it has been the focus of renewed attention with the development of modern climate models. An added sense of urgency has emerged with the realization that the atmosphere, land, and ocean systems are not always capable of benignly absorbing and disposing of the waste products routinely discarded by man.

Factors That Determine Planetary Climate

The amount of solar energy impinging on the Earth per unit area is about 340 watts per square meter (averaged throughout the day). Measurements from satellites indicate that 30 percent of this energy is reflected directly back to space by clouds and other bright features of the Earth-atmosphere system. Hence, about 238 watts per square meter (about the heating capacity of a good reading lamp) are absorbed into the system and can be used for raising the temperature, evaporating water, melting snow, etc. If there were no mechanism to release this heat, the Earth's surface temperature would continue to rise, and liquid water exposed at the surface would continue to evaporate indefinitely.

Infrared radiation acts as a means of dissipating this heat energy into space. This radiation rate to space increases as the Earth's temperature increases. When the Earth's average temperature is 15°C (about 59°F), the outgoing radiation is about 238 watts per square meter, another fact established by satellite measurements. In other words, the planet appears to be close to striking a balance between its absorbed sunlight and its emitted infrared light. Comparison of seasonal temperature data with the satellite infrared measurements suggests that when the surface temperature goes up 1°C, the outgoing radiation increases by about 2 watts per square meter. If the sun were to emit 1 percent more energy, the absorbed solar radiation would increase by 2.4 watts per square meter and the Earth would warm up until the infrared radiation to space again exactly balanced the increased absorbed solar radiation. This would occur as a result of an increase in surface temperature of a little over 1.2°C (2.2°F).

Changing the amount of carbon dioxide in the atmosphere affects the amount of outgoing radiation to space for a given average surface temperature. For a doubling of the amount of carbon dioxide in the atmosphere this radiation rate is reduced by about 4.2 watts per square meter, according to standard atmospheric theory. We estimate that the retention of this additional energy would result in about 2°C of surface

GERALD R. NORTH

warming. This is the so-called greenhouse effect for a carbon dioxide doubling. But how good is this atmospheric theory, and how long does the adjustment take? Both questions are tough—the calculated change of 2°C is only a ballpark estimate (it could be as large as 4°C or maybe as small as 1°C), and the adjustment time could vary from a few years to many decades, depending on the model adopted for the calculation.

Consider a closer look at these two important parameters: the sensitivity of climate to doubling carbon dioxide, and the time required for the system to adjust to the new conditions. A major concern in climate-sensitivity research involves the so-called feedback mechanisms in the atmospheric system. As an example, consider water vapor, which is itself a naturally occurring greenhouse gas. If the climate is warmed by some external agent, the amount of water vapor in an air column will increase (tending to keep the relative humidity approximately constant), which in turn will thicken the atmosphere with respect to the passage of infrared radiation. Hence, as we warm the planet, internal mechanisms deliver more greenhouse gases to the atmosphere in the form of water vapor and thus amplify the warming. Current indications suggest that the water vapor amplifier approximately doubles the sensitivity of climate to any large-scale perturbation such as solar changes or changes in carbon dioxide concentration (IPCC 1990, Chaps. 2, 3). The water vapor feedback mechanism was included in the earlier estimate for increases in emissions to space as a result of increases in solar radiation. Other significant feedbacks are harder to quantify and include clouds, which may amplify the climatic response by as much as a factor of 2 (IPCC 1990, Chap. 3).

It is interesting to note that if there were no greenhouse gases or clouds in the atmosphere, the Earth would radiate heat to space directly from its surface at a rate of 384 watts per square meter, far exceeding the 238 watts per square meter absorbed. Thus, in the absence of the greenhouse gases (mainly water vapor and carbon dioxide), this would lead to a cooling until a new equilibrium at a temperature of about −25°C (−13°F) was established. Under these conditions, the Earth would be ice covered and uninhabitable, like the satellites of planets in the outer solar system. Hence, changes in the Earth's temperature due to increases in the concentration of greenhouse gases is a tiny increment on top of a very large, well-established greenhouse effect that has been in effect for billions of years.

The delay in the establishment of a changed climate after

perturbations are introduced is due mainly to the impact of the oceans (IPCC 1990, Chap. 6). We know that heating a deep pot of water on a stove takes much longer than heating a shallow one with the same setting. The warming of the world oceans by a radiation imbalance is different from the example of heating a pot of water, because in the natural system the heat comes from above and does not lead to the natural convective overturning that would occur in a pot on a stove. And, because this mechanism is not well understood, the rate at which warm water from the surface layers gets stirred naturally to the depths is not known. The more efficient this mixing of heat from the top to the bottom of the ocean, the slower the adjustment will be in the natural climate system.

Finding answers to these questions will depend upon a close interplay between the ever-improving computer models and empirical evidence about the climate system. The next section is a review of some important lines of evidence that suggest that the greenhouse effect is real and is likely to lead to important global climate changes over the next century.

Greenhouse Gases

Several atmospheric gases have the properties of greenhouse gases; i.e., they are transparent to visible rays but highly absorbing to infrared rays. Two of the most significant gases, water vapor and carbon dioxide, are naturally occurring and, under equilibrium conditions, help to maintain a constant planetary temperature. Water readily evaporates into the air from both inert wet surfaces and plants, which draw otherwise isolated water from their root zones and pass it into the air through evapotranspiration. Carbon dioxide emanates from volcanoes in great quantities and is also produced as a byproduct of respiration of living organisms. It is removed from the air by photosynthesis, a process by which plants fix atmospheric carbon in the presence of sunlight. Carbon dioxide is also removed from the atmosphere by absorption in the oceans' cooler surface waters and sometimes carried deep into the ocean by localized downwelling currents in the frigid polar waters. Evidence suggests that these rates of input to and removal from the atmosphere were in balance until the early 1800's, when we began to burn fossil fuels and clear forests at rates greater than the absorption rate capacities of the natural removal mechanisms. In time, the natural cleansing mechanisms probably would remove the excess atmospheric carbon dioxide, but it has been estimated that hundreds of years might be required for such an equilibration to become established.

Another important greenhouse gas is atmospheric methane, a naturally occurring gas which also appears to be increasing rapidly due to man's activity over the last 2 centuries. Although originally present in the atmosphere at less than 1 part per million, its concentration has doubled since preindustrial times and it is about 25 times more powerful per molecule as a greenhouse gas than carbon dioxide. Nitrous oxide, another greenhouse gas, is primarily generated from anthropogenic activities, mainly in connection with modern agricultural practices. The last in the list of greenhouse gases are the chlorofluorocarbons (CFCs), which have been used extensively in the last 2 decades in such applications as refrigeration and in aerosol spray dispensers. The CFCs have come under much scrutiny in recent years because of their implication in the depletion of the ozone layer, an effect unrelated to the greenhouse effect. While the chlorofluorocarbon molecules are scarce compared to carbon dioxide molecules, they are particularly effective because their absorptivity to infrared radiation is of the order of 10,000 times greater than that of carbon dioxide.

The Carbon Dioxide Record

Carbon dioxide concentrations in the air far from population centers have been continuously measured and archived since the 1950's at a high-altitude observatory in Hawaii (IPCC 1990, Chap. 1). Because the mixing time for carbon dioxide is short compared with its lifetime in the atmosphere, trend measurements at a single, unbiased site (away from local anthropogenic sources) are representative of the entire globe, as confirmed by more recent measurements from a variety of locations. Figure 1.1 shows this record from its inception in 1958 to 1990.

The seasonal oscillation and the upward trend are notable features of this record. The seasonal oscillation is due to the annual rhythm of the biosphere. Carbon dioxide is released by decaying matter and then taken up during the growing season. The growing cycle of Arctic tundra is thought to be a particularly important component of this process. For climatologists the upward trend is the more important feature. The Mauna Loa record shows that the carbon dioxide con-

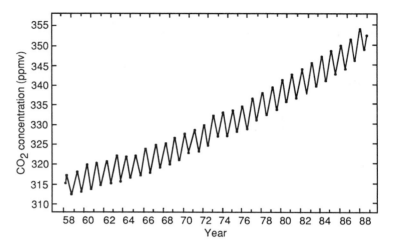

centration is increasing in the atmosphere at a rate of about 0.5 percent per year. If this continues, the carbon dioxide concentration will double every 140 years.

Ice cores are another source of data. Figure 1.2 shows the results of measurements from ice cores drilled from the Greenland ice sheet (IPCC 1990, adapted from Chap. 1). Material from a segment of a deep core drawn from the ice sheet can be easily dated by counting the number of annual snow layerings from the top of the core. Bubbles in the ice contain air from the atmosphere when the snow was originally deposited. Undisputed analyses of these air samples all lead to the conclusion that the concentration of carbon dioxide in the atmosphere is increasing, and that its departure from a steady value coincides with the beginnings of the industrial revolution. These data have also been corroborated by measurements from Antarctic ice cores.

Other Greenhouse Gases

Concentrations of the other greenhouse gases are less well recorded over the last century, but we do have good records for the last decade. Carbon dioxide, methane, and chlorofluorocarbons are all increasing rapidly, although there is some evidence that methane has recently reduced its rate of increase to less than that of the last decade. The records of methane and nitrous oxide are similar to that in Figure 1.2 (IPCC 1990). The results over the last several centuries indicate that the concentrations of these gases also started a dramatic rise from a preindustrial base about 200 years ago.

GERALD R. NORTH

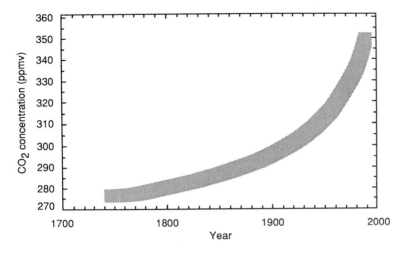

Figure 1.2. Schematic diagram of the increase in CO_2, as recorded in a Greenland ice core. Based on data taken from IPCC (1990).

Atmospheric radiation computations tell us that the global warming potential from the combination of all the other greenhouse gases just about adds up to the contribution from carbon dioxide alone. Hence, although one hears most about carbon dioxide and its production through fossil fuel burning and deforestation, about half the warming potential is due to increases in the other greenhouse gases. Therefore, although it is predicted that carbon dioxide concentrations are likely to double in the next 140 years, predictions for global warming based on this scenario are actually likely to be realized within 70 years.

Finally, climatologists agree that historical records for greenhouse gas concentrations are the least controversial of the components that go into the evidence linking man's activities on the planet and a possible global warming. All of the chemical measurements that go into the record are straightforward, and the interpretation of the results is un-contested in the scientific community. Quantitative values for the sources and sinks of some of the greenhouse gases are less certain because of the poorly understood emission/ab-sorption rates of gases with the terrestrial and aquatic bio-sphere. For example, precise global inventories of the rates of emission/absorption from the ocean surface in remote parts of the world are very difficult.

Climate Models and What They Say

How are we to make concrete forecasts of what climate will be like 50 years from now? How can the back-of-the-envelope estimations given earlier be refined into outlooks that can be used with some confidence in formulating policy? What about specific regions such as the Texas coast, the Hill Country, Big Bend, or the Panhandle? These are problems for the modern, computerized climate model.

Meteorologists have had about 35 years of experience in putting the equations that govern atmospheric motion and related processes onto computers and using them to generate weather forecasts. The forecasts we see every day on television are based mostly on millions of arithmetic calculations made in the previous 24 hours on some of the world's fastest computers. The results of the computations are spread over a distribution network to which our local forecasters and television reporters have access. Not insignificant is the worldwide observing system that collects atmospheric data and reports it to a central location at regular intervals. The data tell the computer the current state of the atmosphere's winds, moisture distribution, pressure distribution, etc. Then the computer advances the governing equations to form the forecast. In a weather forecast we need to report out a short-term (24-hour) forecast on a timely basis. The strategy is to include as much detail in the model as possible, while limiting the computations to a period of 1–2 hours.

Building a model to simulate climate involves dividing the planet into grid squares and developing a set of parameters for each, much like the picture produced on a television screen. Data collected within a grid square are averaged to give a single data point for each parameter. The larger the squares, the less resolution is possible. However, as the grid squares are reduced in size, more data and more calculations are needed for the same simulation of climate. Thus, the easiest way to speed up the computations is to reduce the resolution, that is, to use a coarser grid. State-of-the-art weather forecast models divide the Earth's surface into computational boxes about the size of Arkansas. This enables them to capture small features such as fronts. For climate models, grid squares the size of Texas are used. Figure 1.3 shows two grids commonly used in atmospheric modeling (Washington and Parkinson 1986). The upper panel shows a grid commonly used in weather forecasting, while the lower panel shows the grid commonly used in climate simulation during the 1980's. It is generally believed by atmospheric scientists that the finer the grid the more faith-

GERALD R. NORTH

12

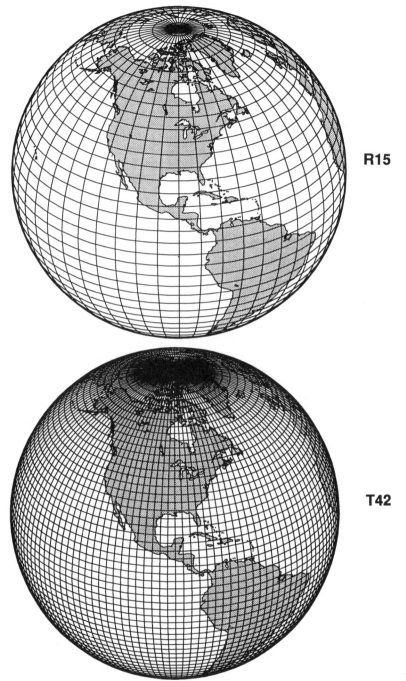

R15

T42

Figure 1.3.
Schematic diagrams indicating grid spacing for typical climate models. The
R15 grid is of approximately the resolution used in most climate model
simulations of the 1980's. The T42 grid is now being introduced into many
numerical experiments.

ful the simulation. A grid like that in the lower panel can produce a 25-year simulation of the atmospheric climate in less than 100 hours of modern supercomputer time. As computers increase their speed, simulations from the intermediate grids shown in Figure 1.3 will become common.

Climate Feedback Mechanisms

The most delicate aspect of climate simulation is the realistic inclusion of feedback mechanisms. These are processes in the system that come into play when the climate is disturbed; these secondary processes, in turn, amplify or diminish the system's response. Perhaps the most important of these is the water vapor feedback mentioned earlier. As the planetary temperature rises—due, for instance, to a hypothetical solar brightness increase—the water vapor in the air column will increase, maintaining a fixed relative humidity and increasing the water vapor greenhouse effect. The result is an increase in global average temperature of about twice as much as the solar increase would cause for a dry planet. Hence, the sensitivity to climate change is dramatically increased by such a positive feedback mechanism. The magnitude of these feedback mechanisms is a subject of controversy, because it is hard to check.

Some other feedback mechanisms are very significant in the 50–100-year time frame. For example, snow and ice are highly reflective to sunlight. If the planet is warmed, by a hypothetical increase in solar brightness, we could expect ice and snow cover to decrease. This would make the planet less reflective to sunlight and more heat would be absorbed, thereby contributing to the heating effect. It is commonly believed that the snow/ice feedback mechanism amplifies climate change by about 10–30 percent.

The most controversial feedback mechanism is cloudiness. Cloudiness may change as climate changes. An increase in cloudiness increases the Earth's reflectivity, causing a cooling of the surface. On the other hand, an increase in cloudiness also leads to a greenhouse-like blanket, causing a warming of the surface. An increase in cloudiness might therefore lead to either a cooling or a warming of the surface, depending upon which of the two effects is larger in magnitude. Moreover, it is not clear whether a warmer planet has more clouds or fewer. Because clouds are formed by subtle rising motions in the atmosphere, coarse resolution models cannot predict them reliably. Certainly a model whose grid

Table 1.1. Model Predictions for Temperature Increases
for a Doubling of CO_2 Concentration

	Global	Midwest, U.S.
Geophysical Fluid Dynamics Laboratory	4.28°C	5.84°C
National Center for Atmospheric Research	3.51°C	3.34°C
Goddard Institute for Space Studies	4.48°C	4.68°C

Source: Grotch and MacCracken 1991.

boxes are the size of Texas cannot be expected to depict with much accuracy the cloud field over the continent.

Because most feedback mechanisms such as cloudiness are at a smaller scale than the typical model grid, it is impossible for the model to calculate the generation of each cloud individually. This means that the models must look at some larger-scale feature and from it deduce that clouds should exist at the smaller subgrid scale. Not surprisingly, each model prescribes cloudiness differently, so the models presently in use differ most in the way they characterize cloud features. Hence, models differ in the magnitude and even sign of the feedback. Clouds are the single most unsettled issue of atmospheric climate modeling.

What the Models Indicate

This is a good time to introduce some preliminary results from climate model experiments. In the 1980's there were three major models contributing to our understanding of climate change. A computer run typically simulates a period of 15–25 years with present conditions, and then runs a second simulation with the amount of carbon dioxide doubled. Each result is an equilibrium result; that is, there is no attempt to model how the climate gets to its new state. The problem of transient climate change is one for the 1990's.

The models were created at the Geophysical Fluid Dynamics Laboratory (GFDL) of Princeton, the Goddard Institute for Space Studies (GISS), and the National Center for Atmospheric Research (NCAR). Table 1.1 shows in its first column the results from estimating the global average temperature increase after equilibration to a doubling of carbon dioxide concentration. All the increases are in degrees Celsius. Note that the models agree that the globally averaged temperatures increase between 3.0 and 4.5°C (5.4 and 8.1°F). The second column shows the corresponding increases for a region in the midwestern United States. Note that these are comparable to the global increases, but that the models differ more from each other in their predictions. This brings us to a general remark based upon experience: The models become less reliable as the spatial scale being examined becomes smaller. For the smallest scale, the models differ from each other in their predictions by more than 50 percent. We do not know to what extent this is a measure of their overall accuracy, because it is possible that they are more like each other than they are like nature.

Including All the Parts of the System

In the discussion so far we have focused only on the atmospheric part of the climate system. The transition to a world with more greenhouse gases will involve interaction with the world oceans. Heat from the atmosphere is absorbed by the surface waters of the oceans. These surface waters may, however, remain cool if the surface water is replaced with cooler waters from the ocean depths. Eventually, the water below will also be warmed and the delaying process will come to an end. As noted earlier, this might mean delays of from a few years to several hundred.

Figure 1.4 shows a schematic graph of how the oceans are thought to delay warming. First, imagine a linear increase in the heating rate due to (exponentially) increasing carbon dioxide concentration. For the calculation, a nominal carbon dioxide doubling rate of 70 years (which effectively includes the effects of all the greenhouse gases) is taken. The top line shows the expected increase in temperature if there were no ocean. In addition to the delaying effect just described, we must add the time of adjustment needed to get onto the increasing straight line (bottom line). Thus, it is likely that the final impacts of global warming will not become apparent for several decades as a result of these two effects.

Computing these lags and adjustment times are the most basic tasks of coupled ocean-atmosphere climate models. Coupling the two media in the calculation is a major obstacle to our complete understanding of global climate change. It will be several more years before the effects of the delaying action of the oceans is understood. The first few runs with

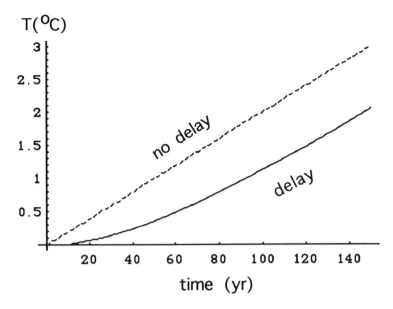

Figure 1.4.
A schematic
diagram of a very
simple ocean
adjustment time
corresponding to
50 years. The graph
illustrates how the
ocean can delay the
effects of warming
on the surface
temperatures.

rather crude ocean models do suggest that the delay and adjustment times are of the order of a few decades as suggested above, but the community of scientists is not yet satisfied that the ocean models are adequate for the task of accurately computing transient effects of time-dependent carbon dioxide changes.

Figure 1.5 shows the results of a computation of the global average temperature based upon a simplified coupled ocean-atmosphere climate model at Texas A&M University, under research sponsored by the U.S. Department of Energy (Kim et al. 1992). The graph shows the model-computed curve of global temperature change, along with the record of temperatures recorded over the last century. This computation suggests that for the next 50 years a global warming of about 1.6°C (2.9°F) might be expected. The model is fairly insensitive compared to the average climate model, since several controversial feedback mechanisms are deliberately omitted. Hence, this calculation is on the low end of the range of likely warming scenarios.

Other parts of the system, such as the ice volume on the planet, are also in need of inclusion. Ice is stored in great continental sheets, such as on Greenland and Antarctica, in mountain glaciers, and in sea ice. Each sheet reflects more sunlight than an exposed dark surface would and therefore acts as a positive feedback. In addition, ice when melted raises sea level. We have witnessed a small increase in sea

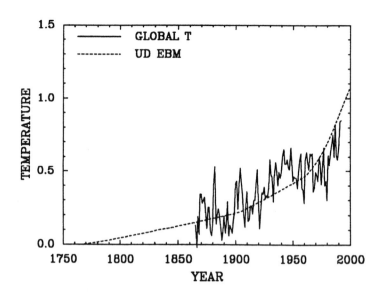

level over the last few decades, and this seems to be attributable to the meltback of mountain glaciers. Sea-level rise is of obvious importance to Texas, with its exposure to the Gulf of Mexico. Some preliminary estimates of sea-level rise due to a doubling of carbon dioxide have been conducted, and they suggest an increase in sea level of 30–100 cm (1–3 feet) (IPCC 1990, Chap. 9).

The Climate Record

Compiling a record of climate change is a formidable task. In this section the record of thermometer readings for the last century is examined in search of evidence for trends.

The Instrument Record

Figure 1.6 shows three records of large-scale average temperatures: the lower panel shows the global average, the upper panel shows the Northern Hemisphere average, and the middle panel shows the Southern Hemisphere average. Records like these have been compiled and published by several internationally recognized groups. There is little difference from one to another, but because they are based essentially on the same raw data, it is not surprising that they are in fairly good agreement with each other. There are problems in compiling an accurate record because a number of significant corrections have to be made. For example, 70 percent of the

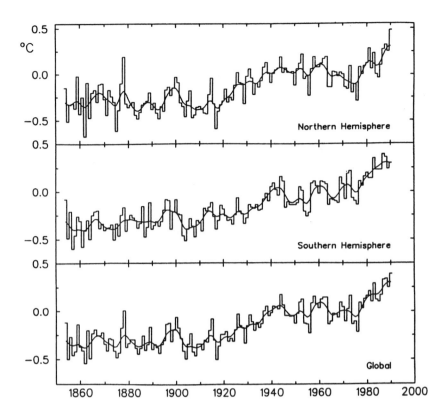

Earth is covered with ocean, and much of the data that go into the spatial averages must come from fairly sparse ship records. Small, seemingly insignificant changes in the practices of commercial vessels that routinely collect data on weather, visibility, etc., can lead to systematic biases in the record and result in artificial trends.

A notorious effect, for which corrections have to made, is the so-called urban heat island bias. This name comes from the fact that observing stations are traditionally located just outside urban areas, typically at airports. It is well known that cities are warmer than the surrounding countrysides due to a host of micrometeorological effects, and because suburban environments make up only a small fraction of the Earth's area, they may not be representative of broad area averages. The main part of the problem comes when a city's margin grows out toward the airport. The temperature readings will show a steady increase, not because of global warming but merely because the warm city is encroaching on the fixed observing station. Such urban heat island effects can account for as much as 0.15°C in the record. Attempts have

Figure 1.6.
Three records of temperature deviations from the average for the last century: the lower panel shows the global average deviation, the upper panel shows the Northern Hemisphere, and the middle panel shows the Southern Hemisphere (Jones et al. 1991).

been made to remove these kinds of effects from the curves in Figure 1.6.

Irregularity in the records is also noteworthy. We do not see a smooth, monotonic rise in temperature for either of the hemispheres or their combined data, but rather we see ups and downs of essentially random periods. This is the so-called natural variability of the system referred to earlier. The most noteworthy of these irregularities is the cooling trend in the Northern Hemisphere beginning in the 1940's and lasting over 20 years. Note that it is absent in the Southern Hemisphere. Examination of temperature-change maps suggests that the cooling was mainly localized in the Arctic and may have something to do with the Arctic Ocean overturning and the corresponding amplification in the surface temperature by sea-ice feedbacks. This appears to be an example of how natural variability can delude us into thinking a trend has slackened or reversed. In fact, at the time some careless spokesmen were suggesting a return to ice-age conditions. These cries ended in the 1970's when it became clear that temperature was on the rise again in the Northern Hemisphere, just as it had been all along in the Southern.

While one cannot be unequivocal about it (there probably is significant natural variability at the centennial time scale after all), we can surmise from the curves of Figure 1.6 that a warming of about 0.5°C (0.9°F) has taken place over the last century. But could such a warming be due to a natural anomaly, as in the cooling from the 1940's to 1970? While there is considerable uncertainty about the amplitude of fluctuations on centennial time scales, the evidence suggests that a global warming of average size 0.25°C (0.45°F) over a century, and increasing monotonically during that century (as predicted by the models), is an extremely rare occurrence. The probability of such an event occurring as a result of natural variability is perhaps less than 1 in 100 (North et al. 1993).

The Eruption of Mount Pinatubo

In June of 1991 a large volcanic eruption in the Philipines resulted in more than 100 deaths. The volcanic debris was sent high into the stratosphere (well above 30,000 feet). The particular combination of sulfur compounds in the gaseous effluent resulted in condensation and aggregation of water droplets into a fine mist that spread throughout the global stratosphere over a period of 6 months. Satellite measurements analyzed by Dr. Larry Stowe of the National Oceanographic and Atmospheric Administration showed that this cloud's opacity to sunlight peaked in the tropics in August of 1991 and began to slowly decay as the aerosol particles coagulated and subsequently fell out.

James Hansen, the director of the Goddard Institute of Space Studies (GISS), seized upon the opportunity to use a naturally occurring experiment to validate his model. Hansen and his group boldly published a paper predicting that the cooling would be about 0.5°C (0.9°F) and last for about a year (Hansen et al. 1992). Such cooling is about as great as the warming induced by greenhouse gases added to the atmosphere since the industrial revolution; it is also three times the standard deviation for annual average temperatures. While the measurements are only partially in at this time, they appear to be bearing out the Hansen prediction. It is extremely significant that the models were able to predict the outcome of a natural experiment before the results were in. Had the experiment been conducted after actual data were available, it would have had much less impact. This represents an acid test for the climate models and their ability to predict the results of perturbations to the radiation budget.

Summary and Conclusion

In this chapter, four lines of evidence were presented to suggest that the Earth is likely to warm in the next 50 years. First, and least controversial, is the fact that the greenhouse gases have been increasing over the last 200 years and the source of the increase is likely to be anthropogenic. Second, simple models of the Earth's climate give reasonable simulations of today's climate and suggest that a rather large greenhouse effect (40°C) is required to give us our present climate. Hence, the argument is not about whether there is a greenhouse effect but rather whether it will change from 40°C to 43°C (72°F to 77.4°F) in the next 50 years. As models improve, we can expect these predictions to become more reliable and useful. This process will, however, be slow, and it depends heavily on improvements in computer technology.

The third line of evidence is the record of the Earth's average temperature over the last 150 years. While irregular, it shows a steady increase of about 0.5°C (0.9°F). The warming over this period could be the result of a natural fluctuation of the climate system, but this seems unlikely. Better information from paleoclimatic research may help to resolve this issue. A fourth piece of recently acquired evidence is based upon the cooling resulting from the eruption of Mount Pinatubo. This provided a valuable opportunity to test existing climate models. Well after the prediction was published, the data appear to be supporting the results.

Although none of these lines of evidence is sufficient to "prove" the global warming hypothesis, all four together provide a strong supporting case. There is no solid evidence in favor of the hypothesis that climate will remain unaffected by a continued buildup of greenhouse gases, nor is there evidence that global cooling will occur. The debate, of course, is over just how fast warming will occur and what the regional and local impacts will be. Temperature changes are likely to be distributed unevenly: some regions will receive increased precipitation, while others will become drier. We also expect changes in the extent of ice sheets and glaciers, some degree of sea-level rise, and changes in the frequency and intensity of storms and hurricanes.

These assertions underscore the importance of climate research, ranging from satellite measurements and paleoclimate reconstructions to the development of better computer-simulation models. This research must be conducted, not only to gradually improve and exploit our current knowledge to make climate projections, but to ensure that we remain on the lookout for the unexpected. The climate system is so complicated, with subsystems that are tightly interlinked, that surprises are inevitable. Every effort must be made to remove the present uncertainties.

The purpose of this book is to examine the impact of inevitable climate change on Texas and its surroundings. Given the limitations of today's climate models, this is an uncertain task at best. On the other hand, most political and economic decisions are actually made with far less-certain information than can be provided by these imperfect models.

The next chapter focuses on the state of Texas, its present climate, and its likely response to global warming.

References

Crowley, T. J., and G. R. North, 1991. *Paleoclimatology*. Oxford University Press, New York.

Grotch, S., 1988. Regional Intercomparisons of General Circulation Model Predictions and Historical Climate Data. U.S. Dept. of Energy, Report DOE/NBB-0084(TR041).

Grotch S., and M. MacCracken, 1991. The Use of General Circulation Models to Predict Regional Climate Change. *Journal of Climate* 4: 286–303.

Hansen, J., A. Lacis, R. Ruedy, and M. Sato, 1992. Potential Climate Impact of Mt. Pinatubo Eruption. *Geophysical Research Letters*, January 15 issue.

IPCC, 1990. *Climate Change: The IPCC Scientific Assessment.* J. T. Houghton, G. J. Jenkins, and J. J. Ephraums (eds.). Cambridge University Press, Cambridge, U.K.

Jones, P. D., P. M. L. Wigley, and G. Farmer, 1991. Marine and Land Temperature Data Sets: A Comparison and a Look at Recent Trends. In: *Greenhouse-Gas-Induced Climate Change: A Critical Appraisal of Simulations and Observations.* M. E. Schlesinger (ed.). Elsevier Press, New York.

Kim, K. -Y., G. R. North, and J. Huang, 1992. On the Transient Response of a Simple Coupled Climate System. *Journal of Geophysical Research* 97: 10,069–10,081.

North G. R., K. -Y. Kim, S. P. Shen, and J. W. Hardin, 1994. Detection of Forced Climate Signals. *Journal of Climate*, 7 (in press).

Washington, W., and C. Parkinson, 1986. *Introduction to Three Dimensional Climate Modeling.* University Science Books, Mill Valley, Calif.

GERALD R. NORTH, GEORGE BOMAR,
JOHN GRIFFITHS, JAMES NORWINE,
AND JUAN B. VALDES

2. The Changing Climate of Texas

This chapter presents a brief survey of the present climate regimes in Texas, emphasizing their diversity, their seasonality, and the interannual irregularity in temperature and precipitation. Such extreme events as hurricanes, tornadoes, floods, and droughts are shown to be part of the natural climate of Texas, even in the absence of global climate change. The importance of external influences, such as the El Niño–La Niña cycle in the Pacific, will be related to the drought/flood cycle in Texas. The past and potential future impacts of the greenhouse effect on Texas' climate will be evaluated, and an attempt will be made to assess the ability of today's climate models to forecast next century's climate changes. Finally, model-inspired scenarios of future climate are presented, and these should be helpful guides in estimating the effects of global warming on topics to be treated in later chapters.

Present Climates in Texas

Texas is a large state composed of a variety of underlying geographical conditions. The Panhandle of Texas is part of the Southern Great Plains, characterized by flat to rolling terrain several thousands of feet above sea level. An extension of the Southern Rocky Mountains crosses extreme West Texas, yielding an elevated, rugged topography. South-Central Texas is dominated by the Hill Country of the Edwards Plateau. Eastern and South-Central Texas are a coastal plain gently sloping to the Gulf of Mexico.

The climate of Texas is dominated by two competing influences—the passage of frontal systems from the north and west, and moist air moving inland from the Gulf of Mexico. As these two factors interact with each other and with the topography, dramatic changes in weather are common, particularly where warm, moist air is forced upward by the Edwards escarpment. The influence of the Gulf of Mexico is particularly important, as it provides a source of moisture and modulates the average seasonal and diurnal cycles, particularly in the coastal regions. In fact, proximity to the coast is the most important factor determining regional climatic differences in Texas.

Another significant geographical feature is the generally northwestern origin of rivers, which flow to the southeast, eventually discharging fresh water into the Gulf of Mexico. Because Texas is a largely arid state, it is heavily dependent on its rivers and their reservoirs as a source of fresh water for agricultural irrigation and municipal supplies. Significant changes in precipitation patterns could have disastrous impacts on the economy and ecosystems of the state. In this chapter we outline some of the major features of Texas' climate and how they might change under global warming. This information provides the groundwork for exploring potential climate-induced changes in the state's water resources, natural and managed ecosystems, and economy.

Regional Climates

The Panhandle and the Rio Grande Valley represent the climatic extremes within the state. The climate of the Panhandle is an elevated continental type characterized by an enhanced seasonal cycle in temperature. Precipitation peaks in summer due to air-mass thunderstorms typical of mid-latitude continental interiors. In contrast, coastal climates tend to have a smaller amplitude to their seasonal cycle, and in this part of the world, their annual cycle of precipitation tends to be flatter (more uniform) throughout the year. In addition to the continental-to-coastal continuum of climate differential across Texas, the latitudinal variation is important. This can be seen in Figure 2.1, a map of the length of the growing season (average length of frost-free periods in days). In addition to these two factors, there is a distinct east-west gradient of precipitation (Figure 2.2), which results in near rain-forest conditions on the upper Gulf coast and desert-like conditions in the extreme west.

Although some climatologies use as many as 10 regions to describe Texas climate (e.g., Griffiths and Bryan 1987), a highly simplified picture of the climate of Texas, with four climatic regions, will be used here. Data taken from two rep-

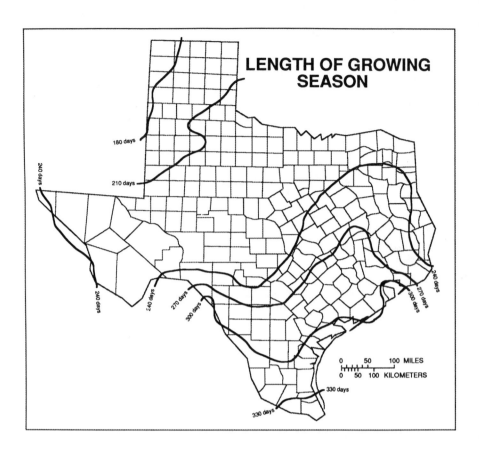

LENGTH OF GROWING SEASON

180 days
210 days
240 days
240 days
240 days
270 days
330 days
270 days
240 days
270 days
300 days
330 days
330 days
330 days

0   50   100 MILES

0   50   100 KILOMETERS

Figure 2.1.
The length of
growing season,
shown as the
number of frost-
free days each year
(Jordan et al. 1984).

G. R. NORTH,
G. BOMAR,
J. GRIFFITHS,
J. NORWINE,
AND
J. B. VALDES

26

resentative stations within each of these regions is presented to demonstrate the regional diversity within the state.

First consider the Southern Great Plains region. Figure 2.3 shows the annual cycle of temperature and precipitation for Amarillo (elevation 3,606 feet) and Abilene (elevation 1,784 feet). The dashed curves show the average daily maximum and minimum temperatures as a function of month. Amarillo has its precipitation peak in summer, as is typical of Great Plains climates farther into the continental interior. The average annual precipitation is 19.3 inches. Proceeding south (about 3 degrees of latitude) to Abilene, the summer peak splits into two maxima, one in the early summer and the other in early fall. The origin of the rainfall here is a mixture of summer convective storms and storms associated with the passage of air masses and their often discontinuous borders (fronts). Abilene's mean annual precipitation is 23.5 inches. The annual swing of temperatures is quite large for both of these sites, ranging from monthly average

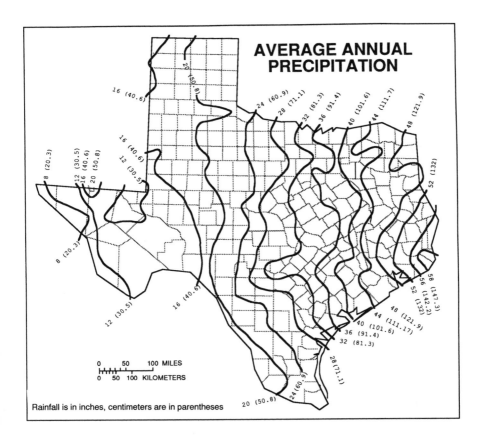

AVERAGE ANNUAL
PRECIPITATION

16 (40.6)
20 (50.8)
24 (60.9)
28 (71.1)
32 (81.3)
36 (91.4)
40 (101.6)
44 (111.7)
48 (121.9)
52 (132)
16 (40.6)
8 (20.3)
12 (30.5)
16 (40.6)
20 (50.8)
12 (30.5)
12 (30.5)
16 (40.6)
20 (50.8)
8 (20.3)
12 (30.5)
16 (40.6)
58 (147.3)
56 (142.2)
52 (132)
48 (121.2)
44 (111.9)
40 (101.17)
36 (91.4)
32 (81.3)
28 (71.1)
24 (60.9)
20 (50.8)

0   50   100 MILES
0   50   100 KILOMETERS

Rainfall is in inches, centimeters are in parentheses

daily highs in the low to mid 90s (°F) in July to monthly average daily minima in the low 20s in January. Annual evaporation from free water surfaces such as lakes exceeds precipitation by approximately 45 inches, a measure of the aridity
of the area. Winds tend to come predominately from the west
in winter, turning to a distinctly (warm) southerly flow in
summer.

To the south and west is the Western Plateau region (Figure 2.4). El Paso (elevation 3,918 feet) is noteworthy for its
lack of precipitation, which averages only 7.8 inches per year
and peaks in late summer. Its high elevation and distance
from the oceans make for a large annual cycle (average daily
highs of 96°F in June to average daily lows of 30°F in January).
Less extreme is San Angelo (elevation 1,903 feet), with an average yearly precipitation of 18.2 inches. The double peak in
its seasonal precipitation pattern blends continuously with
the neighboring Southern Great Plains region. The annual
swing of temperatures is very close to that of El Paso. In this
region the free water surface evaporation exceeds precipita-

*Figure 2.2.
Average annual
precipitation
(inches) (Texas
Department of
Water Resources
1984, p. 16).*

THE CHANGING
CLIMATE OF TEXAS

27

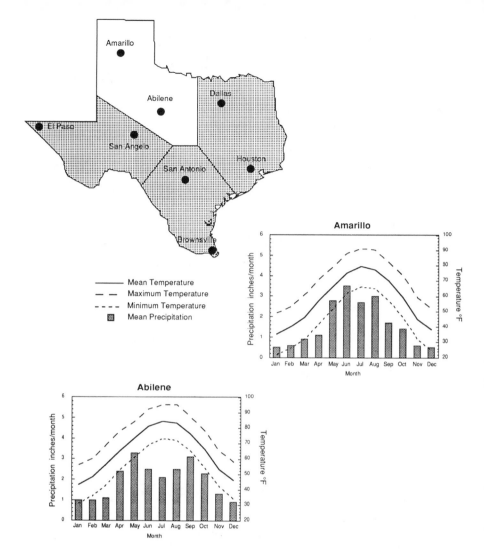

Figure 2.3.
Temperature and
precipitation data
for the Southern
Great Plains (data
from Griffiths and
Bryan 1987).

tion by about 60 inches, making this an extremely arid region. While El Paso's winds show no preference in direction
throughout the year, except for a tendency for westerlies in
the spring, San Angelo has a pattern more typical of eastern
parts of Texas, namely, a strong southerly flow in summer.

The Prairie-Coastal region contains the two major population centers of Dallas and Houston, as depicted in Figure
2.5. For a variety of reasons, the annual cycle of precipitation
in Houston (elevation 41 feet) is nearly flat, with an annual
mean of 42.7 inches. The slight peak in September is due to
hurricanes and tropical storms. As one moves up along the
Gulf Coast to Port Arthur, the mean annual precipitation in-

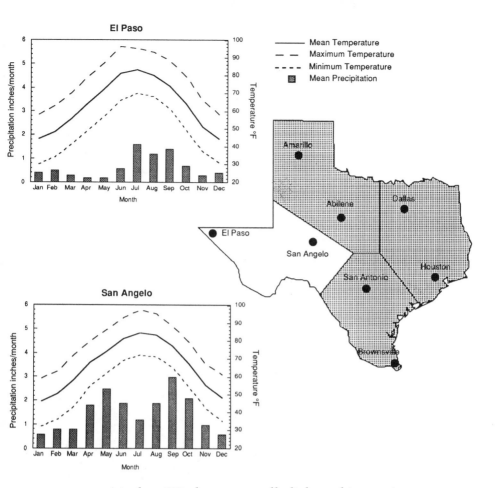

cre, to 55 inches. Winds are generally light and isotropic in the Houston area, with a tendency for the flow to come from the Gulf in warmer parts of the year. The average of daily highs in July is 93°F, while the average of daily lows in January is 46°F.

About 3 degrees of latitude north of Houston lies Dallas (elevation 440 feet), which has a mean annual precipitation of 36.1 inches. A strong peak in precipitation occurs in late spring, when frontal passages are frequent in this region. These are often accompanied by severe weather including tornadoes. Because of its more continental climate, Dallas has larger swings in its annual temperature cycle than Houston, with an average daily high in August of 96°F and an average daily low in January of 36°F. Lake surface evaporation, about 60 inches per year, is nearly exceeded by precipitation in the eastern part of the region. Hence, East Texas has abun-

Figure 2.4. Temperature and precipitation data for the West Texas Basin and Plateaus (data from Griffiths and Bryan 1987).

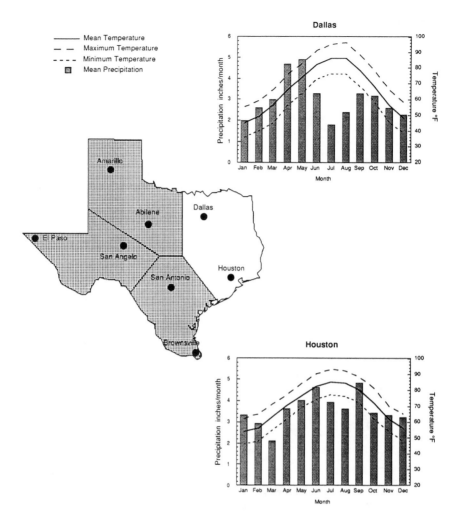

Figure 2.5.
Temperature and
precipitation data
for the Prairies and
Coastal Plain (data
from Griffiths and
Bryan 1987).

dant moisture to support trees and lush vegetation. Winds in
the Dallas area are southerly most of the year, with mon-
soonal flows predominating in summer.

As we examine the precipitation and temperature data
for Dallas in more detail, the interannual variability of precipitation, typical of Texas' climate, becomes apparent. Figure 2.6a shows a histogram of annual precipitation totals for
Dallas using data collected between 1914 and 1991. Note the
rather flat distribution across a large range of annual rainfalls. Twenty-five percent of the years at this station have
rainfall rates above 40 inches, and 25 percent of the years fall
below 28 inches. Figure 2.6b shows a similar histogram for

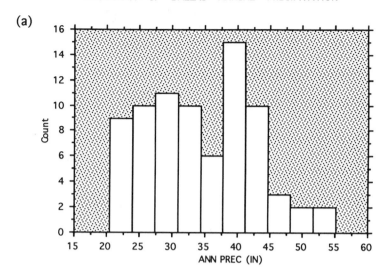

HISTOGRAM OF DALLAS ANNUAL PRECIPITATION

(a)

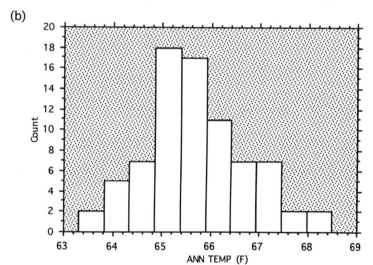

HISTOGRAM OF DALLAS ANNUAL TEMPERATURES

(b)

Figure 2.6.
Interannual
variation in annual
precipitation
(inches) and
temperature (°F)
for Dallas (data
from the Office
of the State
Climatologist).

the 78 years of data for annual average temperature in Dallas. Note how much more bell-shaped this curve is in contrast with the boxlike histogram for precipitation. While the interannual variability in temperature is small, being confined to within 1.5°F of the mean 65.7°F during 80 percent of the years, the corresponding statistics for precipitation are much more variable, with standard deviation one-quarter of the mean (8.2 inches compared to 34.5 inches). Figures 2.7a and 2.7b show the corresponding histograms for the 78 Decembers. As expected, the percentage spread is far greater for a calendar month than for a whole year, with the standard deviation of precipitation for December at about the value of the mean (2.0 inches compared to 2.3 inches). Similarly, the standard deviation of the December temperatures is over three times that for the annual mean (3.6°F compared to 1.1°F). These variability characteristics will be discussed again as we examine climate change in Texas.

Finally, the regional climate of South Texas is shown in Figure 2.8. Near the coast of extreme southern Texas, close to the mouth of the Rio Grande, lies Brownsville, with a mean annual precipitation of 26.9 inches. Maximum precipitation in September–October is attributable to tropical storms. For example, the area received 12.2 inches of rain in 1 day in September 1967 from Hurricane Beulah. Because of the extended frost-free period (exceeding 320 days per year), the climate of this region is suitable for citrus fruit farming. However, occasional hard frosts have caused concern about the viability of this industry. The climate of San Antonio (elevation 788 feet) is characterized by a double-peaked annual cycle of precipitation and represents a transition to the climate farther west. Mean annual precipitation is 28.3 inches. San Antonio's distance from the Gulf and its elevation make for a large annual cycle of temperature: average daily highs in July–August of 95°F, and average daily lows in January of 39°F. Winds in South Texas blow mostly from the Gulf, with the strongest coming in summer.

The types of atmospheric systems that bring about the daily variations in temperature and precipitation vary by season and position in Texas. In spring and fall, weather fluctuations are due mostly to the passages of frontal systems in a generally west-to-east direction. As fronts line up in a generally north-easterly direction, moist air is brought northward from the Gulf, with the advancing front wedging under the warmer, moist air. This leads to frontal precipitation often

G. R. NORTH,
G. BOMAR,
J. GRIFFITHS,
J. NORWINE,
AND
J. B. VALDES

(a)

HISTOGRAM OF DALLAS DECEMBER PRECIPITATION

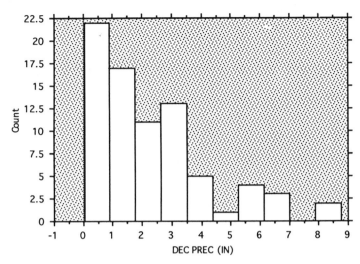

(b)

HISTOGRAM OF DALLAS DECEMBER TEMPERATURES

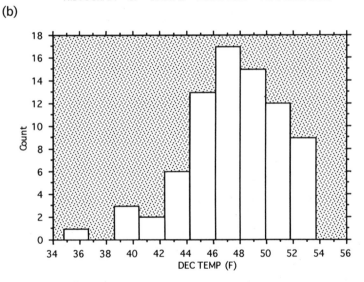

Figure 2.7. Interannual variation in December precipitation (inches) and temperature (°F) for Dallas (data from the Office of the State Climatologist).

accompanied by severe weather. In winter the fronts come more from due north, bringing cold, dry, Canadian air. At some point in the late spring, the last frontal passage occurs in southern parts of Texas, and during summer months there is no relief from the persistent heat. If global warming should

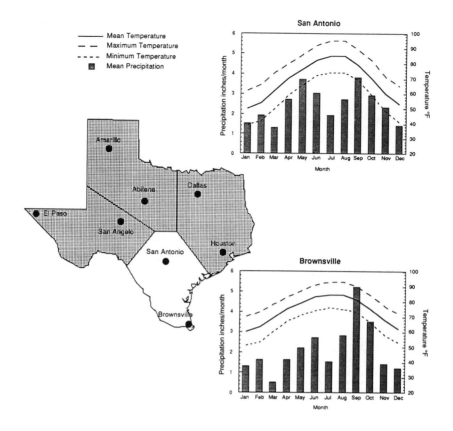

Figure 2.8.
Temperature and
precipitation data
for South Texas
(data from Griffiths
and Bryan 1987).

occur, the seasonal transition to a tropical climate would be
expected to occur earlier in the year and last longer.

Occurrence of Drought

Drought occurs in all parts of Texas, even in the absence of
global climate change. Roughly speaking, drought is a prolonged period in which precipitation is below average and/or
evaporation is elevated. As demonstrated in Figure 2.6, the
frequency distribution for annual precipitation is broad for
most of Texas, with extremes fairly likely. (The ratio of the
standard deviation to the mean for annual precipitation is
32 percent in the Trans-Pecos, 27 percent in South Texas and
the Edwards Plateau, and 19 percent in East Texas; Riggio
et al. 1987.) A major obstacle to recognizing that a drought is
in progress is the fact that rainfall is very erratic from month
to month and a period of several months with below-average
rainfall is common. Usually by the time a drought is fully

G. R. NORTH,
G. BOMAR,
J. GRIFFITHS,
J. NORWINE,
AND
J. B. VALDES

34

appreciated, its repercussions on agriculture, hydrology, and other sectors of the economy have become pronounced.

Texas' proximity to the Chihuahuan Desert suggests that the state will undergo periods of prolonged, below-average rainfall. That great desert continually expands and contracts in response to the long-term migration and strength of the large-scale subtropical ridge of high pressure that surrounds the Earth above the equator for much of the year. The size and strength of that prominent feature depend on a variety of factors, such as the occurrence of El Niño and volcanic eruptions, as well as natural variability of the coupled atmosphere-ocean system.

Every region of Texas experiences drought, with the frequency and duration being irregular and intermittent. Because they are closest to the Chihuahuan Desert, the High Plains and Trans-Pecos regions of the state are the most vulnerable. This is especially true in the colder half of the year, when intrusions of dry polar air are frequent and the return flow of moist Gulf air above the shallow polar air mass fails to reach far enough into the region to produce appreciable rainfall. On the other hand, summer drought can afflict any portion of the state. In any warm season the regions to be affected are determined by the positioning of the subtropical ridge (high pressure) over the southern United States.

At least some portion of Texas has suffered a serious drought in every decade of the twentieth century. The most calamitous dry spell of the modern era was the extreme drought that tortured the whole state for most of the 1950's, breaking dramatically in 1957. That drought is commonly regarded as the benchmark against which all other droughts in the state are compared. The Dust Bowl drought, while more severe in areas of the Great Plains to the north of Texas, was nonetheless severe in most of Texas for several years during the 1930's.

Occurrence of Severe Weather

Texans have had a respect for hurricanes since 1900, when a monster storm struck Galveston and as many as 6,000 lives were lost. Nowadays, no such loss of life is to be expected from such a storm, because of the early warning provided by satellite tracking of tropical storms and the modern computer modeling of their paths. The likelihood of a hurricane reaching land is about equal anywhere along the Texas coast.

The frequency of large Atlantic hurricanes has diminished over the last 2 or 3 decades. Dr. William Gray, a prominent hurricane analyst, thinks that this is part of a cycle of several decades' duration, in which case the return of more frequent Atlantic hurricanes might be expected over the coming decades. This conjecture has nothing to do with global warming, but rather with an empirical connection between rainfall over the Southern Sahara and the incidence of Atlantic storms (Landsea et al. 1992). The rainfall rate in Northern Africa has been low for nearly 3 decades now and is expected to revive toward normal soon. According to Gray's conjecture, when this happens we are likely to see an upsurge in the frequency of intense Atlantic hurricanes.

On the longer time scale, some scientists have conjectured that global warming will lead to a change in the frequency and intensity of hurricanes (Emanuel 1987). While intuition suggests that the changes will include increases in both frequency and intensity of these storms, it must be acknowledged that the theoretical and empirical evidence for such a conclusion is meager and the changes are still being debated in the climate research community. Global climate models are not yet able to simulate the occurrence and intensity of hurricanes, because their grids are too coarse. One goal of the modeling program of the next decade is to improve our ability to look into these questions.

Other forms of severe weather include tornadoes. The northeastern part of the state forms the southwest-most end of the so-called tornado alley, which extends northeast through Oklahoma to the Great Lakes. These storms occur mostly in the spring, but they can happen at any time of the year and at any point in Texas; in November of 1992, a series of tornadoes struck the suburbs of Houston in connection with the passage of a dramatic cold front sweeping from the west. Aside from frontally associated outbreaks, tornadoes and waterspouts also frequently accompany hurricanes.

External Factors Governing Texas Climate

Seasonal to Few Year Time Scale

The climate of Texas is controlled by the same radiation balance factors that govern global climate except that, just as for any subdivision on the planet, account must be taken of the flow of weather into Texas from neighboring regions. In addition, the atmospheric general circulation occasionally sets

G. R. NORTH,
G. BOMAR,
J. GRIFFITHS,
J. NORWINE,
AND
J. B. VALDES

up long stationary waves that encircle the planet. These can lock into place for many months and steer stormy weather across the state more frequently than on the average. When such a situation arises, weather patterns that seem to repeat over many months are established. Recognizing this effect has provided us with the potential to produce useful climate forecasts out to the seasonal and even annual time horizon. Events in the Tropical Pacific have been found to be at the root of many of Texas' climatic anomalies.

It has been known for a century that the temperatures of the Tropical Pacific are highly variable from one year to the next. The sea surface near Peru is usually cool due to the up-welling along the equatorial coast of cold waters from far below. The cool and nutrient-rich upwelling waters are very important to the Peruvian fishing industry, which thrives on anchovy catches. Each year around Christmas this upwelling slows and the coastal surface water tends to warm notice-ably. Periodically, every 2–7 years, there is no upwelling to speak of throughout the year, and the eastern Pacific switches into a prolonged warm state, which may last for more than a year. Because of the small annual slowing of the upwelling, these occasional megaepisodes are called El Niño ("the boy child," named after Christmas).

El Niño is part of a chain of events sequentially unfolding across the Tropical Pacific Basin. Extreme swings in the opposite direction (anomalously cool water in the Eastern Pacific) are also possible, and these are called La Niña by climatologists. Records from coral and from ice cores taken from the high Andes suggest that these cycles have been occurring with about the same frequency for hundreds of years. The El Niño cycle sets up a very large-scale shift in the tropical circulation known as the Southern Oscillation. It is this shift that leads to the "teleconnection" with our North American weather.

Occurrence of El Niño events has a significant effect on the general circulation in the middle latitudes of the world. When an El Niño occurs we see a brief warming of the global average temperature of the order of 0.2°C (0.36°F), which could account for an appreciable part of the variability in the global temperature over the last century. In addition, both the precipitation and temperature of the southeastern part of North America show a statistically significant relationship to the El Niño cycle. Figure 2.9 shows a scatter diagram of raw data for the so-called Southern Oscillation Index (the difference between the atmospheric pressure at Darwin and

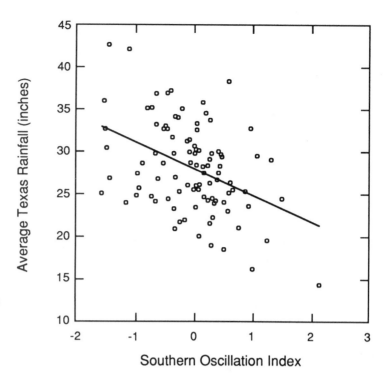

Figure 2.9.
A scatter diagram
of raw data for the
so-called Southern
Oscillation Index
(the difference
between the
atmospheric
pressure at Darwin
and Tahiti) and the
annually averaged
precipitation
in Texas.

Average Texas Rainfall (inches)

Southern Oscillation Index

Tahiti) and the annually averaged precipitation in Texas. Demonstrating this seemingly vague trend (correlation coefficient = 0.40), which makes no use of computer models, shows considerable analytical skill. In principle, models might be used to sharpen the correlation and therefore improve the forecast. However, the potential impact on Texas of these events is illustrated by the fact that a recent (1988) drought in Houston (when rainfall was half of its annual average) coincided with an occurrence of La Niña.

As with hurricanes, there is concern about the frequency and intensity of the El Niño–La Niña cycle under the influence of global climate change. Again, this is an issue for the climate models of the next decade to address. Currently, none are quite capable of reproducing this phenomenon with sufficient reliability and accuracy to trust their predictions about a hypothetical warmer scenario.

Another important occasional influence on continental climates is the eruption of volcanoes, as discussed in the previous chapter. In principle, the cool summer and fall of 1992 could have been predicted, if operational climate models had been ready to take information from satellites on the opacity of the atmosphere and translate it into seasonal predictions.

G. R. NORTH,
G. BOMAR,
J. GRIFFITHS,
J. NORWINE,
AND
J. B. VALDES

The modeling results reported in the previous chapter were only used for research purposes, but calculations of that type will become part of the seasonal outlook in the near future. Each volcanic eruption is different depending on its location, the season of the eruption, the altitude to which the volcanic material is sent, and the composition of the ejecta. Because of these factors, rapid assimilation of the eruption characteristics will enable the initialization of models and the production of forecasts.

Decadal and Longer Time Scales

Global climate changes on all time scales, ranging from years to thousands of millennia. Ice sheets similar to those currently covering Greenland and Antarctica have advanced periodically across Canada into the northern tier of the (present) United States over the last few million years. The largest ice sheet expansions occur with a periodicity of about 100,000 years. As little as 14,000 years ago such a massive ice sheet covered Canada and extended all the way south to the present location of Madison, Wisconsin. The ice sheets decayed in just a few thousand years, resulting in the present interglacial state, itself a replica of many such nearly identical recurrences over the last million years. This interglacial may last another 5,000–10,000 years before the ice sheets again begin their slow buildup (Crowley and North 1991). Evidence suggests that temperatures then in what is now present-day Texas were about 5°C (9°F) cooler than today (Ibid.), a value similar in magnitude to the increase in temperature predicted by some global climate models for a doubling of greenhouse gases. Could it be that our garbage gases could warm the earth by an amount comparable to the amplitude of ice age fluctuations in just the next 50–100 years?

Arguments advanced in Chapter 1 suggest that the anthropogenic contribution to the greenhouse effect is likely to have been gradually warming the planet since the beginning of the industrial revolution. It is reasonable to ask whether there has been a detectable effect in Texas. Figure 2.10 shows a graph of the average temperature in Texas for the last century. Notable, of course, is the large amount of natural variability from one year to the next. Also notable, and somewhat embarrassing for the greenhouse devotee, is the lack of warming as seen in the global curves of Chapter 1. In fact, the time-dependence of the temperature averaged across the

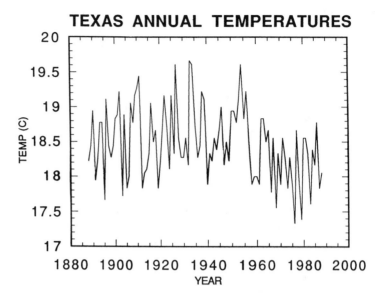

TEXAS ANNUAL TEMPERATURES

Figure 2.10.
Annual mean
temperature
(°F) for Texas,
1888–1989.

United States appears to be quite flat. The entire Southeast exhibits the same anomalous mild cooling that we see in Texas (Plantico et al. 1990). There are several possible explanations:

1. The natural variability of a small (compared to the whole world) region like Texas could have a much larger inter-annual natural variability, and this could easily mask the underlying 0.5°C (0.9°F) per century trend over the last century.

2. Anthropogenic modifications, such as irrigation, clearing, dust, smoke, etc., could have counteracted the greenhouse effect enough to hide it at least temporarily.

3. An anomalous, century-long cooling could have taken place in the Gulf of Mexico due to some slow overturning and exposure of cool water from below.

4. The Gulf Stream could have moved away from the Atlantic shore in a slow but steady meander.

5. The greenhouse warming hypothesis could be false; but then we have a lot of explaining to do to reconcile the curiosities in Chapter 1.

G. R. NORTH,
G. BOMAR,
J. GRIFFITHS,
J. NORWINE,
AND
J. B. VALDES

Any of these reasons could be correct, but the first seems most likely.

Impacts of Global Warming for Texas' Climate

Model Warming Predictions

In Chapter 1 it was argued that an average warming of 1.5–4.0°C (3–7°F) should be expected for the globe between now and 2050 A.D. The models all predict that the poles will warm more and the equatorial regions less. A midlatitude region like Texas can be expected to have about the same warming as the global average. This is borne out by examining maps of the results of warming experiments with the models. Models also suggest that continental interiors will warm a little more than coastal regions, but experience shows that this correction is negligible for Texas; hence, it is neglected here. The models do predict a slight seasonality to the global warming (winters might warm slightly more toward the poles, but less in the subtropics), but the differences between models seems to be as large as the predicted seasonal cycle change itself. Moreover, the seasonality effect is larger at more poleward latitudes than those crossing Texas. Therefore, for the purposes of constructing future climate scenarios for Texas, the seasonality of the expected temperature change will be neglected: the scenario warming will be the same for every month of the year.

Precipitation climatologies are notoriously difficult to compute in a general circulation model; needless to say, changes in the precipitation climatology are even more difficult. This difficulty comes from several sources. First, the highly irregular nature of precipitation makes it difficult to estimate its mean with a short record. For example, the statistical uncertainty in estimating the mean rainfall total for December in Dallas is 10 percent, with only 78 years of record. Unfortunately, there is a nonlinear relationship between the length of the record and our ability to reduce this error term (780 years of record would still lead us to a 3.1 percent error). This means that to obtain the seasonal cycle of rainfall rate from a model would require prohibitively long runs, even if the model were perfect.

In addition to this fundamental limitation, model errors occur because the spatial scales at which precipitation manifests itself are much smaller than the numerical grid spacings used by today's climate models. This means that the precipitation process must be estimated based upon inadequate information. As expected, the calculations for precipitation changes vary greatly from one model to another. They all agree, however, that the global average precipitation (this requires a much smaller record length in the simulation) should increase from 3 to 8 percent for an effective doubling of greenhouse gases (expected to take 70 years). The main questions are, How will precipitation be distributed geographically, and will there be differences by season? And more important, how will soil moisture be affected?

Soil Moisture Changes

The condition of the soil is of extreme importance to agriculture and in the interaction of the Earth's surface with the atmosphere. Most global climate models include only very crude representations of soil variables. In fact, the only variables being considered in virtually all the models are soil temperature and moisture. Most models include some variant on the "bucket" model (e.g., Delworth and Manabe 1993). This model considers the local soil to be a bucket 6 inches (15 cm) deep. When the amount of rain accumulated in the bucket exceeds its capacity, runoff occurs. Evaporation from the top of the bucket is a nonlinear function of the amount of water in the bucket and the temperature. Some newer models are beginning to allow the "field capacity" (depth of bucket) and other parameters to have a geographical dependence. Kellogg and Zhao (1988) have surveyed the soil moisture changes in model simulations of doubled carbon dioxide. They found that the variance from model to model was very large, suggesting that we are far from simulating this phenomenon with any degree of confidence.

Some clues come from a recent simulation with a coupled ocean-atmosphere model by Manabe and colleagues (1992) of the Geophysical Fluid Dynamics Laboratory (GFDL). Using conditions in which there is an effective doubling of greenhouse gases (approximately 70 years from now), they report an increase of about 10 percent in precipitation over middle- and high-latitude land and about 6.6 percent over middle- and high-latitude oceans. However, evaporation in midlatitudes increases drastically, because of the increased surface temperatures (about 4.5°F over Texas). When this is factored into their coupled soil moisture model, they find continuously decreasing summertime soil mois-

G. R. NORTH,
G. BOMAR,
J. GRIFFITHS,
J. NORWINE,
AND
J. B. VALDES

42

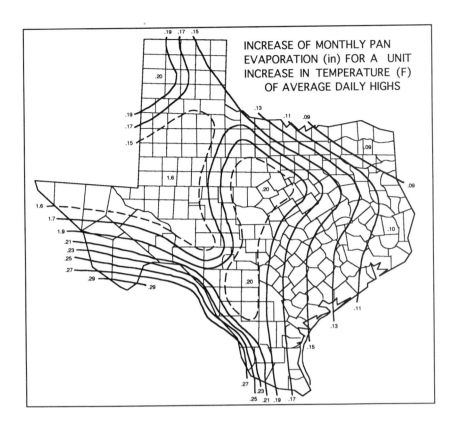

Within the figure:

INCREASE OF MONTHLY PAN
EVAPORATION (in) FOR A UNIT
INCREASE IN TEMPERATURE (F)
OF AVERAGE DAILY HIGHS

ture from 0.2 to 0.6 inches (0.5 to 1.5 cm) as the model run is continued from 50 years of simulation to 90 years. In their model, the soil moisture varies between 1.2 and 2 inches (3 and 5 cm) during these summer months. Hence, the soil moisture decreases are substantial—between 10 and 50 percent.

A simpler, less model-dependent approach to the problem of soil moisture is to rely on measurements of open surface evaporation compiled by Moe and Griffiths (1965). These authors found a relationship between the month-long average of daily high temperatures and the rate of evaporation from open surfaces such as lakes. For a given increase in monthly high temperatures, the corresponding increase in pan evaporation rates can be computed (Figure 2.11). Evaporation rates are given in inches per month, and the temperature changes are in °F. For example, the coefficient for Dallas is 0.15 inches/month/°F. Thus, for a 3°F warming due to the greenhouse effect, we might expect a 0.45 inch/month in-

Figure 2.11.
Expected increases in pan evaporation rates with elevation in temperature (inches/month/°F).

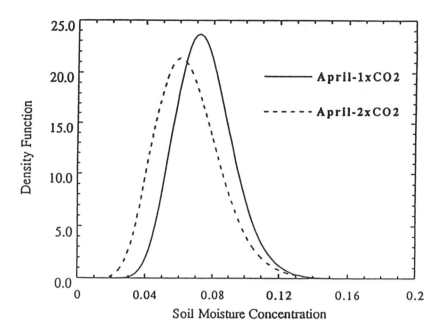

Soil Moisture Concentration

Figure 2.12.
The frequency
distribution of
soil moisture
concentration
for April in San
Antonio for
current ($1 \times CO_2$)
and warmer ($2 \times CO_2$) conditions.

G. R. NORTH,
G. BOMAR,
J. GRIFFITHS,
J. NORWINE,
AND
J. B. VALDES

crease in pan evaporation rate. This is to be compared to the present average rainfall rate of about 3 inches/month. While pan evaporation is not the same as the actual evaporation from soil and plant cover, it is evident that the greenhouse-induced increase in temperature alone will lead to a considerable increase in evaporation, and this is the main cause of the expected drying out of soil.

Another approach has been taken by Valdes et al. (1993). These authors employed a more detailed approach to the analysis of soil moisture (better than the bucket) and allowed precipitation to be stochastic (random, like throwing dice), but with the probability distribution (i.e., mean and standard deviation) matching the climatology. In this way, they could simulate the seasonal cycle, which on the average would look like the seasonal cycles shown for the stations described earlier in this chapter. After finding satisfactory matches to the present climate, they experimented with altered climates such as the scenarios proposed in this chapter. Figure 2.12 shows the histogram of soil moisture for the month of April in San Antonio for a 2°C increase in temperature and a 10 percent decrease in precipitation. In this case the mean soil moisture decreased by 20.9 percent. The average decrease varies by month, from 24 percent in September to 16 percent in December. Annual average decreases vary somewhat over the state (19 percent in Amarillo, 10 percent in Temple).

Changes in Frost-Free Period

One of the interesting possibilities for Texas is that the growing season will be increased by global warming. Such an effect, coupled with the potential fertilizing effects of increased carbon dioxide, could potentially help Texas agriculture. The chapter on agriculture covers this topic. However, some conclusions can be arrived at by a qualitative examination of the present climatology, simply by translating vertically the lower, short-dashed curves in Figures 2.3, 2.4, 2.5, and 2.8. We must be careful not to confuse the monthly average of low temperatures with actual lows that are lower because of natural fluctuations. Hence, the length of the growing season (Figure 2.1) is shorter than the interval between intersections of the short-dashed lines and an imaginary horizontal 32°F line. Nevertheless, we can see that regions with large seasonal cycles will tend to have a smaller change in their growing season lengths than those with small seasonal cycles. Because of its obvious importance, this will be a subject of future research.

It is intriguing that observed data show that over mid-latitude continents the nighttime low temperatures have been increasing steadily over the last 40 years, while daytime highs have held fairly steady, as shown in Figure 2.13 (Kukla and Karl 1992). Most models of the 1980's did not include a diurnal cycle, so it was hard to say what they would have predicted about changes in the frost-free period at a given location. One of the more recent calculations did include a diurnal cycle and predicted no differential between nighttime lows and daytime highs—in contradiction of the observed record. This serves as one more reminder that modeling has a long way to go before the details of global climate change and its regional effects can be predicted with certainty.

The Vulnerable Subtropic Climate of Southern Texas

This section takes as an example one part of Texas and the effects that global warming might have on it. The region chosen is Southern Texas, but any region of Texas might have been singled out for a study of its particular vulnerabilities and likely responses to global warming. Southern Texas is especially interesting because two dividing lines cross it: that between the arid west and the humid east, and the more ambiguous break between the winterless or tropical climates to the south and the seasonal midlatitude regimes to the

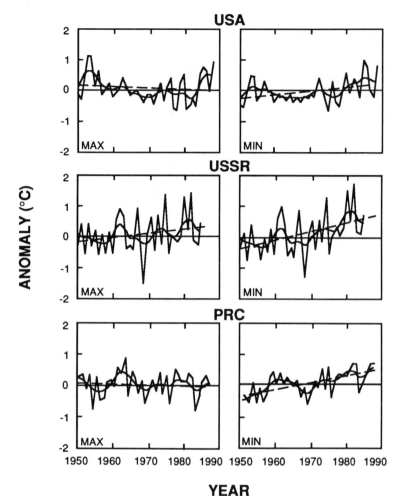

Figure 2.13. Variations in mean annual maximum and minimum temperatures since 1951 for the United States, Soviet Union, and China. Solid line: nine-point binomial filter; dashed line: linear trend.

G. R. NORTH,
G. BOMAR,
J. GRIFFITHS,
J. NORWINE;
AND
J. B. VALDES

north. The existing regional climate—characterized by limited moisture availability, extreme interannual rainfall variability, high temperatures, high evapotranspiration rates, and occasional killing freezes—is consequently a marginal or "problem" climate with respect to intensive human settlement and usage. This is especially true of South Texas: the subtropical regimes that lie roughly within the area bounded by San Antonio, Victoria, Brownsville, and Del Rio. South Texas may experience further climatic deterioration as a consequence of global warming.

Summer might be crudely defined by the number of "hot" (i.e., maxima greater than 90°F) days. According to this definition, from one-third to one-half of the year is summer for

South Texas. For example, the number of hot days is 150 in Kingsville and 180 in Rio Grande City. The mean annual number of hot nights (minima above 80°F) is much less; for example, Houston averages only about one hot night per year. Because the annual temperature curves are so flat for these coastal regions, a small upward displacement of the curves in Figures 2.5 and 2.8, by 1.7–3°C (3–6°F), will lead to a large number of days or nights above the "hot" threshold.

Because of high temperatures and limited rainfall, South Texas' subhumid to semiarid climates are generally moisture deficient. For example, Brownsville currently exhibits an annual deficit in precipitation versus evaporation of about 25 inches. One recent study (Powley and Norwine 1992) suggests that with a typical global warming scenario this deficit might increase by 15 percent. Consider the increase of evaporation rate along the Rio Grande following a temperature rise of 3°C (6°F). As inferred from Figure 2.11, this warming would lead to an increase of 1.7 inches per month in the pan evaporation rate, roughly twice the increase expected for Dallas. This is obviously serious for a region like Laredo, where average monthly precipitation is less than 2 inches.

Interannual variability of precipitation varies from 30 percent in coastal South Texas to 40 percent in the western part near Laredo. These mean variability coefficients, greater than those of any other large semiarid region on Earth other than northeast Brazil, are at least as challenging to regional economies and ecologies as the limited average annual rainfall. An agriculturist or ecologist in Laredo, for instance, must deal not only with mean yearly precipitation of about 20 inches, but also with not-infrequent extremes of 5 and 50 inches. Climate models cannot reliably project changes in interannual variability of precipitation at this time. However, variability is likely to increase if there is more desiccation of the soil and a higher frequency of tropical storms.

Clearly, some changes likely to occur in South Texas will be favorable, as might be expected from a lengthening of the growing season. On the other hand, water resources will be more scarce as a result of increased population pressure as well as a warmer climate.

Scenarios for This Book

The editors of this book have had to make a choice of scenarios to ensure consistency between the assessments of the effects of global climate change on the various economic, ecologic, and geographic sectors of Texas considered in later chapters. Naturally, all of the chapter authors wanted precise values for the expected changes in temperature and precipitation for each month of the year, with some even wishing for regional estimates. Considering the present state of development of climate models, this is simply not achievable with any degree of confidence. A scenario approach was chosen instead, with changes in temperature somewhere in the center of model predictions. In the absence of any reliable information from the models on precipitation, the best that could be done was to choose two values expected to capture the range of possibilities.

Our assessment of the results of the various modeled temperatures is that an increase of 2.0°C (3.6°F) is reasonable for the target date of 2050 A.D. If it turns out in the next decade that experts agree on a higher rate of warming, the effects calculated for 2050 A.D. with the 2.0°C scenario can simply be applied to an earlier point in time. Much more problematic is the amount of change in mean annual precipitation. Since modeled precipitation rates are so unreliable, changes of +/− 20 percent were chosen as two possible scenarios. While this range is large, it is still smaller than the standard deviation of annual rain totals over most of the state. Annual precipitation rates this different from the mean occur in as many as 35 percent of the years, even in today's climate. On the other hand, a persistent shift of this magnitude in the value of the mean will have drastic effects on the hydrology of the state. For this reason, a smaller value was used for the calculations in the chapter on hydrology. Hence, we have taken the models as a guide rather than literally. In this way we hope to bracket the effects of global warming in such a way as to make our results useful without overselling their reliability. We believe this philosophy is consistent with the desires of most climate modelers.

In the course of assembling the material for this chapter, considerable uncertainty has been encountered. The findings suggest that there are many important questions about Texas climate that need to be answered and that investigating these issues should be high on the agenda of researchers and policymakers.

G. R. NORTH,
G. BOMAR,
J. GRIFFITHS,
J. NORWINE,
AND
J. B. VALDES

References

Crowley, T. J., and G. R. North, 1991. *Paleoclimatology*. Oxford University Press, New York.

Delworth, T., and S. Manabe, 1993. Climate variability and land-surface processes. *Advances in Water Resources* 16:3–20.

Emanuel, K. A., 1987. Dependence of hurricane intensity on climate. *Nature* 326:483–485.

Griffiths, J., and J. Bryan, 1987. *The Climates of Texas Counties.* Natural Fibers Information Center, University of Texas at Austin.

Kellogg, W., and Z. -C. Zhao, 1988. Sensitivity of Soil Moisture to Doubling of Carbon Dioxide in Climate Model Experiments. *Journal of Climate* 1:348–378.

Kukla, G., and T. Karl, 1992. Nighttime Temperatures in the Northern Hemisphere. Carbon Dioxide Information Bulletin, Oak Ridge, Tenn.

Landsea, C. W., W. Gray, P. W. Mielke, and K. J. Berry, 1992. Long-Term Variation of Western Sahelian Monsoon Rainfall and Intense U.S. Landfalling Hurricanes. *Journal of Climate* 5:1528–1534.

Manabe, S., M. J. Spelman, R. J. Stouffer, 1992. Transient responses of a coupled ocean-atmosphere model to gradual changes of atmospheric CO_2. Part II: Seasonal response. *Journal of Climate* 5:105–126.

Moe, R., and J. Griffiths, 1965. A Simple Evaporation Formula for Texas. Texas Agricultural Experiment Station, Report MP-795.

Plantico, M. S., T. R. Karl, G. Kukla, and J. Gavin, 1990. Is recent climate change across the United States related to rising levels of anthropogenic greenhouse gases? *Journal of Geophysical Research* 95:16,617–16,637.

Powley, J., and J. Norwine, 1992. Effects of Carbon Dioxide-Induced Global Warming on Water Budget in Southern Texas. In: *Managing Water Resources During Global Change.* Amer. Water Res. Assn., November.

Riggio, R. F., G. W. Bomar, and T. J. Larkin, 1987. *Texas Drought: Its Recent History.* Texas Water Commission, Report LP 87–04.

Valdes, J. B., R. Seone, and G. R. North, 1994. A methodology for the evaluation of global warming impact on soil moisture and runoff. *Journal of Hydrology.* (in press).

3. Greenhouse Gas Emissions

As outlined in Chapter 1, the warming of the Earth is directly related to the atmospheric concentrations of greenhouse gases, notably CO_2. Released at the current rate, for example, the concentration of CO_2 in the atmosphere is likely to double some time in the next century. The Intergovernmental Panel on Climate Change (IPCC), under its "Business-As-Usual" scenario (which assumes only modest CO_2 controls), estimates that a doubling of 1990 CO_2 levels will occur by the year 2080. According to IPCC calculations, global mean temperature will rise by 1°C (1.8°F) by 2025 and by 3°C (5.4°F) by 2100. The IPCC (1990) concluded that at least a 60 percent reduction in CO_2 emissions was necessary to prevent a further buildup in its atmospheric concentration.

Such a reduction in emissions could totally change our current lifestyles. The developed world has a very energy intensive way of life, and this is particularly true of the United States, which uses approximately twice the amount of energy per unit of gross domestic product as do Japan and France (Goldemberg 1992, p. 225). However, this discrepancy alone illustrates that significant opportunities exist for reducing the amount of energy consumed, without a significant deterioration in living standards. In response to the 1973 oil embargo, some attempts to reduce energy consumption were initiated by the U.S. government, but the return of low energy prices in the 1980's removed a lot of the motivation. Recent attempts at developing a national energy policy illustrate the difficulties, as various interest groups, including producers and environmentalists, are pitted against each other. With the Clinton administration in office, some of the elements of the debate have changed. Already (as of January 1993), the possibility of increasing energy taxes has started to gain some momentum, partly in response to the need to increase federal revenues.

Overall, the federal government has made little effort to address the issue of global warming, and in general, policies that would reduce emissions are primarily aimed at reducing energy use. At the federal level there have been some attempts to encourage energy efficiency, but most of the implementation and development of new initiatives has taken place at the state level. In this chapter we examine the potential problems and opportunities for Texas as we move toward an era of increasing pressures, both economic and regulatory, to reduce emissions, improve energy-use efficiency, and limit greenhouse gas production. A few states have already adopted programs aimed at increased energy-use efficiency, and an analysis of some of these programs is included.

The Contribution of Greenhouse Gases in Texas to Global Warming

Nature of Greenhouse Gases

The Earth's atmosphere is 99 percent oxygen and nitrogen; the other 1 percent is made up of a number of "trace" or "greenhouse" gases. These gases include carbon dioxide (CO_2), carbon monoxide (CO), methane (CH_4), nitrous oxide (N_2O), ozone (O_3), and, for the last 30–40 years, chlorofluorocarbons (CFCs). The majority of shortwave solar radiation passes through the atmosphere and is absorbed by the Earth's surface. The longwave radiation emitted by the Earth's surface interacts with the gases in the atmosphere, resulting in the absorption of some and the reemission of the balance. As trace gases increase in relative amount, the quantity of heat retained by the atmosphere increases.

The most predominant of the greenhouse gases is CO_2. In nature CO_2 is a part of an integrated carbon cycle, in which plants absorb CO_2 from the atmosphere, storing the carbon and releasing oxygen. In turn, CO_2 is released back into the atmosphere as a result of respiration, organic decay, combustion, and chemical diffusion. A steady state results if these processes are in equilibrium. However, human activity has caused the acceleration of many of these processes, resulting in a disproportionate increase in the production of CO_2. One of the more significant causes is the rapid release of CO_2 from fossil fuels that have acted as a *carbon sink* over a very long period of time. A second major contributor is the destruction of forests, which not only release their existing carbon, but no longer have the capacity to contribute to the carbon cycle by removing CO_2 from the atmosphere (Graedel and Crutzen 1989). Currently, fossil fuel combustion releases approximately 5.4 GtC (Gigatons of carbon) per year, and deforestation and changes in land use add an additional 0.6–2.6 GtC per year (Watson *et al.* 1990).

Methane is a naturally occurring gas that makes up approximately 18 percent of the current greenhouse gas contribution from human activity. It is generated naturally by bacteria breaking down organic matter in the absence of oxygen. Methane may be produced by natural wetlands, flooded rice fields, ruminant livestock, landfills, coal mining, biomass burning, and deforestation. The concentration of methane has more than doubled since the industrial revolution (Graedel and Crutzen 1989).

First introduced into the atmosphere in the 1930's, CFCs were originally discovered in 1928 and manufactured by DuPont under the trade name *freon*. Chlorofluorocarbons have served as refrigerants, coolants, insulators, and precursors of various foam materials. They are used in an estimated 90 million car and truck air conditioners, 100 million refrigerators, 30 million freezers, and 45 million home and building air conditioners (Machado and Piltz 1988). These gases have received considerable attention in recent years as a result of their role in the depletion of stratospheric ozone, a critical element in screening ultraviolet rays of the sun (Graedel and Crutzen 1989; Watson *et al.* 1990).

In 1987 the Montreal Protocol, which aimed to reduce CFC emissions, was signed by representatives of more than forty industrialized countries. It was revised in June 1990, with the goal of banning the production of CFCs by the year 2000, with a ten-year extension for less-developed countries. The 1990 amendments to the Clean Air Act provide the legal basis for the implementation of these provisions in the United States, by outlawing CFCs by the year 2000 (Joint Select Committee on Toxic Air Emissions and the Greenhouse Effect 1991, p. 68). However, CFCs' very long lifetime will facilitate stratospheric ozone destruction for as much as 100 years.

Unlike stratospheric ozone, which is being destroyed, the concentration of ozone in the lower atmosphere is increasing. Here it acts as an infrared absorber, contributing to global warming. It is produced mainly as a result of emissions from fossil fuel combustion and is the main component of photochemical smog.

The atmosphere also contains certain additional trace

Table 3.1. Carbon Emissions per Unit of GSP—Ten Highest States

State	Total Emissions (million metric tons)	Oil	% of Total Coal	Nat. gas	Tons of Carbon/ $million GSP
West Virginia	28.42	16.9	77.0	6.1	1179
Wyoming	11.63	18.0	72.3	9.7	996
North Dakota	10.39	21.7	74.7	3.7	968
Louisiana	51.73	50.5	8.3	41.2	695
Indiana	49.13	30.0	58.4	11.6	579
Kentucky	30.01	29.4	62.4	8.3	565
Montana	6.32	38.3	52.5	9.2	520
Texas	154.87	50.8	18.7	30.5	510
New Mexico	12.01	32.5	50.3	17.2	509
Arkansas	14.62	41.8	38.4	19.8	462
U.S. TOTAL	1275.30	47.6	33.7	18.7	306

Source: Machado and Piltz 1988, p. 6.

gases that cumulatively make up about 13 percent of the total greenhouse gas composition. These include halon-1211, halon-1301, methyl chloroform, and carbon tetrachloride. These chemicals can be produced in photochemical processing, fire extinguishers, solvents, and CFC production. The atmospheric lifespans and heat absorption capacities of these gases vary, but all are increasing at a rate greater than 1 percent per year.

Greenhouse Gas Emissions in Texas

The underlying cause of global warming is the growing volume of greenhouse gases emitted into the atmosphere. Emissions of these gases are particularly high in Texas, which produces nearly twice as much CO_2 as any other state and more than 10 percent of the U.S. total. If Texas were an independent nation, it would rank seventh in the world in CO_2 production, the same as the United Kingdom, which has more than 3 times the population (Lashof and Washburn 1990). However, when the states are ranked according to tons of CO_2 per unit of gross state product, Texas ranks eighth (Table 3.1).

Table 3.1 includes data on the contribution of each fossil fuel to CO_2 emissions. This information is important, because different fuels produce different amounts of CO_2 per unit of energy generated. For instance, natural gas produces approximately twice as much energy for the same CO_2 emissions as coal. Thus, states that rely heavily on coal have relatively higher CO_2 emissions, and an interim strategy for reducing these emissions could be an increase in the use of natural gas.

In 1988 the industrial sector produced more than one-third (37 percent) of Texas' CO_2 emissions, primarily from the combustion of fossil fuels. Emissions from electric utilities and transportation accounted for 23 and 21 percent, respectively. A further 14 percent of CO_2 emissions came from fuel production, including extraction and refinement of oil and natural gas. However, a significant portion of these emissions are from the petrochemical industries, which account for more than 50 percent of total U.S. petrochemical production. Thus, part of the emissions from extraction and production of these fuels results from producing fuels on behalf of other states.

Oil, which is the major fuel for Texas' industries and transportation, is the source of over half of Texas' CO_2 emissions. Oil extraction, refinement, and combustion produced 52 percent of Texas' carbon emissions in 1988, with natural gas contributing 32 percent and coal 16 percent. In Texas from 1980 to 1988 the use of coal for electricity production doubled, while natural gas use declined. This trend occurred nationally in response to doubts about the sufficiency of natural gas reserves, and government policies that discouraged the use of natural gas. Many of the states that rank higher than Texas in terms of CO_2 production per unit of gross state product also have a large petrochemical industry; others are heavily dependent upon coal (see Table 3.1). California, which ranks second in total carbon emissions, has approximately one-half of the national average when adjusted to tons of CO_2/$million GSP. Seventy-two percent of its emissions are produced from oil; less than 2 percent come from coal (Machado and Piltz 1988).

A detailed inventory of the sources of the major greenhouse gases in Texas has been compiled (Schmandt et al. 1992). The primary sources of the data were the 1988 Renew America report *Reducing the Rate of Global Warming: The State's Role,* and *National- and State-Level Emissions Estimations of Radiately Important Trace Gases from Anthropogenic Sources,* published in 1990 by the U.S. Environmental Protection Agency. Data were also available from reports published by California and Oregon. Some discrepancies were evident between these different sources; for example, between estimates for carbon emission factors for different fuels.

Carbon emissions were estimated using energy consumption figures published in the Energy Information Administration's 1989 *State Energy Data Report* and multiplying these figures by the carbon emission factors calculated by Renew America. Methane emission factors for fuel consumption were taken from the California data. Carbon and methane emissions associated with the mining and production of fuels were also computed. Other greenhouse gas emissions were harder to estimate. For instance, methane emissions from animals were based on the quantity of livestock, as these were the only numbers available; estimates for natural-gas transmission losses varied from 1.59 to 2.37 percent; and methane emission rates for landfills varied greatly in different reports. Other, less significant sources of greenhouse gases that could not be accurately estimated were not included.

A summary of the inventory data compiled for Texas is shown in Table 3.2. The largest source of methane, accounting for more than 50 percent of production in 1988, is leakage incurred in the production and transmission of natural gas. The second largest source is domestic animals, which release methane as a byproduct of digestion, and the third largest source is landfills. Methane emissions declined slightly from 1980 to 1983, with decreasing natural gas production, and have remained fairly constant since that time. CFC-12, used primarily in refrigeration and air conditioning, is Texas' largest source of CFCs. Other types of CFCs are used as blowing agents and in air conditioning.

Greenhouse gases differ in their longevity in the atmosphere and in their ability to trap heat. This makes it difficult to compare the greenhouse effects of similar quantities of different gases, unless the warming potential of each gas is indexed relative to CO_2. In Table 3.2 the total tonnage of carbon, methane, and CFCs has been converted to CO_2 equivalents, assuming a 500-year time horizon. Such a scale accounts for the different atmospheric lifetimes, heat-trapping abilities, and chemical reactivity of each of the gases. The conversion factors were based on those devised by the IPCC (1990).

Table 3.3 shows estimates for emissions in Texas for the years 2000 and 2010 using EPA projections for the rate of in-

Table 3.2. 1988 Greenhouse Gas Emissions in Texas

	Million Short Tons	CO_2 Equiv. Million Short Tons[a]	% of Total CO_2 Equiv. Emissions
Carbon			
Natural gas	68.8	252.2	27.6
Petroleum	113.6	416.6	45.6
Coal	35.1	128.8	14.1
Other	1.6	5.9	0.6
Carbon subtotal	219.1	803.5	88.0
Methane			
Livestock and humans	0.90	8.08	0.9
Landfills	0.57	5.09	0.6
Natural gas leaks	2.00	18.04	2.0
Other	0.39	3.55	0.3
Methane subtotal	3.86	34.76	3.8
CFCs			
CFC-11	0.006	9.6	1.1
CFC-12	0.012	51.9	5.7
HCFC-22	0.006	3.3	0.4
CFC-113	0.004	7.9	0.9
Other CFCs	0.002	2.5	0.3
CFC subtotal	0.030	75.2	8.2
TOTAL		913.5	100.0

[a] Based on a 500-year time horizon.

crease in each of these gases nationally. In predicting these rates of increase, the EPA has taken into account the 1990 Clean Air Act Amendments, Department of Energy initiatives to encourage energy conservation, and other federal initiatives that will affect greenhouse gas emission rates. When the gases are compared on a carbon equivalent scale, it is apparent that CO_2 production is, and will continue to be, the primary contributor to global warming in Texas. Despite population increases, advances in energy efficiency for automobiles and appliances resulted in a constant level of CO_2 emissions in Texas between 1980 and 1988. It appears that this trend is likely to continue. According to Table 3.3, Texas' greenhouse gas emissions are expected to increase 10 percent by the year 2000 and 16 percent by 2010, while population is projected to increase by 40 percent by 2010 (Texas Water Development Board 1990, p. 3-2). With this increase

JUDITH CLARKSON

Table 3.3. Projections for Texas Greenhouse Gas Emissions
(500-Year Time Horizon)

	CO_2 Equivalents (million tons)		
	1987	**2000**	**2010**
Carbon	771.1	884.7	957.7
Methane	33.8	29.9	30.5
CFCs	78.1	54.5	40.0
Total	883.0	969.1	1028.2

in population, it seems likely that greenhouse gas emissions will increase at rates substantially higher than national rates of increase.

Policy Options for Reducing Greenhouse Gas Emissions

Although most environmental legislation is federal, much of the responsibility for implementing the regulations has been transferred to the state level. The federal government will set standards and then rely on individual states to develop their own strategies to meet them. This is particularly true in the area of pollution control and also applies to several programs that encourage more efficient energy use. In response to the 1973 Arab oil embargo, Congress passed the Energy Policy and Conservation Act of 1975, which included the following:

1. created a national infrastructure of state energy offices;

2. set broad national goals and provided funding, but delegated implementation to the states; and

3. required states to document energy savings achieved (NASEO 1991).

This action is significant from two respects. First, while providing a general policy framework, Congress has made it clear that improving energy efficiency and exploring other options for energy generation is primarily the responsibility of the states. In addition, the requirement that energy savings be documented has resulted in a considerable body of knowledge that can now be used by other states in the development of their programs. This approach has merit from several perspectives. In addition to providing flexibility, an advantage in a country as climatically diverse as the United States, it allows for small-scale, state-level experiments in energy conservation that can provide the framework for more extensive programs.

Individual states have the authority to promote energy efficiency through utility regulation, building codes, mass transit, urban planning, and state taxes/rebates. States also have the ability to regulate vehicle emissions, encourage sequestration of carbon dioxide, and promote fuel switching. Through statewide education programs, states can inform the public about the threat of global warming and the part that the individual can play in dealing with the problem. In addition, individual state governments can set an example through their own buying policies, e.g., by buying recycled and recyclable materials wherever possible and ensuring that state car fleets use the most fuel-efficient vehicles. This approach is particularly effective because it contributes to the creation of markets that might otherwise be too small for an effective response from producers. Finally, state congressional delegations can try to influence national policy, by supporting increased Corporate Average Fuel Economy (CAFE) standards or an environmentally sound national energy policy.

In 1989 the EPA awarded a grant to the National Association of State Energy Officials (NASEO) to evaluate some of the programs currently in place. Criteria used in the evaluation were energy savings, CO_2 production avoidance, and cost-effectiveness. The most successful programs were found to be cost-effective, frequently with a pay-back period considerably less than the life of the project. Under these conditions, the programs can be justified on economic terms alone, and the savings in CO_2 emissions are realized at no cost (NASEO 1991). Here we describe and evaluate some examples of the actions taken by other states to increase energy use efficiency and reduce air emissions. The extent to which Texas has implemented similar programs is also discussed.

Transportation

Motor vehicles produce a variety of greenhouse gases. The major component is CO_2, but several other components of vehicular emissions are produced in significant quantities. The most important of these, for the purposes of the current discussion, are nitrogen oxides and volatile organics, which combine to form ozone. Ozone is a major component of smog and also contributes to global warming by acting as an infra-red absorber. Another component, carbon monoxide, pro-longs the life of methane in the atmosphere and is eventually converted to carbon dioxide.

In 1988 Texas consumed 202 million barrels of motor gasoline, putting it second only to California (Energy Information Administration). As a result, Texas emitted 38.8 trillion tons of CO_2 in 1988 from vehicle usage (21 percent of Texas CO_2 emissions). In 1986 Texas' vehicles averaged only 14 miles per gallon of gasoline (Machado and Piltz 1988). Several mechanisms are available for reducing greenhouse gas emissions from vehicles, including reducing the amount of fuel consumed and controlling gaseous emissions. The former includes increasing the fuel efficiency of vehicles, en-couraging multiple occupancy of vehicles, and considering a wider range of criteria in transportation planning.

Currently, manufacturers of new passenger cars sold in the United States are subject to CAFE standards, which require that the vehicles meet a fuel economy standard of 27.5 mpg. Various proposals have been considered in Con-gress, including one to increase this level to 40 mpg by the year 2001. Economic analyses have shown that there are less-expensive ways to achieve energy conservation and reduce greenhouse gas emissions. It has been estimated that a gaso-line tax of 27.5 cents imposed over 5 years would achieve the same petroleum and CO_2 savings through 2003 at less than one-quarter the cost. A carbon tax reaching $20 per ton of carbon would have a comparable effect on CO_2 emissions at an even lower cost, because it spreads the burden over a larger number of consumers and producers. Still more cost-effective are transportation management policies that dis-courage driving alone. Such policies could save as much as 100,000 barrels of petroleum per day and are especially ame-nable to implementation at the state level (Charles River Associates Inc. 1991, p. 7).

Connecticut has decreased traffic congestion, reduced air pollution, cut CO_2 by 83,000 tons per year, and saved almost 9 million gallons of gasoline annually—all through car pool-ing. Three ride share organizations have set up 12,000 car pools and 180 van pools (EPA 1991). Washington State is also promoting alternatives to riding alone. Employers must pro-vide incentives for employees to move away from single oc-cupancy vehicles—through encouragement of car pools, van pools, and bicycles, and through increased parking charges. Washington is also providing high-occupancy-vehicle lanes and park-and-ride facilities. As of 1987, 16 states funded ride-sharing programs (Ibid.). While Texas was the first state to develop a ride-share program, it has given it little attention since the mid 1980's, when low oil prices resulted in a reduction in public demand.

A program implemented in California and evaluated by the NASEO is a traffic flow management scheme that involved the retiming of 1,535 traffic signals. The program is estimated to have saved 6.4 million gallons of fuel (6 percent), $8 million (as compared with program costs of $2 million), and, assuming all of the fuel was gasoline, nearly 625 tons of CO_2 emissions. Other, indirect societal savings associated with less vehicular wear and reduced travel time could amount to as much as $424 million (NASEO 1991). Statewide, Texas has spent approximately $10 million on programs designed to synchronize traffic lights in metropolitan areas.

Another means of reducing greenhouse gases from transportation sources is through use of alternative fuels. However, fuels vary in their effectiveness in reducing greenhouse gases and this is highly dependent on how they are produced. For example, electric vehicles that are recharged primarily from coal plants will increase greenhouse gas emissions. Those fuels reducing emissions include natural gas, electric vehicles recharged from natural gas plants or renewable energy, and fuels produced from biomass—methanol or ethanol. Use of solar energy and fuel cells can also produce net reductions in greenhouse gases, but their use is dependent upon continued technological improvements over the next 10–20 years. Alcohol fuels (methanol and ethanol) range from no improvement to increased greenhouse gas emissions, depending upon how they are produced. Methanol is generally produced from natural gas and results in a slight reduction in greenhouse related emissions. Ethanol produced from biomass greatly reduces emissions, but ethanol produced from corn or grain, as is the general practice, results in no net improvement (DeLuchi et al. 1988).

Currently, many fleet vehicles in Texas are in the process of being converted to natural gas. Legislation passed by the Texas legislature in 1989 requires school districts, state agencies, and metropolitan transit authorities to convert 30 percent of their fleet by 1994. If the TACB determines that this policy is effective in reducing air pollution and that more conversions are necessary to improve air quality, 50 percent of the vehicles must be converted by 1996, and 90 percent by

1998 (Senate Bill 740). In addition, local governments and private fleets in nonattainment areas will be required to convert 30 percent of their fleet by 1998 (Senate Bill 769). If these programs were adopted by other states, Texas would benefit from the expansion of the compressed natural gas market—a key growth industry for Texas.

Industry

As the emission inventory shows, industrial processes are the largest producers of CO_2 in Texas, producing more than one-third of the state's CO_2 emissions. State government can promote reductions in industrial emissions by encouraging industrial energy conservation, requiring mandatory CO_2 offsets, or regulating greenhouse gases as pollutants.

If Texas industry can be encouraged to introduce improved energy efficiency programs that cut production costs—and coincidentally CO_2 emissions—then Texas would increase its competitiveness, both within the United States and with the Japanese and the Europeans, who are already further advanced in energy efficient production. Currently, the United States uses 50 percent more energy to make a ton of crude steel than Japan, and twice as much energy to make a ton of cement as West Germany (World Resources Institute 1990). Cost-effective energy efficiency improvements have the potential to cut U.S. industrial energy use by 10 percent through more efficient equipment (motors, lights, pipes, and pumps) and manufacturing processes.

Several states have already begun programs to advise industries about energy efficiency opportunities. Particularly noteworthy is the New York State Energy Advisory Service to Industry. Under this program, all businesses are eligible to receive technical energy audits (usually conducted by retired engineers) and recommendations for energy efficiency improvements. A zero-interest loan program for making these improvements is financed by the state oil overcharge fund. This successful program has saved industry $50 million annually in energy costs (EPA 1991). The New York State Energy Office once estimated a benefit-cost ratio of 20:1 and savings in CO_2 emission of 400 tons annually (NASEO 1991).

Agriculture

Using oil overcharge funds and the state's agricultural extension service, Georgia has developed programs to help the agriculture industry save energy. An energy efficiency audit program for irrigation has helped farmers save more than $3.5 million annually and has eliminated 50,000 tons of CO_2 each year. Another program helps farmers use "waste" heat in fresh milk to heat wash water in the dairy. Together, Georgia's agriculture energy programs have helped to avoid the generation of an estimated 95,000 tons of CO_2 per year (EPA 1991).

Several agricultural demonstration projects are currently being funded by the Governor's Office in Texas. In the Texas High Plains, average overall efficiencies of irrigation pumps were found to be 32 percent below optimal, and most irrigators could lower energy use by 25 percent through equipment adjustment and repairs. The current program will determine to what extent these improvements could be realized in areas outside the High Plains. Other programs are designed to improve the performance of various production systems, including the cleaning and drying of cotton, crop harvesting, and pecan production, through more informed pest-management decisions.

Saving energy in field operations often results in savings in other agricultural inputs such as water, pesticides, and fertilizers. Reducing the quantity of these inputs not only generates additional cost savings but has significant environmental benefits.

Electricity Use

Utilities are the second largest source of Texas' CO_2 emissions (23 percent). Recent studies demonstrate that U.S. electricity demand could be reduced by at least 25 percent using currently available technologies. Texas could promote electricity conservation through rate restructuring and improvements in the energy efficiency of buildings and appliances. Many of these policies could be financed, at least in the short term, through the Oil Overcharge Fund, which currently provides money for the Low Income Weatherization Assistance Program, the State Energy Conservation Program, the Energy Extension Service, and the Institutional Conservation Program.

There must be incentives for electric utilities to invest in programs that increase generation efficiency and reduce consumer demand. In California, for example, a utility's rate of return depends on its progress in promoting end-use efficiency and acquiring cost-effective sources of generating capacity (Ibid.). Currently, electric utility rates in Texas are set by the Public Utility Commission. And, while provisions do exist to encourage the promotion of end-use efficiency by utilities, few have implemented aggressive programs to this end. In addition, integrated resource planning, which includes energy conservation programs, has not been adopted by all utilities in Texas. This approach would, however, benefit from an integrated statewide effort initiated by the Public Utility Commission.

The energy efficiency of existing buildings can be improved by encouraging improvements in heating, lighting, air conditioning, and insulation efficiency through loans, rebates, tax credits, or information programs. An Illinois program that provides grants and low-interest loans for home energy efficiency improvements has reduced CO_2 emissions by more than 5,200 tons per year. Iowa is working to install all cost-effective energy efficiency improvements in the state's schools, hospitals, nonprofit organizations, and state and local government buildings. In 1990, Iowa's program decreased CO_2 emissions by 86,167 tons—an average of 125 tons for each of 691 school buildings (National Governors' Association 1991).

In Arizona's Seniors Helping Seniors program, senior citizens weatherize homes for other senior citizens. Since 1982, over 10,000 homes have been weatherized, saving an estimated $2 million in utility costs. Financed by oil overcharge and utility funds, Ohio's weatherization program relies on community organizations to weatherize homes of low-income families. In a 3-year period, 23,000 homes were weatherized, resulting in a 14 percent energy savings with weatherization alone, and an additional 7 percent with the education of homeowners in energy efficient practices (EPA 1991). As of 1987, Texas had weatherized only 3 percent of its low-income homes (Machado and Piltz 1988).

State governments can save tax dollars by making government buildings models of energy efficiency. It is estimated that Texas could save $20 million a year in the state budget if state buildings were completely retrofitted. Texas has, in fact, made considerable progress in improving energy use efficiency in a number of significant areas. The New York technical energy audits described earlier were modeled on a similar program initiated in Texas in the early 1980's. At this time, federal funds were available to assist in the development of energy conservation programs, and both the private and public sector were beneficiaries. With a reduction in federal funds during the Reagan administration, the scope of the program was reduced, and since 1987, only the public sector has received this type of assistance, financed by oil overcharge funds. To date, $300 million in state funds has been dedicated to this effort.

Policy Options for Texas

State action, however crucial, is not a substitute for federal action. As the report *Reducing the Rate of Global Warming: The States' Role* concludes: "States can initiate models of effective programs, but a strong federal presence is required to ensure that all states implement effective policies" (Ibid.). In addition, there are certain policy options that states cannot take unilaterally and remain economically competitive; these policies are best pursued by the federal government. For example, a charge based on the carbon content of specific fossil fuels would most likely be passed on to the consumer in the costs of finished products and would place an unfair burden on any one state instituting such a carbon tax on its own. (Indeed, such a charge may have to be part of an international system.) Similarly, standards regarding the fuel efficiency of vehicles or the energy efficiency of household appliances would be most easily applied at the point of manufacture by the federal government.

However, as the previous section demonstrates, there is a whole range of energy-saving measures that are cost-effective, even if the only benefit considered is the avoided energy cost. In many cases the projects pay for themselves long before the effective life of the program or equipment expires, and the additional benefit of reducing CO_2 emissions is literally without cost. Often all that is needed to implement such programs is a pool of money for capital expenditures or low-interest loans. Texas has had a number of state-financed revolving funds, and these could be used as a model for similar energy-conservation programs.

Texas has made a good start in developing energy-saving measures. Many programs were initiated by the Governor's Energy Office in the early 1980's, and some of them continue to realize significant energy savings throughout the state. Some of the programs died as federal funds were withdrawn, and others were victims of low energy prices in the 1980's.

JUDITH CLARKSON

64

Nevertheless, the 1991 Energy Savings Report, submitted to the Department of Energy as a requirement of the Energy Policy and Conservation Act of 1975, documents statewide annual savings of 211 trillion BTU (equivalent to 36 million barrels of oil). Nineteen program areas were evaluated, of which four account for the largest savings: industrial efficiency program (16.0 percent); local government energy program (20.5 percent); thermal efficiency standards (31.2 percent); and lighting efficiency standards (14.9 percent).

With increasing energy costs and fewer resources, at both the personal and government level, saving energy is not only wise environmental policy but also good economics. Reducing input costs for the agricultural and industrial sectors of the state will improve the competitiveness of Texas' products in the marketplace. Our competitors in Japan and Europe use less than half the energy we use for some manufacturing processes. One of the factors contributing to the high energy-intensity of this society is the considerable subsidies associated with energy use. The many examples of this include government expenditures for defense to protect oil imports, infrastructure maintenance associated with transportation, and the failure to account for the health and environmental costs of air pollution.

As pressure to improve energy efficiency and reduce greenhouse gas emissions increases, Texas has an opportunity to evaluate the role that it can play in the policy debate. By taking an active part, Texas can help to shape the policy options with its own interests in mind. The Texas economy is heavily dependent on the energy sector, and energy taxes that affect producers could have an adverse impact. On the other hand, an interim strategy for reducing CO_2 emissions is the increased use of natural gas. As a major exporter of natural gas, Texas would be a beneficiary of policies aimed at substituting natural gas for other fuels in vehicles, steam generators, and heating units. In addition, Texas could position itself to take advantage of opportunities to develop and manufacture new, energy-efficient technologies. Texas is well placed to take advantage of new markets, especially those likely to open up in Mexico with the implementation of the North America Free Trade Agreement.

The United States, which produces more than 20 percent of worldwide anthropogenic CO_2 emissions, has an obligation to develop policies to limit its reliance on fossil fuels. Reducing CO_2 emissions through energy conservation is a realistic goal. Many states have demonstrated the economic feasibility of such measures, and Texas could take a more aggressive approach to the problem. Until such time as national and international policies are implemented, however, emphasis should be placed on cost-effectiveness and overall economic benefits.

References

Charles River Associates Inc., 1991. Policy Alternatives for Reducing Petroleum Use and Greenhouse Gas Emissions, Final Report.

DeLuchi, M. A., R. A. Johnston, and D. Sperling, 1988. Transportation Fuels and the Greenhouse Effect. *Transportation Research Record* 1175:33–44.

Energy Information Administration, various years. Selected excerpts from *State Energy Data Report*.

Environmental Protection Agency (EPA), 1991. *Selected Summary of Current State Responses to Climate Change.*

Goldemberg, J., 1992. Global Climate Change: The Role of Developing Countries. In: *The Regions and Global Warming, Impacts and Response Strategies*, J. Schmandt and J. Clarkson (eds.). Oxford University Press, New York.

Graedel, T. E., and P. J. Crutzen, 1989. The Changing Atmosphere. *Scientific American* 261(3):58–68.

IPCC, 1990. *Climate Change: The IPCC Scientific Assessment.* Cambridge University Press, Cambridge, U.K.

Joint Select Committee on Toxic Air Emissions and the Greenhouse Effect, Interim Report Presented to the 72d Legislature, January 1991. Austin, Texas.

Lashof, D., and E. Washburn, 1990. *The Statehouse Effect: State Policies to Cool the Greenhouse.* Natural Resources Defense Council, Washington, D.C.

Machado, S., and R. Piltz, 1988. *Reducing the Rate of Global Warming: The State's Role.* Renew America, Washington, D.C.

National Association of State Energy Officials (NASEO), 1991. *Energy Efficiency and Renewable Energy: Economical CO_2 Mitigation Strategies.* Report on the Pilot Phase, EPA/NASEO Joint Project.

National Governors' Association, 1991. *Environmental Research and Technical Assistance Report*, Winter report.

Schmandt, J., S. Hadden, and G. Ward, 1992. *Texas and Global Warming: Emissions, Surface Water Supplies and Sea Level Rise.* University of Texas at Austin.

Texas Water Development Board (TWDB), 1990. *Water for Texas: Today and Tomorrow.* TWDB, Austin.

JUDITH CLARKSON

66

Watson, R. T., H. Rodhe, H. Oeschger, and U. Siegenthaler, 1990. Greenhouse Gases and Aerosols. In: *Climate Change: The IPCC Scientific Assessment.* Cambridge University Press, Cambridge, U.K.

World Resources Institute, 1990. *The Greenhouse Trap*, a World Resources guide to the environment. Beacon Press, Boston.

4. Water Resources

Texas exhibits a variety of climates, soil types, and vegetational communities, all of which combine to result in a concomitant variety of subregional water resources. As available water resources determine the limits of water supply, and thereby circumscribe human activities, this is a fundamental aspect of the Texas environment. These water resources are also directly affected by climate change. It is the potential alterations in water supply due to a change in climate that are of greatest concern for Texas. As we will show, much of Texas is already exploiting the available water resource to its limit; any further limitation or diminishment will have profound economic and social impacts.

The central or driving factor in water planning and management in Texas is the drought. Water supply is predicated on what can be dependably available during the "worst" drought condition. The volume of water that can be removed from a water-supply source during drought conditions is its *firm yield*, and water is allocated on a firm yield basis. The key notion is the *worst drought*, which present practice defines as the most intense drought that has occurred during the period for which weather data are available, the *drought of record*.

From an engineering and water-management viewpoint, this has the considerable advantage of basing water management on real events—for which meteorological and hydrological measurements are available, and whose effects have been actually demonstrated—rather than on a theoretical construct. Using a recorded event for planning purposes is particularly advantageous from a policy standpoint. Water development is also highly political, involving large expenditures and the sacrifice of land for the creation of reservoirs. It is far easier to argue such actions based upon a real drought event rather than an abstract possibility.

However, use of the drought of record also presents an important disadvantage: we are effectively assuming that the most intense drought to have occurred in our relatively short period of data collection (about 50 years for most rivers in Texas—at most, 100 years) is the very worst that nature can bestow upon us. If our assumption is correct and we design our reservoirs and water supplies to accommodate that level of drought severity, then we will be all right. However, given the existing variability of Texas climate, this assumption may be untrustworthy, and climate change may well increase the severity of extreme drought. For most of Texas, the drought of record is in the 1950's. During this decade, especially during the first 6–7 years, rainfall events were sparse in time and limited in magnitude, leading to a cumulative surface-water shortage that was an economic disaster for the state. Any drought is measured by the combination of its intensity, i.e., the deficit below normal of rainfall, and its duration (the period over which the rainfall deficit is prolonged). The 1950's drought was especially severe because of both its intensity and its duration of nearly 7 years.

Availability and Disposition of Fresh Water

Sources of Water

The present chapter focuses on availability of fresh water, i.e., water with sufficiently low dissolved solids that it can be used for human and animal consumption, for the various agricultural and industrial enterprises, and for the wide suite of biological processes that require water of this quality. Water sources in Texas are broadly categorized into surface water and groundwater. Surface water encompasses all of the watercourses on the surface of the land in which water flows or is accumulated. This includes streams and rivers, lakes and reservoirs, and under certain conditions may even include the coastal embayments.

One implication of the basic character of Texas' climate is that most of the precipitation in Texas is of convective origin. Texas does not accumulate a winter mass of snow which slowly melts in the spring, feeding lakes and rivers, nor is Texas subjected to long-lasting stratiform weather systems that sustain moderate-intensity but prolonged rainfall over large regions. Rather, Texas' precipitation is derived from deep-convecting storm systems and individual thunderstorm cells. Precipitation, consequently, is locally intense but short-lived: rainfall is intense when it occurs, but of brief du-

GEORGE WARD
AND
JUAN B. VALDES

Figure 4.1.
Location of major
reservoirs in Texas
(Texas Department
of Water
Resources 1984).

ration. As this precipitation falls on the surface and is orga-
nized into stream and river channels, the corresponding river
flows are "flashy," with pronounced peaks in flow separated
by long periods of low stream flow.

Because river flows are not dependable, this variability
poses a major problem in using surface water for water
supply. At any time, there may be too much or too little river
flow to provide a supply of water. This problem is dealt with
through the construction of dams, which impound reservoirs
that capture some of the higher flows of the rivers and hold
this water for use during dry periods. The reservoir is the cor-
nerstone of Texas' water resources. Nowhere in Texas is
there any significant use of uncontrolled, run-of-the-river
flow as water supply. Texas has 188 existing major reservoirs
and 3 under construction, each with a storage capacity of
more than 5,000 acre-feet. They have a total storage capacity
of 37.1 million acre-feet (maf), allocated for various purposes,
including water supply. A total of 17.9 maf (48 percent) is
used for flood protection. (This flood-protection allocation of

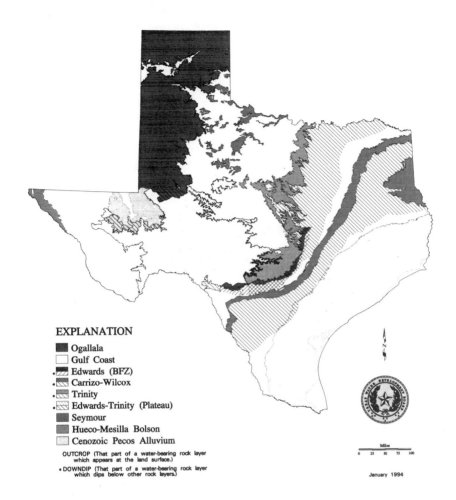

EXPLANATION

- ■ Ogallala
- ☐ Gulf Coast
- .▨ Edwards (BFZ)
- .▨ Carrizo-Wilcox
- .▨ Trinity
- .▨ Edwards-Trinity (Plateau)
- ■ Seymour
- ■ Hueco-Mesilla Bolson
- ☐ Cenozoic Pecos Alluvium

OUTCROP (That part of a water-bearing rock layer
  which appears at the land surface.)
• DOWNDIP (That part of a water-bearing rock layer
  which dips below other rock layers.)

Miles
0   25   50   75   100

January 1994

capacity is based upon a design flood of some prescribed rarity, with the result that the reservoir may not provide protection for a flood of arbitrary size, as the recent floods of 1989, 1990, and 1991 have shown.) The dependable water supply is about 11 maf, which is 30 percent of the total storage capacity available (Texas Water Development Board 1990). Figure 4.1 shows the location of major reservoirs in Texas.

Groundwater is the water contained in permeable rock formations, called *aquifers*. Nine major and 20 minor aquifers provide important water-supply sources in Texas (Ibid.). The major aquifers are shown in Figure 4.2. The influx of water to an aquifer, referred to as *recharge*, comes from infiltration and percolation from the surface. The extent to which an aquifer is recharged is strongly dependent upon the over-

Figure 4.2.
Location of major aquifers in Texas (Texas Department of Water Resources 1984).

lying strata, the nature of the land surface and soils, and the hydroclimatology of the recharge area.

Water Use

In discussing water use, we distinguish between withdrawal and consumption. *Withdrawal* means the removal of water from a surface water or groundwater resource for some purpose (the term *diversion* is synonymous). Once water is withdrawn and used, it may be returned to the water resource as a *return flow*. For example, municipal water use entails a withdrawal for water supply and a return flow of treated wastewater. Of course, the quality of the two may be very different, and contamination can delimit further use of the water. This discussion views water supply in Texas from a broad perspective with the focus on water volume; we therefore disregard water quality issues and consider a return flow to be a credit to the available water resource. (This will be qualified further in discussion of specific uses.) Water *consumption* means that the water is permanently removed from the water resource. The difference between withdrawal and return flow for a specific use is the water consumption of that use. Water that is consumed generally is emitted back to the atmosphere in some form and may find its way back into the water supply through precipitation. But the accounting of water supply disregards such consumed water for the simple reason that it is no longer available for water supply.

Many human activities require the use of water in large volumes. For present purposes, these are treated in three broad categories. The first is combined municipal and industrial use. These are combined because the two are generally associated with large population centers in Texas. This category includes personal water consumption and domestic use, as well as water used as part of an industrial process. The principal return flow is treated wastewater. Advancements in wastewater treatment technology have resulted in significant improvements in the quality of such return flows.

The second broad category is agriculture, including both crop production and ranching. The dominant water use in this category on a statewide basis is irrigation, which involves the diversion of enormous volumes of water for placement on soil. Some of this returns to the surface water system through the process of runoff (see below), but much of it ends up in the atmosphere, evaporating directly from the soil or being transpired as a byproduct of plant metabolism.

GEORGE WARD
AND
JUAN B. VALDES

(Some of Texas' most insidious water quality problems are associated with agricultural return flows, which contain elevated nutrient and pesticide levels.)

The third category of water use is electric-power generation, or more specifically, steam-electric generation. Steam-electric generation is the dominant form of power generation in Texas and involves exploiting the thermodynamics of evaporation and condensation of pure water to create high-pressure steam for spinning turbines. In the process, this steam is recondensed by the use of large volumes of cooling water drawn from the surface water supply. Cooling water returned to the surface resource is altered only by its increase in temperature. This excess heat is quickly dissipated to the atmosphere, and the water can be reused for cooling. In fact, many of the steam-electric plants in Texas are situated on a dedicated reservoir, continuously reusing the water for cooling, a closed-cycle process.

There are, of course, other uses of water, such as recreation, but the three categories listed above dominate water use in Texas. We also note that these categories refer strictly to water used by people. The maintenance of natural ecosystems, notably the rivers and lakes in the interior of the state and the estuaries along the Texas coast, requires a dependable flow of water. Maintaining the integrity of these ecosystems is also important for the economy of the state. This issue is explored in more detail in Chap. 5.

Regional Water Budgets

A valuable technique for analyzing the uses of water is a *water budget*. As the name implies, this is an accounting of water transfers, analogous in many respects to financial management, in which the sources and disposition of money are identified. A water budget similarly analyzes the different compartments or accounts of water and the transfers among them. A water budget is carried out for some well-defined region in space and integrated over some definite period of time. In this context, we will present water budgets closed over the entire state or in large subregions of the state. Clearly, water budgets can be closed for smaller and smaller units, e.g., a river basin, a county, a city, or even an agricultural field or house and lot, depending upon the purposes of the analysis.

Unlike a financial budget, however, there is little documentation of the transfers of water, nor are there records of

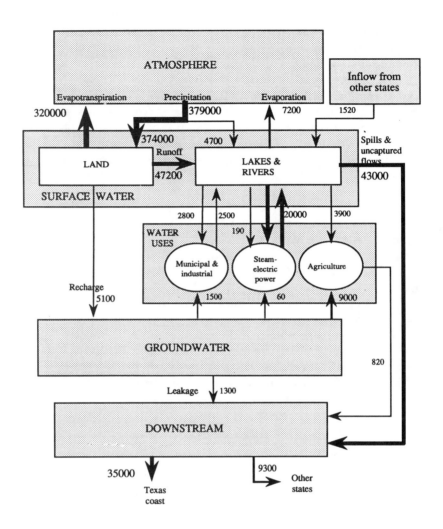

ATMOSPHERE

Inflow from
other states

Evapotranspiration   Precipitation   Evaporation
320000   379000   7200   1520

374000   4700   Spills &
Runoff   uncaptured
LAND   LAKES &   flows
47200   RIVERS   43000

SURFACE WATER

2800   2500   20000   3900

WATER
USES   190

Municipal &   Steam-
industrial   electric   Agriculture
power

Recharge
5100   1500   60   9000

GROUNDWATER

820

Leakage   1300

DOWNSTREAM

35000   9300
                                            Other
Texas   states
coast

Figure 4.3.
Water budget
transfers
(thousands of acre-
feet), aggregated
for entire state
of Texas.

GEORGE WARD
AND
JUAN B. VALDES

74

the balance in the different water accounts. These must be
discovered by direct measurement, by inference from meteorological or hydrological principles, or by posing and testing
alternative assumptions. Closing a water budget can become
a challenging scientific endeavor, and the results are frequently unexpected.

An approximate water budget for Texas is shown in Figure 4.3. The principal pools or compartments of water are the
large rectangles. The atmosphere is, of course, the ultimate
source of water, through precipitation. Groundwater and surface water are the two sources of water supply. The land,
which includes the surface of the earth and the soil, plays an
extremely important role in the disposition of precipitation,

though its water retention is too transient and diffuse to act as a water supply source; water contained in the soil is sub-surface water, but is distinguished from groundwater for this reason. In the present context, we regard the land compart-ment as a "processor" of water.

The transfer of water from one compartment to another is indicated in Figure 4.3 by the arrows, and the magnitude of that transfer is shown by the number attached to the arrow. The units are thousands of acre-feet per year, but the units are less important for this discussion than the relative size of the transfers. To emphasize this, the larger transfers are shown by larger and bolder numerals. Details on the sources of data and the analyses underlying this water budget, as well as more technical information on the transfers themselves, are given in Ward (1992).

Rainfall supplies roughly 379 maf of water to Texas per year, of which about 1 percent falls directly on lakes and riv-ers. The remainder of the influx to the lakes and rivers of the state must traverse the land surface, a process referred to as *runoff*. Most of the precipitation falling on the land surface—nearly 90 percent statewide—does not make it to a surface water body but is intercepted by a complex of processes, most importantly direct evaporation back into the atmo-sphere or uptake by plants and subsequent transpiration. The efficiency of the runoff process is very low, therefore, and is a strong function of terrain, soils and near-surface geology, vegetation, and antecedent conditions. With respect to the last, the runoff produced from a rainstorm is greatly reduced if the surface is desiccated, a characteristic of arid regions and of drought conditions when there are long separations between storm events. One measure of this efficiency of run-off is the ratio of runoff per unit of rainfall for a watershed area. Figure 4.4 displays the distribution of this runoff:rain-fall ratio for the state. Clearly, as one progresses westward into the more arid sections of the state, the ratio drops pre-cipitously. Of course, this figure is based upon data averaged over many years. In a drought situation, the contours of this ratio would shift eastward.

A small amount of the precipitation incident upon the land, about 10 percent of the runoff, eventually infiltrates to the groundwater. However, approximately twice this amount is withdrawn from the groundwater for human con-sumption. On balance, then, there is a net overdraft of the state's groundwater resource. Since the volume of water po-tentially available from groundwater is finite, this chronic

Figure 4.4.
Runoff: rainfall
ratios across the
state of Texas.

GEORGE WARD
AND
JUAN B. VALDES

76

overdraft is of great concern for future water planning in the state.

Water demand is shown in Figure 4.3 by the ovals corresponding to the three broad categories discussed above: agriculture, which includes ranching; municipal and industrial, combined because the two are usually associated with population centers; and steam-electric power generation. An inspection of this water budget, crude as it is, reveals several, perhaps surprising facts about water use in Texas. First, of the total runoff flowing into the reservoirs, only about 10 percent is removed for all human uses (a net 4,390 thousand acre-feet per year withdrawn, compared to 47,200 runoff). This is because the reservoirs are able to capture only a portion of the flood flows of the rivers; the rest flows through (or over) the dams and, ultimately, to the Gulf of Mexico. Next, we note that municipal (and industrial) withdrawals are offset by a return flow of over 80 percent of the volume withdrawn. We also note that there is an enormous withdrawal required for steam-electric generation (roughly 20,000 thousand acre-feet per year). This is, in fact, the largest single diverter of water in the state, but this water is almost entirely returned to the surface water resource. Thus, while the actual consumption of water for power generation is minuscule in comparison to total consumption, electric power requires the availability of a large volume of throughflow. The next largest category of withdrawal is for agricultural purposes. This is the dominant consumer of water in the state, approximately six times the total consumption of all other uses combined.

Two of the most significant inferences to be drawn from this water budget merit special comment. The first is that, from a water supply viewpoint, Texas is primarily a groundwater state: in terms of net withdrawals (i.e., with credit for agricultural, municipal, and industrial return flows), the groundwater withdrawal is over twice that from surface supplies. The second is that runoff is more than ample to meet the surface water requirements of the state. Both inferences are misleading. The problem is the geographical variation in the elements of the water budget. This is demonstrated by performing a similar water budget on subregions of Texas.

For this purpose, following Ward (1992), the state has been subdivided into four regions based upon climate, hydrology, and economic activity, as shown in Figure 4.5. While each of these regions is far from homogeneous in climate, vegetation, and hydrology, as a group they generally characterize the range in hydroclimatology of the state. Separate water budgets for each of these regions are presented in Figures 4.6–4.9. A quick inspection of these figures will make the differences in the water budgets immediately apparent. (The names of the regions apply only in the present context and only poorly approximate the usual geographic terminologies.)

The High Plains region, Figure 4.6, accounts for 70 percent of the groundwater withdrawal of the entire state, predominantly for agriculture. With only 7 percent of the population, the other uses in this region are minor at best. The source for this enormous volume of groundwater withdrawal is a single remarkable resource, the Ogallala formation. The recharge is negligible compared to the withdrawal. Thus, the Ogallala is a finite resource, from a water supply viewpoint, that can only decline monotonically until depleted. There are also reservoirs in the High Plains, but runoff is quite low as a consequence of the arid climate. The reservoirs principally supply some of the municipal demands of the region. Clearly,

HIGH
PLAINS

EAST

CENTRAL

SOUTH

Figure 4.5.
Hydroclimatological
regions of Texas
used in water
budget analysis.

the available runoff, even if totally captured (probably a physical impossibility), cannot begin to replace the Ogallala. Once the Ogallala is exhausted, the economy of this region will change drastically. The High Plains region is virtually isolated from the rest of the state's water budget, both as a source and a sink of water, but its inclusion in the state averages of Figure 4.3 greatly distorts the interpretation of that water budget. If the High Plains groundwater withdrawal is deleted from Figure 4.3, then Texas is revealed to be very dependent upon surface water.

At the other extreme of the spectrum, the East Texas region, shown in Figure 4.7, has about the same population as that of the High Plains, virtually no groundwater usage, and about 15 times the runoff. Indeed, on an areal basis, this region has the greatest runoff rate of the state and is, therefore, the most water rich. Some of the water captured in reservoirs, and most of the electric power, is exported to the more populous regions of the state. The central concern, amounting to a fixation, of water supply engineering in Texas for at

GEORGE WARD
AND
JUAN B. VALDES

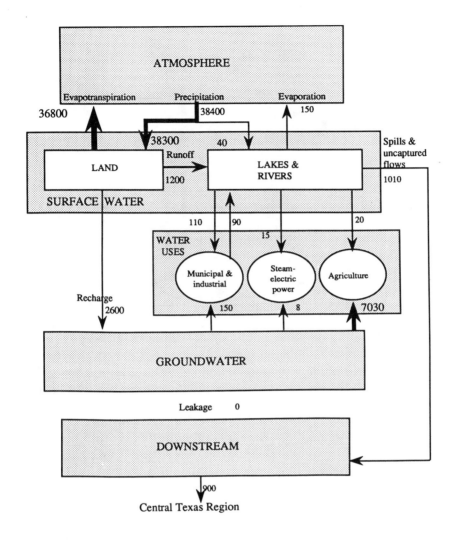

least 4 decades has been devising a means of transporting water from this water-rich region to regions where demand exceeds supply.

The Central Texas region, Figure 4.8, contains the principal population centers of the state and most of its industrial capacity. The groundwater withdrawal for agricultural and municipal use is dominated by one formation: the Edwards aquifer in south-central Texas. (The Edwards is the sole municipal water supply for the city of San Antonio, a fact that has erupted as a political issue in recent years because of competing demands for this water, both for agricultural irrigation farther west and for maintenance of spring and river

Figure 4.6.
Water budget transfers (thousands of acre-feet), High Plains region.

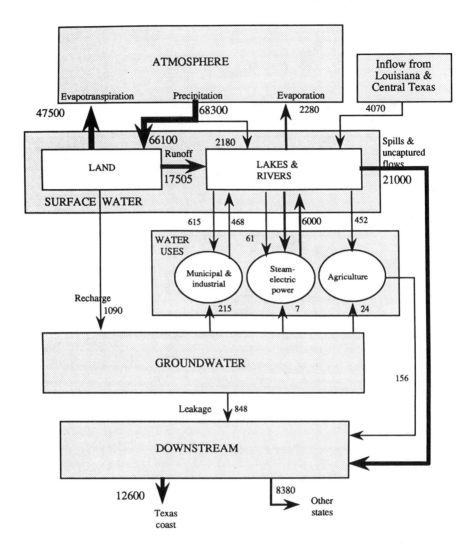

ATMOSPHERE

Inflow from
Louisiana &
Central Texas

Evapotranspiration   Precipitation   Evaporation
47500   68300   2280   4070

66100   2180
Runoff   LAKES &   Spills &
LAND   RIVERS   uncaptured
17505   flows
                                         21000

SURFACE WATER

615   468   61   6000   452

WATER
USES

Municipal &   Steam-   Agriculture
industrial   electric
                power

Recharge
1090   215   7   24

GROUNDWATER

156

Leakage   848

DOWNSTREAM

12600   8380
                              Other
Texas   states
coast

Figure 4.7.
Water budget
transfers
(thousands of acre-
feet), East Texas.

GEORGE WARD
AND
JUAN B. VALDES

80

flow.) While the runoff in total volume exceeds that of the East Texas region, the runoff per unit area is considerably less. Reservoirs are the essential element of water supply in this region.

Finally, South Texas (Figure 4.9) includes the vast semitropical areas of the Nueces and Rio Grande basins and is the most arid region of the state, with substantial areas of desert in the west. Groundwater usage for agriculture is dominated by withdrawals from the Edwards aquifer in the Winter Garden. Agricultural irrigation in the Rio Grande Valley is the dominant use of surface water, supplied mainly from the Rio

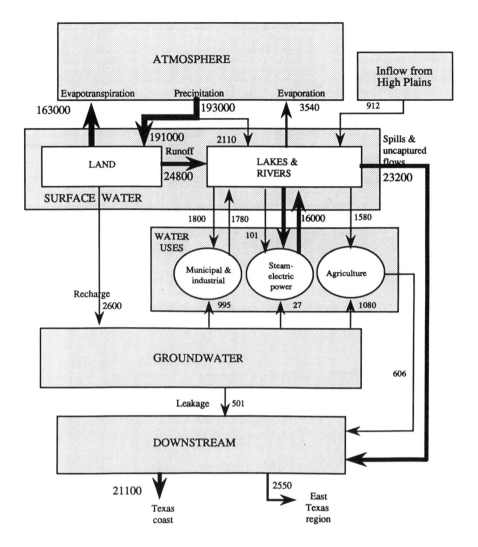

Figure 4.8.
Water budget
transfers
(thousands of
acre-feet),
Central Texas.

Grande reservoir system of Falcon and Amistad. The most significant feature of this region's water budget is the high ratio of reservoir supply to runoff. In other regions, this ratio is at least an order of magnitude, e.g., somewhat less than 10 percent in Central Texas. In South Texas, net surface water withdrawal is over 50 percent of the runoff. Unlike the other regional water budgets, this one cannot be closed reliably for influxes from out of state. Most of the watershed is located in Mexico, and the majority of the flow of the Rio Grande is from the Rio Conchos. Good data are not available on Mexican diversions, and diversions from the Rio Grande

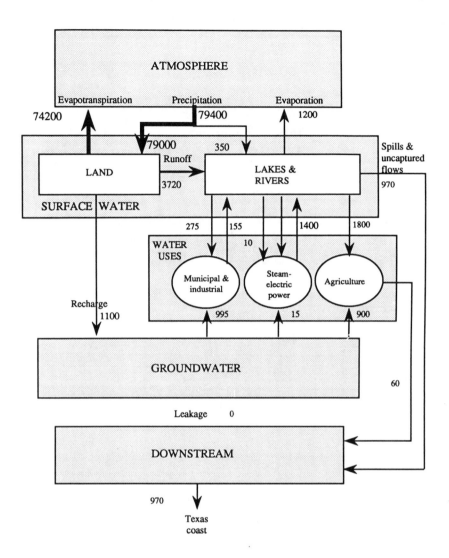

ATMOSPHERE

Evapotranspiration — 74200

Precipitation — 79400

Evaporation — 1200

79000

350

LAND

Runoff 3720

LAKES & RIVERS

SURFACE WATER

Spills & uncaptured flows 970

275 | 155 | 1400 | 1800

WATER USES

10

Municipal & industrial

Steam-electric power

Agriculture

Recharge 1100

995 | 15 | 900

GROUNDWATER

60

Leakage 0

DOWNSTREAM

970 → Texas coast

Figure 4.9.
Water budget
transfers
(thousands of acre-
feet), South Texas.

GEORGE WARD
AND
JUAN B. VALDES

to Mexico are not included. The water budget of Figure 4.9 considers only the sources of runoff within Texas and the withdrawals for Texas users.

Several facts about Texas water supply emerge from the foregoing analysis. First, there is a substantial regional variation in the water budget, from the water-rich, low-usage East to the arid South, where water demands approach a major portion of the runoff. Second, Texas is critically dependent upon its surface water resources for meeting water demands. Third, much of the runoff in all regions of the state flows uncaptured to the coast or to other states, a consequence of the flashiness of runoff in the convective-dominated climatology. Moreover, these water budgets were closed for the long-term average conditions in the state. Under drought conditions, the Central, South, and High Plains regions become even more stressed. Detailed analyses of the 1950–1956 drought period are given in Ward (1992), who finds a 65 percent reduction in runoff statewide and over 60 percent reduction in flows to the coast, as compared with average conditions. The present water demands are at the very limit of what can be met under such drought conditions, and in some regions exceed the firm yield supply. A paper analysis is not necessary to demonstrate this. During the 1980's, local droughts that occurred throughout the state were of far less intensity than the drought of record but sufficient to require severe water rationing and trucking of water supplies. This crisis also ignited acrimonious public debate between competing interests for water. The prolific and unusual rains that began in 1989 have removed water supply from the public forum for the present time. But the crisis will return.

Potential Impacts of Climate Change

Most water budgeting in the state is based fundamentally upon measurements of precipitation, stream flow, and diversions. While hydrologists readily acknowledge that the ultimate controls are atmospheric, it is far easier, and in many respects more precise, to measure the manifestations of these controls in rainfall and stream flow and to extend these results statistically than to measure and calculate the direct effect of atmospheric processes on hydrology. So long as climate is stable over the long term, this is certainly a valid and fruitful approach to hydrology. We now inquire how the hydrology of the state might be altered if climate changes. This draws upon the calculations reported in Ward (1992) based upon recasting the state water budget in terms of direct functions of temperature and precipitation.

Global warming is expected to increase the intensity of the global hydrologic cycle (e.g., MacCracken and Luther 1985; Mitchell 1989; AAAS Panel 1990; IPCC 1990). The impacts are quantified by application of global climate models and by reasoning from historical and prehistorical associations between climate indicators. As discussed elsewhere in this book, there is considerable uncertainty in any such quantitative climate forecast, especially as applied to the hydrological cycle, which is the end product of a chain of complex physical processes. Generally, an increase in tempera-

Table 4.1. Texas Water Budget Projections for Global Climate Change Scenarios

	1000 acre-feet per year	Relative to 1980 norm	1000 acre-feet per year	Relative to 1980 norm
	Normal conditions		Drought conditions	
Land evapotranspiration	317000	0.98	280000	0.87
Lake evaporation	8060	1.12	8360	1.17
Runoff	34700	0.74	12400	0.26
Net consumption (all uses)	4110	1.16	4280	1.21
Spills/uncaptured flows	28400	0.67	4660	0.11
Flows to Texas coast	22300	0.64	5700	0.16

ture is indicated for the entire midwestern U.S., with reduced precipitation and drier soil conditions for the Texas area (Webb and Wigley 1985; Kellogg and Zhao 1988). Ward (1992) selected a changed-climate scenario of +2°C increment in temperature and 5 percent decrease in precipitation as a consensus forecast for a 50-year planning horizon. His results, for both normal and drought conditions accumulated over the state, are summarized in Table 4.1. (The original data are presented on a regional basis.) In addition to the magnitudes of the principal components of the state water budget, the ratios of those values to those of 1980 are also given in Table 4.1, as an indicator of the alteration relative to "present" conditions.

Although the postulated alterations in temperature and precipitation for the climate change scenario are modest, their effect on the state water resources is dramatic: a reduction of 25 percent in runoff and 35 percent in flows to the coast under normal conditions, and reductions of 75 and 85 percent, respectively, under drought conditions. The reason for this dramatic impact on water resources is that the physical processes of the water budget act in such a way as to amplify the effects of these changes in temperature and precipitation. The water budget in Ward (1992) includes the following effects:

GEORGE WARD
AND
JUAN B. VALDES

1. Explicit dependence of runoff production rate on rainfall, therefore partially including the effect of watershed desiccation;

2. Dependence of municipal water consumption on temperature;

3. Dependence of natural lake evaporation on temperature;

4. Dependence of power generation load on temperature;

5. Dependence of forced evaporation of cooling lakes on temperature.

There are other temperature-precipitation effects not included in the water budget, such as the effects of increased temperatures on watershed desiccation and vegetational water demand. Moreover, these results are for 1980 populations and water demands. Projections of population growth and increased demands will further exacerbate the reductions in flow and water supply.

Regional Impacts

A more detailed analysis of water availability under conditions of global warming is described in Schmandt and Ward (1991) for three river basins. Using the water budget methodology described above, demand projections for the year 2030 (based on TWDB population and use data) were used to determine an aggregated value for reservoir levels in portions of the Trinity, Colorado, and Rio Grande basins. Surface water availability was based on historical data for the period 1951–1960, which includes the drought of record, in order to determine whether water needs could be fulfilled under the most stringent conditions. The results obtained from this scenario for each river basin were compared with those for a drought of similar intensity under conditions of global warming, i.e., an increase in temperature of 2°C and a reduction in precipitation of 5 percent.

The Trinity River, located in east Texas, receives an abundance of rainfall but serves some of the largest metropolitan areas of the state, including Dallas and Houston. For Zone 1, which includes Dallas, reservoir levels would decline rapidly under drought conditions. By the sixth year of the drought, annual municipal reservoir levels could fall to less than 53 percent of conservation capacity, while power reservoir levels could fall to 79 percent. With global climate conditions superimposed on these 2030 drought conditions, these values fall to 22 and 40 percent respectively. However, under

Table 4.2. Annual Reservoir Volumes of the Rio Grande (Percent of total)

Year of drought	1	2	3	4	5	6	7	8	9	10
2030 demand scenario	92	75	57	48	34	12	−11	−4	10	6
2030 demand scenario with climate change	90	69	47	33	14	−10	−39	−37	−24	−36

these conditions, municipal reservoir levels do not recover readily as the drought subsides, and the level continues to drop to a low of 13 percent in year 9. Less dramatic results were obtained for the lower reaches of the Trinity, where reservoir levels never drop below 67 percent of capacity.

With a more westerly location, the Colorado River originates in an arid part of the state. The main water uses are municipal, including the City of Austin, and agricultural. Assuming a continuing increase in municipal demand and a decline in agricultural demand for the year 2030, municipal reservoirs would be depleted for years 8–10 of a drought like that of the 1950's. Under the global climate change scenario, reservoirs are depleted by year 6. Depending on how irrigation demand is computed under drought conditions, a crisis is also likely in Zones 2 and 3.

Similar results were obtained for the Rio Grande. The Rio Grande is already over appropriated, and agricultural demand is met only in the wettest years. Using projections for the year 2030, the combined capacity of Falcon and Amistad reservoirs would drop to 35 percent of capacity by year 5 of a drought and be depleted by year 7. (Results for the year 2000 were very similar.) Under conditions of global climate change, these conditions would be realized a year earlier, and levels would not recover for the duration of the decade (Table 4.2). To some extent these figures mask the extent to which water supplies are stressed in the Rio Grande Valley. Currently, economic incentives are resulting in the transfer of agricultural water rights to municipalities, and this trend is expected to continue. Thus agriculture, which is a primary component of the valley's economy, is being affected by water availability, and it is likely that there will be continued pressure on agricultural users to reduce their consumption.

These data demonstrate the extent to which Texas is vulnerable to changes in climate. The drought of the 1950's is within living memory, and yet it is evident that population

GEORGE WARD
AND
JUAN B. VALDES

growth alone would make it extremely difficult to cope with a similar drought; many water uses would have to be curtailed. When the consequences of global warming for Texas' climate are included in the equation, the situation is even more serious. Managing our water supplies so that economic goals and ecological objectives can be maintained under such conditions will be a real challenge.

References

AAAS Panel on Climatic Variability, 1990. *Climate Change and U.S. Water Resources.* P. E. Waggoner (ed.). J. Wiley and Sons, New York.

IPCC, 1990. *Climate Change: The IPCC Scientific Assessment,* J. Houghton, J. Jenkins, and J. Ephraums (eds.). Cambridge University Press, Cambridge, U.K.

Kellog, W. W., and Z. Zhao, 1988. Sensitivity of Soil Moisture to Doubling of Carbon Dioxide in Climate Model Experiments. *Journal of Climate* 1:348–378.

MacCracken, M. L., and Luther, F. M. (eds.), 1985. Projecting the Climatic Effects of Increasing Carbon Dioxide. U.S. Dept. of Energy, Publication DOE/ER-0237.

Mitchell, J. F. B., 1989. The Greenhouse Effect and Climate Change. *Reviews of Geophysics* 27(1): 115–139.

Schmandt, J., and G. Ward, 1991. *Texas and Global Warming: Water Supply and Demand in Four Hydrological Regions.* University of Texas at Austin.

Texas Department of Water Resources, 1984. *Water for Texas, A Comprehensive Plan for the Future,* Vol. 1. TDWR, Report GP-4-1, Austin.

Texas Water Development Board (TWDB), 1990. *Water for Texas.* TWDB, Austin.

Ward, G. H., 1992. A Water Budget for the State of Texas with Climatological Forcing. Center for Research in Water Resources, University of Texas at Austin, Tech. Memo. CRWR 92–3.

Webb, T., and T. M. L. Wigley, 1985. What past climates can indicate about a warmer world. In: *Projecting the Climate Effects of Increasing Carbon Dioxide,* M. MacCracken and F. M. Luther (eds.). U.S. Dept. of Energy. Publication DOE/ER-0237.

WILLIAM L. LONGLEY

5. Estuaries

The purpose of this chapter is to describe the relationships that exist between climate and estuaries and, using those relationships, to project the changes that will likely occur in estuarine habitats under the climate change scenarios briefly discussed in Chapter 2. Estuaries are generally characterized as drowned river mouths and are dependent on freshwater flows from streams and rivers for the maintenance of a salinity gradient. The first portion of this chapter presents information concerning the relationship between climate and the physical form of the estuary, the salinity of the waters, and the relative abundance of various wetland and aquatic habitats. The second portion discusses changes in freshwater inflow and water depth that are expected under the various climate scenarios. It also describes a method that can be used to project changes in relative habitat areas as the result of climate change. The third portion of the chapter uses this method to provide estimates of change in the relative areas of estuarine habitats that would result from these various climate regime scenarios.

Texas Estuaries

The Texas Gulf shoreline stretches 370 miles from the Sabine River at the Louisiana state line to the Rio Grande at the Mexican border. Except for two areas along the upper coast, narrow barrier islands and peninsulas separate the Gulf of Mexico from the shallow estuaries. Pritchard (1967, pp. 3–5) defines *estuary* as a semienclosed coastal body of water that has a free connection with the open sea and within which sea water is measurably diluted with fresh water derived from land drainage. The estuaries behind the barrier islands and peninsulas project inland from the Gulf shoreline as much as 30 miles. The land surrounding these aquatic systems is low and flat; one must travel 30–50 miles inland from the Gulf shoreline to reach a land elevation of just 100 feet above mean sea level. The environments of the coastal region can be looked at from several scales of view: the region as a whole, individual estuaries, and habitats. Each viewpoint is useful in understanding the effects of climate and climate change upon estuaries.

River Basins

River basins, the inland land areas from which runoff drains to rivers, can be delineated on topographic maps through careful consideration of land elevation and slope. One or more river basins may drain to an estuary on the coast. The amount of fresh water that flows to an estuary has a strong influence on the shape and form of the estuary, as well as on the habitats and organisms there and in the surrounding wetlands. A regional viewpoint that considers the river basins of the entire state is illustrated in Figure 5.1, which shows the outlines of river basins that drain to the state's eleven estuaries.

Drainage basins for rivers that flow into the Brazos, Colorado, and Rio Grande estuaries extend across the entire state. Flows of water to these estuaries are influenced by rainfall and runoff from a large area, much of which is far removed from the coastline. The basin for the Rio Grande even extends into Mexico, New Mexico, and southern Colorado. Thus, climate changes that may occur a long distance from Texas estuaries may nevertheless have a profound influence on the amount of fresh water that flows into them.

The Sabine-Neches, Trinity–San Jacinto, Guadalupe, and Nueces estuaries have smaller river basins that extend only partway across the state; the Sabine-Neches Estuary also receives some runoff from Louisiana. These smaller river basins are not directly affected by precipitation in the western half of the state. The San Bernard, Lavaca–Tres Palacios, Mission-Aransas, and Laguna Madre estuaries have the shortest river basins; they reach inland no more than about 100 miles from the Gulf shoreline. Runoff to these estuaries is most strongly influenced by the climatic conditions close to the coast.

The lower portion of Figure 5.1 shows the average annual runoff per mi² of the basins that drain to the state's estuaries (Texas Department of Water Resources 1984). The runoff

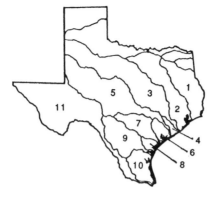

River Basin Runoff (acre-ft/mi^2)

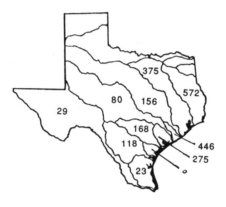

Figure 5.1.
Location of the major river basins in Texas (above), with values for annual runoff averaged over the entire basin (below).

rates vary by more than an order of magnitude between the basins bordering Louisiana and those bordering Mexico. Differences in runoff rates are the result of the interaction of the east-west precipitation (Figure 2.2) and evaporation gradients in the state, the north-east to south-west location of the basin along the coastline, and the distance the drainage basin extends inland from the Gulf shoreline. In general, the more a basin is restricted to the area near the coast, or the farther to the northeast it is located, the greater the average runoff per square mile. Basins that extend farther across the state or are located more to the southwest have lower rates of runoff.

WILLIAM L. LONGLEY

90

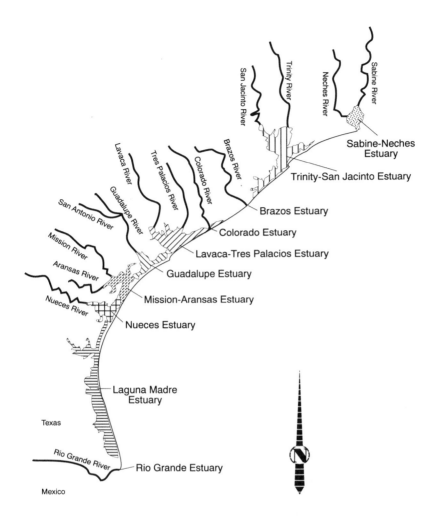

Texas

Mexico

Figure 5.2.
Location of the
major estuaries
in Texas.

Estuary Forms and Climate

The development and configuration of estuaries on the Texas coast is closely bound to climatic changes that have taken place over the period from the last ice age to the present. Three major shapes or forms of estuaries can be seen in Figure 5.2, a medium-scale view of the Texas coast. The first is the classic estuarine configuration such as the Trinity–San Jacinto Estuary, which juts far inland and has an opening to the sea toward its southern tip. Rivers discharge at the most inland end of the estuary, and the axis between the river

ESTUARIES

mouth and the openings to the sea allows the establishment of a long gradient of salinity ranging from low to high levels. Most of the land that surrounds this estuary and others with the same physical form (Sabine-Neches, Lavaca–Tres Palacios, Guadalupe, Mission-Aransas, and Nueces) is of Pleistocene age (Fisher et al. 1972) and was formed 60,000–1 million years before present (B.P.). During the last ice age (Late Wisconsin glaciation), which began about 50,000–60,000 years B.P., sea level declined as water was captured in the ice sheets that covered part of the northern hemisphere. As sea level fell to its lowest point, 300–400 feet below its present level, the land where today's estuaries and near-shore gulf are located was completely exposed; surface sediment eroded, creating deep river valleys. Rivers flowed through these valleys at levels 100–130 feet lower than today's mean sea level. As the climate began to warm, about 20,000 years B.P., sea level started to rise and began to flood the river valleys. The deeper portions of the valleys gradually filled with sediment originating in upland runoff, offshore currents, and eroding valley walls. Offshore sediments that were transported onshore also contributed to the formation of barrier islands and peninsulas, which formed within the past 2,500 years. The processes of transport, deposition, and erosion have continued to the present, slowly filling the deeper areas of the estuaries and widening the edges of the Sabine-Neches, Trinity–San Jacinto, Lavaca–Tres Palacios, Guadalupe, Mission-Aransas, and Nueces estuaries.

Baffin Bay, which was formed in the same manner, should also be included with this group. Today, however, it receives only intermittent inflow and very little sediment from the small creeks that drain into it because of the low level of runoff from watersheds in its basin (Figure 5.1). River basins that drain to these classic-form estuaries are generally midsized or coastal basins and do not extend more than halfway across the state. The existence and shape of these estuaries is clearly a result of the climatic shift that occurred during the ice ages, the subsequent rise of sea level, and the transport and erosion of sediment affected by varying climatic conditions throughout the river basin area.

A second estuarine configuration is illustrated by the Brazos, Colorado, and Rio Grande river mouths. The Brazos River and the Rio Grande now empty directly into the Gulf rather than into a bay. The Colorado River has recently been artificially diverted into the eastern portion of Matagorda Bay and no longer flows directly to the Gulf. During the last ice age, these rivers cut deep river valleys just like rivers flowing into the classic estuaries described above. As the climate warmed and sea level rose, however, these rivers carried so much sediment that their deltas expanded, completely filling their river valleys. This deposition continued all the way to today's Gulf shoreline, allowing the rivers to discharge directly into the sea. The great sediment load of these three rivers resulted from the large areas of their drainage basins, which extend across the entire state. The land immediately surrounding these estuaries was formed very recently; the rapid land growth and direct discharge into the Gulf of the river estuaries is the result of the interaction of climate, physiography, and soil type in the river basins over the past 5,000–10,000 years.

Initially, the San Bernard Estuary seems to be an exception to the generalization that the form of the river estuaries is the result of sedimentation in the large river basins that stretch across the state. Today the San Bernard Estuary has a very small basin, located between the present Brazos and Colorado river basins. The San Bernard River is most likely an abandoned channel of one or the other of these major rivers. When sea level approached its present level, about 2,800 B.P., the Colorado and Brazos rivers emptied into a common estuary and filled it in about 1,200 years (McGowen et al. 1976a). Because the present San Bernard River basin is entirely within the area affected by the Colorado and Brazos river sedimentation, this estuary and the land surrounding it were only recently formed by the large sediment loads of these two great river basins.

The third form of estuarine system on the Texas coast is the lagoon typified by the Laguna Madre. The water body is narrow, and the major axis runs parallel to the shoreline rather than perpendicular to it. Except for the area close to the Rio Grande, the land on the inland side of the laguna was formed as fluvial-deltaic deposits or strandplain during the Pleistocene (Brown et al. 1977; 1980). The barrier island side of the laguna was formed over the past 2,500 years, as sea level rose to its present position. Thus, even the current configuration of the Laguna Madre is the result of a rise in sea level as the climate returned to its present, interglacial state.

Estuarine Salinity and Climate

The discussion above has shown that the geologic history and current form of Texas' estuaries are largely the result of climatic variation and the interaction of climate with land shape and soil character over a period of several thousand years. Climate also plays a dominant role in the chemical nature of the environment in which estuarine organisms live. Salinity is a measure of the concentration of dissolved inorganic matter in estuarine water. The fluids in bodies of aquatic plants and animals also contain dissolved salts and organic materials; the internal concentrations of these materials may be less than, equal to, or greater than the concentration of materials in the water in which they live.

The cells and organs of aquatic species are adapted to work best at particular internal osmotic concentrations. At the same time, water and certain ions can pass through or be transported through their cell walls. Various organs of aquatic species, such as gills, are continuously in contact with the water of the external environment, so organisms are always involved in a metabolic balancing act to maintain acceptable internal osmotic levels, while countering the tendency of their bodies to gain or lose water due to the difference between internal and external osmotic concentrations. Estuarine organisms have developed specialized organs to preserve this balance, but they must expend energy to accomplish it. Different species vary in the range of salinities over which their osmoregulation is successful. Euryhaline species can regulate their osmotic balance over a wide range of salinities and may be found throughout an estuary or over the entire range of estuaries on the Texas coast. Stenohaline organisms have much narrower ranges of salinity over which they can regulate their osmotic balance and are found only in certain areas within an estuary, and may not be found at all in some estuaries.

The quantity of salt in Texas estuaries generally ranges from 0 to about 4 percent by weight. Concentration of salt is measured as salinity in parts per thousand (ppt), which is the percent salt multiplied by 10. Environments in which freshwater plants and animals thrive generally have salinities less than 0.5 ppt. The salinity of a marine environment such as the Gulf of Mexico or the Pacific Ocean is generally about 35 ppt. Estuaries generally have salinities that range between these extremes. Figure 5.3 shows the mean salinity and standard deviations about the mean at locations in several Texas estuaries. Standard deviations range from 5 to 14 ppt, so it is clear that salinities can vary over a wide range through time.

The order of the estuaries in Figure 5.3 is by latitude, from north to south. Several zones are shown within each estuary,

WILLIAM L. LONGLEY

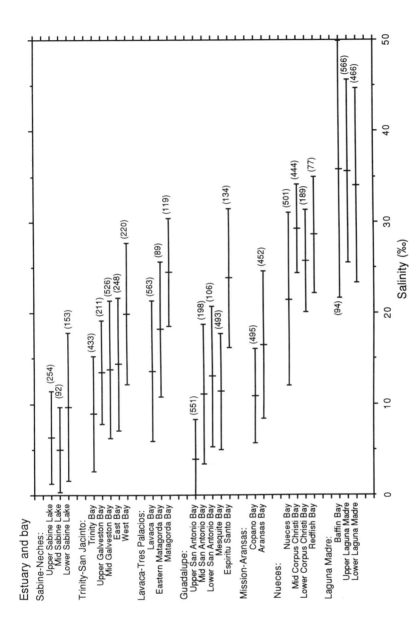

Figure 5.3.
Mean and standard deviation of salinity of Texas' estuaries; number of samples in parentheses.

listed in order of their distance from the river mouth. The figure shows that salinities vary within an estuary and tend to be lower near the river mouth and higher toward the sea. By comparing estuaries, a trend in estuarine salinity can be seen based upon latitude. Except for the Guadalupe Estuary, and to a lesser extent the Mission-Aransas Estuary, salinity tends to increase the farther south the location of the estuary. Salinities correlate well with river basin runoff, as shown in the bottom portion of Figure 5.1. Estuaries that receive flow from river basins with high runoff rates tend to have lower ranges of salinities, while those with lower runoff rates have higher salinities. Thus, the climate of the state strongly influences the total ionic concentration of the aquatic environment of Texas estuaries, which in turn influences the metabolism and distribution of many organisms.

Habitats Associated with Estuaries

Habitats provide the most detailed view of the estuarine environment and its relationship with climate. Maps of environments and biologic assemblages of the Texas coast were prepared by Fisher et al. (1972; 1973), McGowen et al. (1976a,b), and Brown et al. (1976; 1977; 1980). Environment and assemblage units were delineated from aerial photographs from the mid 1950's. Although some areas had already been modified as a result of human activity when the maps were prepared, the degree of change was certainly less than is apparent today. By lumping various mapped units from these studies together, 36 environments and biological assemblages from the studies above were reduced to 9 general habitat areas including wetland, aquatic, and barrier island portions of Texas estuarine systems (Table 5.1).

Figure 5.4 is a schematic diagram that shows a typical spatial arrangement of these habitats. The river carries freshwater flows toward the estuary and supports the fish and invertebrates characteristic of freshwater streams. Along the edge of the river are freshwater marshes with reeds, cattails, water hyacinth, and freshwater fauna. Behind the river bank there may be areas of swamp with water-tolerant hardwoods such as bald cypress and tupelo. These areas are regularly flooded a few times each year and may contain standing water for periods of several months. Occasionally they may be flooded by estuarine water during very high tides resulting from major storms or hurricanes.

At some point, the river changes character and becomes a

WILLIAM L. LONGLEY

96

Table 5.1. Habitat Areas in the Estuaries of Texas (mile²)

	Laguna Madre	Nueces	Mission-Aransas	Guadalupe	Lavaca–Tres Palacios	Trinity–San Jacinto	Sabine-Neches
Fresh Marsh	16.2	9.0	5.7	17.7	21.4	19.4	26.6
Swamp	0.0	0.0	0.3	1.5	0.1	34.6	36.3
Salt-Brackish Marsh	2.3	7.0	25.2	27.9	29.6	116.6	118.0
Wind-Tidal Flat	344.0	19.2	23.4	12.4	5.6	6.5	0.0
Seagrass	220.1	12.4	9.5	8.4	5.7	8.0	0.0
Beach-Barrier	156.1	17.3	23.6	25.9	27.9	61.0	14.3
Reef	0.0	3.2	13.6	18.7	8.4	88.8	0.0
Bay	266.1	157.6	184.6	206.9	366.1	493.6	49.0
Spoil	30.7	9.7	3.9	4.7	10.7	11.2	16.7

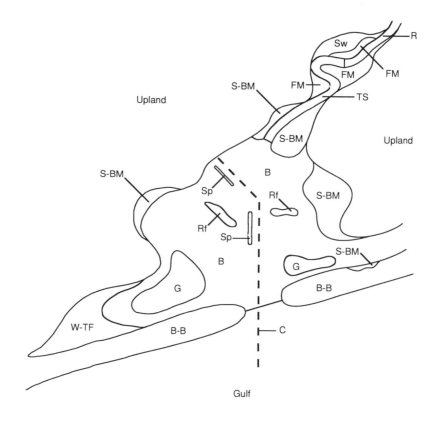

B: Bay
B-B: Beach-barrier
C: Channel
FM: Fresh marsh
G: Grassflat
R: River

Rf: Reef
S-BM: Salt-brackish marsh
Sp: Spoil
Sw: Swamp
TS: Tidal stream
W-TF: Wind-tidal flat

Figure 5.4.
Types of aquatic
and wetland habitat
found in Texas'
estuaries.

WILLIAM L. LONGLEY

98

tidal stream. Tidal streams usually have some degree of bi-directional flow, with fresh water flowing downstream at the surface, saline water flowing upstream along the bottom, and a zone of mixing in the middle. The fauna of tidal streams may include a mixture of freshwater and estuarine species due to the dual direction of flow. Freshwater marshes can still be found along the edge of a tidal stream because the surface waters are nearly fresh. As the tidal stream enters the lower portion of the delta the water becomes measurably brackish due to mixing; wetlands are common, and the plant communities are brackish to saltmarsh in character. Wetland plant species include needle rush and Olney bulrush near the source of low salinity water. The outer edges of the wetland area have typical saltmarsh vegetation such as smooth cord-grass, saltgrass, and glasswort.

Seaward of the delta is the upper portion of the bay where estuarine and river water mix. Salinities are often highly variable, but tend to become more marine as one moves farther away from the river toward the Gulf. Bay constitutes 25–75 percent of the area of the estuaries and is usually the largest habitat type. Oyster reefs are generally present if the salinity characteristics of the estuary are in the range of 10–30 ppt and the estuary has occasional freshenings below 20 ppt. The reefs build perpendicular to the direction of water flow and maximize the frontal surface exposed to flowing water. Reefs are generally found in the mid regions of the estuary.

Natural channels are located near the openings to the sea, but artificial channels have been dredged across the length and breadth of nearly every estuary. While the depth of the bay bottom in most estuaries is usually only 3–15 feet, natural and dredged channels can be much deeper, as much as 50–70 feet. Spoil, a byproduct of dredging, is a habitat usually in close proximity to channels. Subaqueous spoil deposits become indistinguishable from bay bottom with time. Subaerial spoil is usually a disturbed type of habitat, with new materials periodically heaped upon the land surface. The biotic community inhabiting spoil banks is characterized by invading species and a few others that are highly mobile.

There may be small pockets of salt-brackish marsh along the lateral edges of the estuary, particularly in low-lying areas with small creeks and bayous. These wetlands typically have marsh species such as smooth cordgrass and seashore saltgrass, and in areas of higher elevation may contain marshhay cordgrass and Gulf cordgrass. Salt-brackish marsh plants tend to inhabit a zone that ranges from slightly below mean sea level to several feet above mean high water. Distribution of these plants is determined largely by the moisture level and salinity of the soil. Toward the lower end of the estuary, inundation from astronomical and wind tides provides the moisture levels for the hydric soils needed by the marsh plants. Species tolerant of higher soil salinities are found here. At the upper end of the estuary, where tidal inundation is damped, inundation from freshwater flooding is required to maintain hydric soils. Species tolerant of lower salinities are more prevalent here.

Toward the beach-barrier island area, there may be pock-

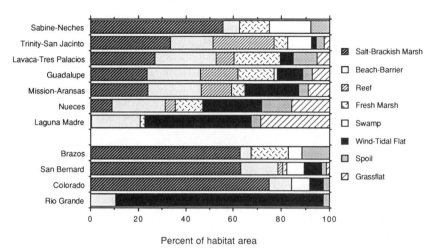

Figure 5.5.
Relative area of wetland and aquatic habitat, excluding bay. The upper portion of the figure shows the relative proportion of habitats in the classic and lagoonal estuaries; lower portion shows rivers that empty directly into the Gulf. The order of the estuaries is from north to south.

ets of submerged seagrasses such as widgeongrass, shoalgrass, and turtlegrass. The latter two species prefer higher salinity conditions, while the first does well in lower salinities. Light penetration is a critical controlling factor for seagrass habitats.

Areas of exposed sediment that are occasionally inundated by the force of wind or tides make up the wind-tidal flat. Macrophytic vegetation is very sparse in these areas, presumably because the soil salinity is too high for survival. However, blue-green algae mats or microscopic diatoms may be found, depending upon whether the flat is muddy or sandy.

Beach-barrier is the habitat that separates the estuary from the Gulf. The back side of the beach-barrier habitat is the vegetated barrier flat with salt-tolerant upland vegetation. At the estuarine shoreline, there may be areas of salt-brackish marsh. Toward the Gulf side, the beach-barrier habitat usually has sand dunes with specialized plants, such as sea oats and railroad vine, that are suited to drier, sand dune conditions.

The schematic in Figure 5.4 is generalized for the whole coast; actually, there is a good deal of variation in habitat area from one estuary to another. Figure 5.5 shows the relative area of various habitats for which measurements are available. Because the area of the bay habitat tends to dominate all of the others, the percentages for this figure were calculated based upon the total area of habitats other than bay.

WILLIAM L. LONGLEY

100

The upper portion of the figure shows the relative proportion of habitats in the classic and lagoonal estuaries; the order of the estuaries is from north to south. It is immediately clear that the relative areas of salt-brackish marsh and swamp decrease toward the south. The same is true of fresh marsh, although the trend is not as obvious. At the same time, the relative proportion of wind-tidal flat and seagrass increases toward the south.

The lower portion of Figure 5.5 shows the relative habitat areas for the river estuaries. The relative area of salt-brackish marsh is similar for the Brazos, San Bernard, and Colorado river estuaries, but drops to zero for the Rio Grande Estuary. An opposite trend occurs for wind-tidal flat. It makes up the majority of the habitat area in the Rio Grande Estuary, but decreases to nil or a very small fraction of the area for the river estuaries of the upper coast.

Relationship of Habitats to Inflow

Changes in area of habitat types for classic and lagunal forms of estuaries become even clearer when the relative habitat areas are compared with a measure of inflow. Figure 5.6 presents the relative area of each habitat type versus the inflow:volume ratio for the estuary. This ratio measures the frequency of turnover of the water in the estuary and is calculated as the average annual inflow (Solis 1992, p. 18-3) divided by the average volume of the estuary (Diener 1975). The inflow:volume ratio varies by a factor of 144, from a high of 53.3 volumes per year for the Sabine-Neches Estuary, to a low of 0.37 volumes per year for the Laguna Madre. On average, the water in the Sabine-Neches system is replaced every 7 days from inflow, while Laguna Madre water is replaced every 2.7 years. Figure 5.6 shows relative habitat area as a function of inflow:volume ratio.

The pattern of relative area versus inflow:volume ratio is similar for fresh marsh, swamp, and salt-brackish marsh. It is known that the abundance and distribution of these wetland habitats is related to the level of soil moisture. Fresh marsh and swamp require fresh water because the plants are less salinity tolerant than salt-brackish marsh species. The latter can tolerate marine salinities, but are limited by higher salinity levels that result from evaporation of water from the soil. From north to south, precipitation and inflow decrease while salinity increases, so it is not surprising that the relative areas of these habitats also decrease.

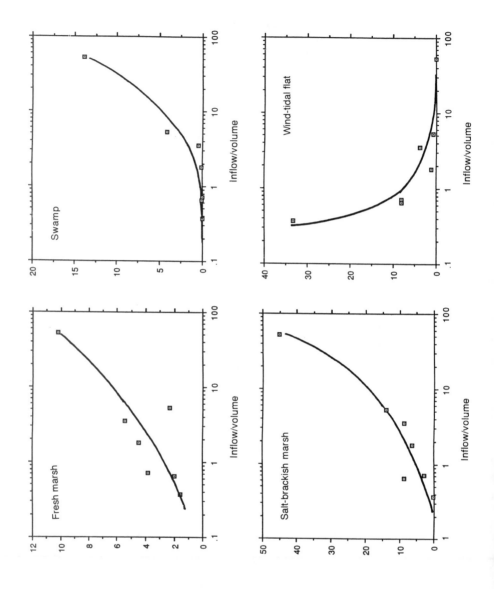

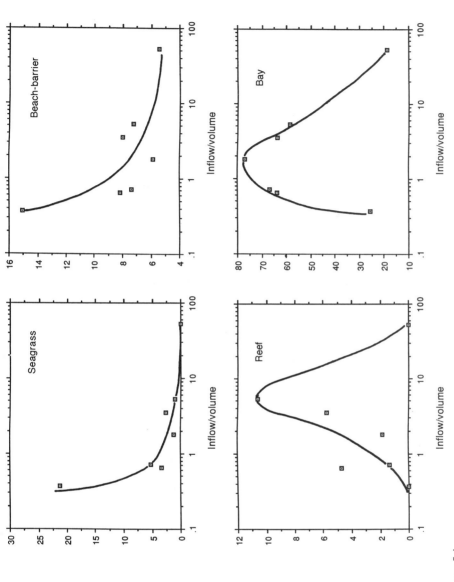

Figure 5.6.
The area of each habitat type (shown as percent of total area) under different salinity regimes. Salinity is represented as annual freshwater inflow/estuarine volume. Note the increase in marsh and swamp habitat and the decline of seagrass and beach barrier with decreasing salinity.

The relative areas of submerged seagrass, wind-tidal flat, and beach-barrier island are inversely related to the inflow: volume ratio. Most submerged seagrasses prefer higher salinity environments where the water is relatively clear. As inflow increases, so does the load of suspended clay particles that causes turbidity in the water. Consequently, areas with higher inflows reduce the light penetration that is vital for seagrass growth and survival. The soil of wind-tidal flats is too saline or is periodically too dry for macrophytic plant establishment. If wind-tidal flats were more regularly inundated or had lower soil salinities due to increased freshwater inflow, they would probably support salt-brackish marsh vegetation. The width of the beach-barrier habitat does not vary much over the whole coastline, but the length of the shoreline associated with each estuary generally decreases from south to north. When combined with the relative areas of the estuaries, the relative proportion of beach-barrier area decreases with increasing latitude.

Reef and bay areas show a very different pattern, with maximum relative areas at inflow:volume ratios ranging from 1 to 10, but decreasing at the extremes of high and low inflow:volume ratios. In the case of oyster reefs, the pattern is clearly related to the physiology of the oyster, which cannot tolerate salinity extremes and tends to grow and survive better in estuaries with salinity variations in the middle range.

The shape of the relative bay habitat area curve cannot be explained by a direct physiological mechanism, as is the case for most of the other habitat types. However, if the relative areas of the other habitats described above for which there is an inflow- or salinity-related pattern are summed, the resulting curve is the inverse of the relative bay habitat area curve. Thus, the relative bay habitat area curve represents the habitat area remaining after the other habitats establish their aerial extents according to the inflow gradient. The Lavaca–Tres Palacios Estuary has the middle value for the inflow:volume ratio of all the estuaries, and the sum of the values for the relative areas of fresh marsh, swamp, salt-brackish marsh, wind-tidal flat, seagrass, and beach-barrier is the lowest for all the estuaries (19 percent). Thus, it is not surprising that relative area of bay habitat is the highest of all the estuaries (77 percent).

WILLIAM L. LONGLEY

Differences in relative habitat area shown in Figure 5.6 are the result of ecological and geological processes that act over long periods of time and are strongly influenced by climate.

For example, natural development of wetlands on existing soils requires time scales of a few decades; development of large oyster reefs may take decades to hundreds of years. No regular pattern of area with respect to the inflow:volume ratio is evident for the spoil habitat. This is probably because spoil production depends solely upon the navigational needs of the region, not long-term ecological adjustments to the inflow pattern. The relative area of spoil tends to be higher for shallower estuaries (Sabine-Neches and Laguna Madre) and lower for deeper estuaries (Trinity–San Jacinto and Lavaca–Tres Palacios).

Over time, habitat areas adjust to new conditions. Portions of beach-barrier, salt-brackish marsh, and wind-tidal flat may be converted from one habitat to the other depending upon precipitation, inflow, and salinity. Areas of reef and bay, and bay and seagrass, may be converted back and forth, largely as the result of salinity variation. Finally, swamp and fresh marsh may be converted from one to the other or to upland.

Projecting Habitat Area Changes from Altered Inflows and Bay Volumes

The graphic relationships between relative habitat area and inflow:volume ratio shown in Figure 5.6 provide the basis for assessing the kinds of habitat changes that may take place with large-scale climate change. To use these graphic relationships, it is first necessary to estimate the magnitude of change in inflow that will occur under various climate change scenarios. Inflow may change as the result of increased water use through population growth, decreased runoff resulting from increased evaporation at higher temperatures, and increased or decreased runoff depending upon statewide changes in precipitation. Once inflow changes are determined, estuarine volumes must be adjusted to account for the rise in sea level that is projected to occur over the same period. These values will provide new inflow:volume ratios that can be used with the curves from Figure 5.6 to estimate the direction and magnitude of habitat shifts in each estuary resulting from climate change.

Inflow Changes

Three independent estimates of change in freshwater inflow under the climate change scenarios defined in Chapter 2 are

Table 5.2. Estimates of Percent Change in Inflow to Texas Estuaries (compared to the 1941–1987 average) under Four Climate Change Scenarios for the Projected 2040 Population; ΔT is Change in Temperature, and ΔP is Change in Precipitation

	Percent change			
			Water	
		Trinity–	budget	Value
	Mission-	San	model of	used in
	Aransas	Jacinto	Ward	this
Case	basin	basin	(1992)	analysis
Case 0: ΔT = 0°C, ΔP = 0%	0	+1	−3	−1
Case 1: ΔT = +2°C, ΔP = 0%	0	−1	−8	−3
Case 2: ΔT = +2°C, ΔP = +20%	+36	+32		+34
Case 3: ΔT = +2°C, ΔP = −20%	−65	−40	−87	−64

presented in Table 5.2. Inflow estimates for the Mission-Aransas and Trinity–San Jacinto basins were made by Texas Water Development Board (TWDB) staff for a study in progress (Dr. R. Solis, TWDB, Austin, pers. comm.). The third estimate comes from a statewide water budget spreadsheet model prepared by Ward (1992). This budget model allows the user to compute the water budget, given population growth relative to 1980 and changes in air temperature, precipitation, and reservoir area compared to 1980 norms. In assessing future water use, Schmandt et al. (1992) recommended using the TWDB's low series forecast for population estimates. Thus, the 2040 population projection used in this analysis is 27,982,904 (B. Bloodworth, TWDB, Austin, pers. comm.).

Case 0 in Table 5.2 represents the inflow change resulting from population growth only; there is no change in temperature or precipitation. The inflow change to the Mission-Aransas basin is 0 percent. This basin is largely rural, with rangeland on which cattle are grazed, and cropland which produces grain and cotton. There is little surface water irrigation, and municipal and manufacturing water largely comes from outside the basin. Since additional water for municipal and industrial use will come from outside the basin (TWDB 1990), reduction in flow to the estuary will be slight. The percent change for the Trinity–San Jacinto basin for Case 0 is +1 percent. The 1990 Texas Water Plan (Ibid.) projects that water demand will increase by 50 percent in this basin, which includes urban, agricultural, and forest areas. Additional supplies will be developed by 2040, and imports from other basins are expected to rise (Ibid.), which explains the 1 percent increase in inflow. The −3 percent change in inflow from the water budget in Ward (1992) is entirely attributable to increased demand throughout the state.

The Case 1 scenario is similar to Case 0 except that it includes a 2°C temperature increase. The models used for the TWDB estimates of inflow are not very sensitive to the effects of temperature change and include only the effect of the thermal increase in reservoir evaporation. Since there are no reservoirs in the Mission-Aransas basin, no decrease in inflow from increased temperature was calculated; a small, 2 percent decrease was computed for the Trinity–San Jacinto Estuary. Ward's budget added inflow reductions of 8 percent as a result of increased evaporation of cooling water at power plants, additional electric generating capacity, and additional per capita municipal and industrial water use.

Case 2 adds a 20 percent increase in precipitation to the 2°C temperature increase. The Mission-Aransas and Trinity–San Jacinto basins are projected to provide a 32–36 percent increase in inflow from a 20 percent precipitation increase. Ward's water budget model is calibrated for precipitation decreases and does not provide a good estimate for a 20 percent increase.

Case 3 represents the most extreme scenario, with a 2°C temperature increase and a 20 percent precipitation decrease. All three estimates show reductions in inflows to the estuaries, ranging from 40 to 87 percent. The values used in this analysis are shown in the last column of Table 5.2; they represent the means of the individual increases or decreases for each scenario.

Sea-Level Rise

In addition to the changes in inflow accompanying climate change, a clearly observable rise in sea level is expected. Schmandt et al. (1992) discusses the various estimates and reasons for the sea-level rise. Estimates of the rise differ according to various experts and range from very small to more than 2 meters by the year 2100 (Ibid.). For the calculations that follow, a rise of 1.5 feet was selected.

Sea-level rise has a direct and indirect effect upon estuarine habitats. Fresh marsh, swamp, and salt-brackish marsh will be particularly vulnerable as rising sea level causes more frequent inundation of these areas by estuarine water. Fresh marsh and swamp will become more saline and may be converted into salt-brackish marsh, wind-tidal flat, or bay; salt-brackish marsh will be flooded and become open bay. In many areas with gentle land slopes, the salt-brackish marsh can migrate landward as sea level rises. Zimmerman et al. (1991) suggest that if the rate of rise is slow, saltmarsh and brackish-marsh migration may be able to keep up with sea-level rise. If the rise exceeds 0.4 inches per year, however, inland establishment of wetlands may not be able to keep pace. Schmandt et al. (1992) state that wetlands are unlikely to be able to compensate for sea-level rise, since land slope increases inland, and reduced inflow will result in reduced sediment for wetland nourishment. In addition, erosion and human activities on or around the areas to which wetlands could move will limit their migration.

Wind-tidal flat will be able to spread inland as the water rises, subject to the same land slope restrictions as salt-brackish marsh. Rising water will increase depth, further limiting light penetration to seagrasses. Because light availability is a strong determinant of seagrass distribution, the plants will have to migrate to shallower waters to compensate for the rise. Sea-level rise will probably decrease the requirements for dredging, so spoil habitat areas will probably not increase at their past rate as the rise occurs.

Indirectly, the rise in sea level increases the volume of the bays, thereby altering the inflow:volume ratio. Consequently, more freshwater inflow is necessary to provide the same salinity gradient as in the unaltered estuary. A rough estimate of the increase in volumes can be made using the volume and depth measurements from Diener (1975, Table 3). Expected volume increases for a 1.5-foot sea-level rise range from 26 percent to 156 percent for the seven major estuaries (Table 5.3). The deeper estuaries show the smallest volume increase, while the shallower estuaries show greater increases. The volume of the Laguna Madre would more than double for this sea-level rise.

Projected Habitat Area Changes in Major Texas Estuaries

Using the percent change in freshwater inflow values from Table 5.2, and the inflow:volume ratio and percent volume increase values in the second and third columns of Table 5.3, new inflow:volume ratios were calculated for each bay and

WILLIAM L. LONGLEY

Table 5.3. Historical Inflow-Volume Ratio (Inflow/Volume), Increase in Estuarine Volume with a 1.5-Foot Sea-Level Rise, and Projected Inflow-Volume Ratios Under Each Scenario for the Seven Classic and Lagunal Texas Estuaries

Estuary	1941–1987 Inflow/Volume	% volume increase	Case 0 Inflow/Volume	Case 1 Inflow/Volume	Case 2 Inflow/Volume	Case 3 Inflow/Volume
Sabine-Neches	53.31	43.2	36.86	36.11	49.89	13.40
Trinity–San Jacinto	5.3	31.8	3.98	3.90	5.39	1.45
Lavaca–Tres Palacios	1.78	25.8	1.40	1.37	1.90	0.51
Guadalupe	3.51	50.1	2.32	2.27	3.13	0.84
Mission-Aransas	0.64	47.2	0.43	0.42	0.58	0.16
Nueces	0.71	28.1	0.55	0.54	0.74	0.20
Laguna Madre	0.37	156.2	0.14	0.14	0.19	0.05

climate scenario combination. The new values are also shown in Table 5.3. Case 2, where precipitation increased by 20 percent, is the only scenario where the inflow:volume ratio did not decrease for every estuary: the ratio increased marginally for the Trinity–San Jacinto, Lavaca–Tres Palacios, and Nueces estuaries, but decreased for all the others. The effect of sea-level rise clearly exacerbates the reductions in inflow due to rising temperature and decreasing precipitation (Case 3) and effectively cancels the effect that a 20 percent increase in precipitation (Case 2) would have upon coastal habitat distribution.

General Habitat Trends

Fresh marsh, swamp, and salt-brackish marsh all decline in relative abundance as the inflow:volume ratio decreases. Except for the three estuaries in the Case 2 scenario noted above, the general trend for these wetland habitats will range from no change to significant decreases in relative area.

Wind-tidal flat and seagrass beds tend to increase in relative area as the estuarine inflow:volume ratio decreases. Except for the three estuaries in the Case 2 scenario, the general trend for these habitats will range from no change to a significant increase in relative area. The beach-barrier habitat has the same trend as wind-tidal flat and seagrass beds and would also show an increase in relative area with decreasing inflow:volume ratio. But there is a problem. The aerial extent of this habitat depends in part upon the supply of sediment from the Gulf. Currently, a large portion of the shoreline of the beach-barrier island habitat is eroding, which indicates a deficit in sediment supply for the habitat. There is no reason to expect that the change in freshwater inflow or sea-level rise will increase the supply of sediment from the Gulf. Sea-level rise will directly decrease the aerial extent of the beach-barrier habitat, unless there is an increased sediment supply. Consequently, it is unlikely that the relative area of this habitat will increase according to the graphic pattern of Figure 5.6.

Reef and bay habitats have their lowest relative areas in estuaries with extreme high and low inflow:volume ratios, and their highest proportions in estuaries with midrange ratios. Because the inflow:volume trend is downward for almost all estuary-scenario combinations, the trend for relative area of reef and bay in the lower coast will be to decrease, while the trend in the upper coast will be to increase, with a middle region of no discernible trend.

Spoil showed no clear trend with inflow:volume ratio. Climate change, however, will probably reduce the relative area of this habitat because there will be a slight reduction in demand for maintenance dredging. This assumes that vessels requiring the same depth continue to operate in coastal channels and passes. If there is a trend toward accommodating deeper-draft vessels, the relative area of spoil might not change or could even increase.

Analyses of Specific Scenarios

For each scenario, the relative change in habitat area for each estuary was estimated using the relationships from Figure 5.6 and the inflow:volume ratios corrected for sea-level rise in Table 5.3. Tables 5.4–5.6 show the results of the analysis. Projected changes less than 10 percent were considered to be no change; increases up to doubling or decreases to half are indicated by single signs, while greater increases or decreases are shown with double signs. A few blanks in the tables indicate estuaries where that habitat is not present and is not expected to develop under the altered climate regime. No results are presented for the beach-barrier habitat because of the sand deficit problem described above.

Because the inflow:volume ratios for Case 0 (population increase and sea-level rise) and Case 1 (population increase, sea-level rise, and temperature increase) are so similar, the Case 1 results will be the only ones presented (Figure 5.4). The only differences are that for Case 0, fresh marsh showed no change in the Trinity–San Jacinto Estuary, and the decrease in reef in the Mission-Aransas Estuary was in the range of 10–50 percent rather than greater than 50 percent. The main effects of these two scenarios upon habitats are the result of increasing population and rising sea level. In general, wetland habitats decrease in area over the entire geographical range of estuaries, with the biggest decreases in the Laguna Madre (swamp habitat is not found south of the Mission-Aransas Estuary). Wind-tidal flat and seagrass will generally increase throughout the coast where these habitats exist; the biggest increases in relative area will occur in the Laguna Madre. Relative area of reef will decrease from the Lavaca–Tres Palacios Estuary southward, but increase in the Sabine-Neches Estuary. Bay area will decrease from the

Table 5.4. Change in Relative Area of Habitats for Scenario Case 1, ΔTemperature = +2°C and ΔPrecipitation = 0%

	Laguna Madre	Nueces	Mission-Aransas	Guadalupe	Lavaca–Tres Palacios	Trinity–San Jacinto	Sabine-Neches
Fresh Marsh	–	–	–	–	–	–	–
Swamp			–	–	–	–	–
Salt-Brackish Marsh	–	–	–	–	–	–	
Wind-Tidal Flat	++	+	+	+	+	+	–
Seagrass	++	+	+	+	+	+	
Reef	–	–	–	–	–	0	++
Bay	–	–	–	+	0	+	+
Spoil	–	–	–	–	–	–	–

0   Change 10% or less.
+   Increase of 10% to 100%.
++   Increase greater than 100%.
–   Decrease 10% to 50%.
—   Decrease greater than 50%.

Table 5.5. Change in Relative Area of Habitats for Scenario Case 2, ΔTemperature = +2°C and ΔPrecipitation = +20%

	Laguna Madre	Nueces	Mission-Aransas	Guadalupe	Lavaca-Tres Palacios	Trinity-San Jacinto	Sabine-Neches
Fresh Marsh	–	0	0	0	0	0	0
Swamp			–	–	+	0	0
Salt-Brackish Marsh	–	+	–	0	0	0	0
Wind-Tidal Flat	++	0	0	+	–	–	
Seagrass	++	0	+	0	0	0	
Reef		0	–	–	0	0	0
Bay	–	0	0	0	0	0	0
Spoil	–	–	–	–	–	–	–

0   Change 10% or less.
+   Increase of 10% to 100%.
++ Increase greater than 100%.
–   Decrease 10% to 50%.
—   Decrease greater than 50%.

Table 5.6. Change in Relative Area of Habitats for Scenario Case 3, ΔTemperature = +2°C and ΔPrecipitation = −20%

	Laguna Madre	Nueces	Mission-Aransas	Guadalupe	Lavaca-Tres Palacios	Trinity-San Jacinto	Sabine-Neches
Fresh Marsh	–	–	–	–	–	–	–
Swamp		–	–	–	–	–	–
Salt-Brackish Marsh	–	–	–	–	–	–	–
Wind-Tidal Flat	++	++	++	++	++	++	++
Seagrass	++	++	++	++	++	++	++
Reef	–	–	–	–	–	–	++
Bay	–	–	–	0	–	+	++
Spoil	–	–	–	–	–	–	–

0 Change 10% or less.
+ Increase of 10% to 100%.
++ Increase greater than 100%.
– Decrease 10% to 50%.
— Decrease greater than 50%.

Mission-Aransas Estuary southward, with no change or small increases to the north. Changes in bay habitat area will most likely be related to the changes in relative amounts of seagrass and reef habitats.

There are not many projected changes in relative habitat area for Case 2 (increase in population, sea level, temperature, and precipitation). This is not surprising, because the inflow:volume ratios for this scenario are so similar to the historical case. Habitats in the Sabine-Neches, Trinity–San Jacinto, and Nueces estuaries will hardly change at all. The Mission-Aransas and Guadalupe estuaries will lose some wetland area, while the Lavaca–Tres Palacios Estuary may gain some. The increased precipitation will not be great enough to offset the effects of sea-level rise in the Laguna Madre, however. It will lose large portions of its wetlands and open bay area and gain large areas of wind-tidal flat and seagrasses.

The inflow decrease for Case 3 (increase in population, sea level, and temperature, and decrease in precipitation) is substantially larger than for Case 1, although both scenarios show the same basic pattern of change. The magnitude of the projected changes for Case 3, however, is more extreme. The relative areas of wetlands will have large decreases throughout most of the coast. Seagrasses and wind-tidal flats will experience large increases coastwide. Reef areas will decrease everywhere but the Sabine-Neches Estuary, where they will increase, and bay areas will generally decrease as seagrasses expand.

On the basis of these analyses, which assume a sea-level rise of 1.5 feet, it is clear that only under circumstances of significant increases in precipitation will the relative areas of estuarine habitats remain as they are now. Sea-level rise will result in an increase in bay area, so significant increases in precipitation will be necessary to maintain current salinity levels. Even with substantial precipitation increases, Laguna Madre salinities would continue to rise, and the distribution of estuarine habitats in the Laguna Madre would change, losing wetlands and gaining seagrass and wind-tidal flats.

Under any other climate change scenarios where precipitation decreases, remains the same, or only increases marginally, there will be a decline in relative wetland areas and an increase in seagrass and wind-tidal flats. These habitats are already more abundant in the central and southern estuaries. Reef areas will decrease except in the Sabine-Neches Estuary, where they will increase. It seems almost certain that salinity levels will increase in all estuaries. For the most extreme case of precipitation decrease, the relative habitat areas of each estuary will become more like their southern neighbors: Sabine-Neches habitat proportions will approach those of the Trinity–San Jacinto; Trinity–San Jacinto habitats will trend toward Lavaca–Tres Palacios; Lavaca–Tres Palacios and Guadalupe relative habitat areas will become like Mission-Aransas; Mission-Aransas and Nueces relative habitat areas will become like the Laguna Madre; and Laguna Madre habitats will become even more arid in character.

Implications of the Effects of Climate Change on Estuarine Fisheries

Commercial fishery species include the brown shrimp, white shrimp, American oyster, blue crab, and black drum. Red drum and spotted sea trout were commercially fished until a few years ago, but are now recreational species only. Other estuarine species caught for recreation include Atlantic croaker, pinfish, southern flounder, and stone crab. The salinity of the water in which these animals live and the availability of vegetative cover are probably the two most important variables influencing their abundance. Under the Case 2 scenario (increase in population, sea level, temperature, and precipitation), salinities and wetland habitat areas will not change substantially except in the Laguna Madre. Fishery production will probably not be strongly affected except in the Laguna, where brown shrimp, white shrimp, and blue crab production would decrease. Production of pinfish, black drum, and red drum might increase in the Laguna Madre, because seagrass beds are favored habitats for these species.

All of the other scenarios, however, would result in increased salinities, decreased wetland and reef areas, and increased seagrass habitats. Oyster production would increase only in the Sabine-Neches Estuary; production of brown and white shrimp, oysters, and blue crabs would probably be reduced in all other estuaries. Case 3, with a large decrease in precipitation, would probably cause a major decline in commercial fishery production, hitting oyster, white shrimp, and blue crab yields the hardest. Brown shrimp would probably decline, but not as drastically. While the commercial shellfish would be hard hit by climate changes as great as in Case 3, some finfish species could benefit. Finfish usually have wider ranges of salinity tolerance than the shellfish and are able to move in and out of suboptimal environments to feed. Seagrass habitats are preferred by predators like black

WILLIAM L. LONGLEY

116

drum, red drum, southern flounder, pinfish, and spotted sea trout, which would benefit from increases in this habitat type in all estuaries. Consequently, global climate changes that do not increase inflow to estuaries will probably result in declines in most shellfish species, the mainstay of the commercial fishing industry. However, finfish species associated with recreational fishing may not be negatively affected by climate change and may even benefit if their preferred habitats significantly expand.

References

Brown, L. F., Jr., J. L. Brewton, T. J. Evans, J. H. McGowen, W. A. White, C. G. Groat, and W. L. Fisher, 1980. *Environmental Geologic Atlas of the Texas Coastal Zone — Brownsville-Harlingen Area.* Bureau of Economic Geology, University of Texas at Austin.

Brown, L. F., Jr., J. L. Brewton, J. H. McGowen, T. J. Evans, W. L. Fisher, and C. G. Groat, 1976. *Environmental Geologic Atlas of the Texas Coastal Zone — Corpus Christi Area.* Bureau of Economic Geology, University of Texas at Austin.

Brown, L. F., Jr., J. H. McGowen, T. J. Evans, C. G. Groat, and W. L. Fisher, 1977. *Environmental Geologic Atlas of the Texas Coastal Zone — Kingsville Area.* Bureau of Economic Geology, University of Texas at Austin.

Diener, R. A., 1975. *Cooperative Gulf of Mexico Estuarine Inventory and Study — Texas: Area Description.* NOAA Tech. Report NMFS Circ.-393.

Fisher, W. L., L. F. Brown, Jr., J. H. McGowen, and C. G. Groat, 1973. *Environmental Geologic Atlas of the Texas Coastal Zone — Beaumont–Port Arthur Area.* Bureau of Economic Geology, University of Texas at Austin.

Fisher, W. L., J. H. McGowen, L. F. Brown, Jr., and C. G. Groat, 1972. *Environmental Geologic Atlas of the Texas Coastal Zone — Galveston-Houston Area.* Bureau of Economic Geology, University of Texas at Austin.

McGowen, J. H., L. F. Brown, Jr., T. J. Evans, W. L. Fisher, and C. G. Groat, 1976a. *Environmental Geologic Atlas of the Texas Coastal Zone — Bay City–Freeport Area.* Bureau of Economic Geology, University of Texas at Austin.

McGowen, J. H., C. V. Procter, Jr., L. F. Brown, Jr., T. J. Evans, W. L. Fisher, and C. G. Groat, 1976b. *Environmental Geologic Atlas of the Texas Coastal Zone — Port Lavaca Area.* Bureau of Economic Geology, University of Texas at Austin.

Pritchard, D. W., 1967. What is an Estuary: Physical Viewpoint. In:

Estuaries, G. H. Lauff (ed.). American Association for the Advancement of Science, Publication No. 83, Washington, D.C.

Schmandt, J., G. Ward., and S. Hadden, 1992. *Texas and Global Warming: Emissions, Surface Water Supplies and Sea Level Rise.* Lyndon B. Johnson School of Public Affairs, University of Texas at Austin.

Solis, R. S., 1992. Patterns of Inflow and Salinity. In: *Freshwater Inflows to Texas Bays and Estuaries: Ecological Relationships and Methods for Determination of Needs,* W. L. Longley (ed.). Texas Water Development Board and Texas Parks and Wildlife Department, Austin.

Texas Department of Water Resources, 1984. *Water for Texas: Technical Appendix,* Vol. 2. TDWR, Report GP-4-1, Austin.

Texas Water Development Board (TWDB), 1990. *Water for Texas: Today and Tomorrow — 1990.* TWDB, Austin.

Ward, G. H., 1992. A Water Budget for the State of Texas with Climatological Forcing. Center for Research in Water Resources, University of Texas at Austin, Tech. Memo. CRWR 92-3.

Zimmerman, R. J., T. J. Minello, E. F. Klima, and J. M. Nance, 1991. Effects of Accelerated Sea-Level Rise on Coastal Secondary Production. In: *Coastal Wetlands Coastal Zone 1991 Conference-ASCE,* H. S. Bolton and O. T. Magoon (eds.). Long Beach, Calif.

WILLIAM L. LONGLEY

JANE PACKARD

6. Biodiversity

The rich biological diversity of Texas is matched by few other states. Ten major natural regions are currently recognized within Texas (Figure 6.1). Within each natural region, the landscape is further subdivided into different vegetation types corresponding to variations in land and water features (Hayes et al. 1987). The concept of *biodiversity* refers to (1) the number of different types of natural regions in the state, (2) the number of native species within each natural region, and (3) the genetic variation within species (Reid and Trexler 1991).

This priceless natural heritage of biodiversity in Texas could change as a consequence of global warming. To date, no detailed studies have been done on the potential effects of climate change on the distribution of native species of plants and animals in Texas, so no predictions can be made about whether biodiversity will increase or decrease with global warming. However, it is certain that the assemblages of native plants and animals that we know today would change in distribution and/or composition as a result of global warming. Exactly how these changes are likely to occur would require an analysis beyond the scope of this chapter.

Therefore, this chapter first outlines some general principles about the potential effects of climate change on biodiversity in terrestrial landscapes. Then the different natural regions of Texas are described to give the reader an appreciation of both the richness of the natural heritage of the state and the reasons ecological changes would be expected to differ for each region. Although aquatic communities are an important part of biological diversity, only the terrestrial landscape will be considered as an illustration of the principles involved.

To be consistent with other chapters, this preliminary application of theory will be based on a scenario of an increase of 2°C in mean annual temperature (Chap. 2). However, the

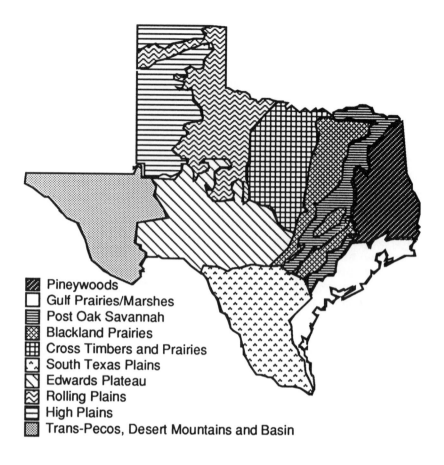

Pineywoods
Gulf Prairies/Marshes
Post Oak Savannah
Blackland Prairies
Cross Timbers and Prairies
South Texas Plains
Edwards Plateau
Rolling Plains
High Plains
Trans-Pecos, Desert Mountains and Basin

Figure 6.1.
The rich biological diversity in Texas is represented in the landscapes of natural resource parks within ten major natural regions that have been further subdivided by ecologists according to distinctive vegetation and geology within each region (Hayes et al. 1987).

discussion will show that many other factors interact in determining changes in the distribution of native plants and animals. In particular, uncertainties regarding associated changes in rainfall, the rate of climate change, and climatic variability (e.g., drought and freezes) make it very difficult in this preliminary analysis to make statewide predictions about changes in biodiversity.

At the conclusion of the chapter, recommendations will be made regarding the types of studies and strategies needed to manage the existing mosaic of protected areas. This mosaic provides a living museum of the natural heritage of the state; however, in contrast to the usual image of museum collections, these natural areas represent a dynamically changing interplay between the past and the present. The very essence of interpreting these processes of change is invaluable for citizens of the state, because in reading the prints of the past, they are encouraged to explore the paths of the future.

General Principles: Ecology and Climate Change

Four general principles are recognized regarding the effects of climate change on ecological systems (Peters and Darling 1985; Peters 1989).

1. As the earth warms, species tend to shift to northern latitudes and higher altitudes.

2. Loss of biological diversity is likely to result from the interaction of climate change and increasing isolation of habitat fragments due to human land-use practices.

3. The rate at which species are lost from protected areas depends on both their intrinsic abilities to migrate and the existence of continuous habitat along gradients of climate change.

4. Factors influencing species distribution are more complex than just mean annual temperature; other factors to be considered include precipitation, evaporation, soil and substrate, soil moisture retention, extremes in temperature and precipitation, carbon dioxide stimulation, and relations between species.

These four general principles are explained below to establish a conceptual framework. In the subsequent section, specific hypotheses about potential landscape changes in Texas will be derived from this general framework. Since very little research has actually been done on the effects of recent climate change on native plant and animal communities in this part of the continent, these statements should be interpreted as hypotheses rather than fact.

Shift to Higher Latitudes and Altitudes

Paleontological studies of plants during warmer, interglacial periods enable us to make the generalization that an increase in temperature is likely to result in shifts in species distribution (Emanuel et al. 1985; Webb 1987). For example, some trees currently typical of southern forests (e.g., sweet gums)

a. Schematic distribution of a species relative to altitude prior to climate change

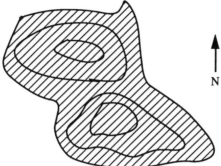

b. After global warming, the same species is limited to higher elevations

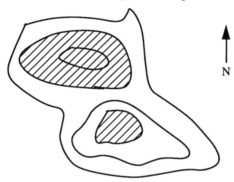

Figure 6.2.
Vegetation zones
are likely to move
up mountains and
toward the north
with global
warming.

JANE PACKARD

122

grew in Ontario during warm interglacial periods that ended more than 100,000 years ago (Peters 1989). Trees such as hemlock and white pine were found 1,150 feet (350 m) higher on mountains during a period that was 2°C warmer than to-day (middle Holocene 4,000–7,900 years ago; ibid.). During the same period, the Chihuahuan Desert supported grass-lands in an area that had been oak-juniper woodland in an earlier, cooler period, the early Holocene (7,900–11,000 years ago; Van Devender 1983).

In general, a reasonable estimate of the shift in vegetation belts is 60 miles (100 km) north (or a 550 foot [170 m] increase in altitude) for each 1°C increase in temperature (Peters 1989). These factors are interactive, such that a patch of evergreen trees may persist on a mountaintop long after conditions favoring surrounding forest at lower elevations have shifted northward (Figure 6.2).

The ability of species to respond to changes in climate is inhibited by increasing isolation of ecological communities resulting from human land-use practices. Two factors are important regarding human impact on landscape: (1) habitat fragmentation and (2) corridors of dispersal between fragments (Noss 1991).

Habitat fragmentation refers to the process by which stands of native vegetation become smaller and discontinuous as a result of clearing for purposes such as agriculture, residential, and commercial use (Brothers and Spingarn 1992). The effects of habitat fragmentation vary depending on the life requirements of the isolated species, the size and shape of the fragment, existing seed banks for plants, and the different abilities of native and nonnative species to move between fragments.

Parks and reserves tend to represent fragments of previously extensive natural vegetation, either because areas with native vegetation were targeted as high priority for protection, or because human development eventually occurs up to the boundaries of protected areas (Wauer 1983). However, fragments of native vegetation may also occur on private lands, depending on land-use practices of the owners. Biologists refer to the "mosaic" of different vegetation types in a given landscape, including those in various stages of cultivation and succession of native vegetation.

Dispersal corridors are relatively long, thin areas connecting habitat fragments (Figure 6.3a), within which the vegetational structure is more favorable for the movement of native species than adjacent areas impacted by human use. For example, native vegetation often is allowed to remain along the banks of rivers. If two biological reserves (habitat fragments) are adjacent to the river, then animals and the seeds of plants may move along the river corridor between the two habitat fragments. However, many factors influence the suitability of strips of native vegetation with regard to the function of corridors linking larger habitat patches. Behavior of each species must be considered in assessing whether a vegetation strip will function as a movement corridor.

Systems of several reserves connected by corridors have been proposed as more likely to protect biological diversity than isolated protected areas (Noss 1991). The logic behind this principle is the same as the old saying, "Never put all

BIODIVERSITY

a. Before climate change

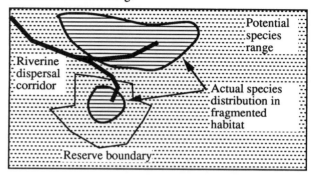

b. After climate change

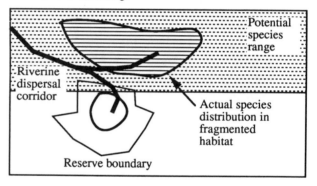

Figure 6.3.
Extinction is likely to be due to an interaction between (1) isolation of habitat fragments and (2) movement of favorable climatic conditions outside of protected fragments.

your eggs in one basket." If a species becomes extinct in one area, the area may be recolonized from connected habitat fragments (Saunders and de Rebeira 1991). In general, the smaller the fragment, the higher the probability of extinction due to loss of genetic diversity, catastrophes, or an imbalance in relations of competing species, predators, and their prey (Soulé et al. 1988).

Isolation of a biotic community due to human-related fragmentation may increase the probability of extinction of species as the climate changes (Figure 6.3b). If barriers exist between two fragments of habitat, and one fragment declines in quality, it is unlikely that a species will cross a barrier to another fragment that is better for it (Peters 1989). This generalization obviously depends on the dispersal abilities of species, as discussed below.

Species Extinction and Disappearance of Communities

Global warming could cause the disappearance of communities and species from areas where they occur today. This could happen as a result of several factors: (1) existing microclimatic conditions may move outside the boundaries of protected areas, (2) species may not be able to migrate as fast as conditions move, and (3) as different species move into the specific location, new interactions may result.

Theoretically, if a protected area is at the southern edge of the distribution of an endangered species, that species may disappear from the area as climatic conditions required by the species move northward or toward the tops of mountains (Figure 6.3b). In an undisturbed system, where habitat fragmentation has not occurred, species that have their center of distribution farther south are likely to invade protected areas to the north as climate warms. However, extinction is likely if the means of dispersal do not exist between old, declining fragments and new, improving patches. Furthermore, endangered species adapted to a very specialized, narrow set of conditions are more likely to be adversely affected by climate change than those that have a wide tolerance of climatic conditions and are endangered due to human impacts such as overharvesting.

Currently, endangered species are viewed by managers as indicators of the health of ecosystems, and attention has shifted from single-species management to management of the community of plant and animal species upon which the endangered species is dependent in a given landscape. However, this perspective raises many questions. Is the current assemblage of species in a community likely to remain constant with global climate change and simply shift to a new location? If not, and the species composition of a community shifts, will invading species fulfill the same functions as those that are left?

The emerging perspective for analysis of such questions deals with the relative rate at which new fragments of habitat become available for a given species as old fragments decline in a habitat mosaic. As climatic conditions change, the suitability of existing habitat is expected to decline, and

a. Habitat change along a continuous gradient of climate change

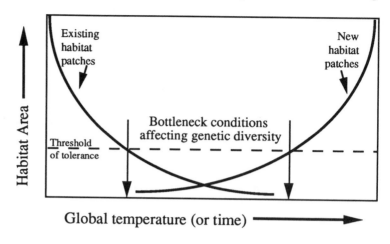

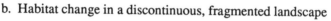

Figure 6.4.
The probability of
extinction related
to climate change is
related to (1) the
changes in old and
new fragments rel-
ative to a threshold
of habitat suitability
and (2) the lag in
disappearance of
old fragments and
appearance of new
fragments in a
landscape mosaic
(adapted from
T. Cook, pers.
comm.).

b. Habitat change in a discontinuous, fragmented landscape

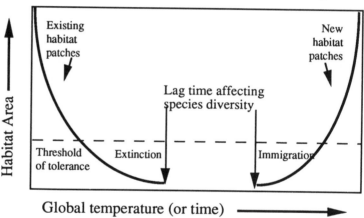

the suitability of new habitat is expected to increase (Figure 6.4a). The bottleneck period for extinction of a species
from a habitat mosaic will be when conditions in the old
habitat fragments drop below a threshold of tolerance, and
conditions in the new habitat fragments have not yet reached
this threshold. This is when genetic diversity is likely to be
lost. The longer the lag time between decline of old fragments and improvement of new fragments, the higher the
likelihood of extinction (Figure 6.4b; T. Cook, pers. comm.).
    The rate of habitat change projected under the global
warming scenario will be many times greater than the rate at

which plant species responded in previous epochs related to glacial periods (Vitousek 1989; Risser 1990). Furthermore, plant and animal species may move at different rates (Davis and Zabinski 1991). Plant species that have windblown seeds will invade new areas more rapidly than those that reproduce vegetatively or whose heavy seeds fall below the parent plant (Brothers and Spingarn 1992). Likewise, animals that can fly or otherwise migrate long distances between suitable habitat patches will be more resilient than those unable to do so. Some scenarios project movement rates of vegetation zones that are faster (4.5 miles [7 km] per year) than rates of range expansion documented for vertebrates such as deer (1-2 miles [2-3 km] per year; Peters 1989). In addition, those species that produce many offspring are more likely to invade newly suitable habitats than those producing few offspring. Theoretically, this latter principle is analogous to playing a lottery: When the payoff is big and few are likely to win, those who purchase many tickets have a higher probability of winning than those who purchase few.

Even for migratory species the picture is complicated. With global warming, vegetation changes are projected to be greater near the poles than near the equator (Kellogg 1990). Thus, loss of tundra nesting habitat may threaten the migratory shorebirds, ducks, cranes, and geese that winter in Texas (Peters 1989).

Extinctions can occur as a result of the invasion of antagonistic species that affect the quality of habitat fragments. For example, a warmer climate may favor invasions of insect species previously limited in their northward expansion by the freeze line (threshold of temperature tolerance for most plants). Such range expansions can affect the viability of native species in the locations invaded. The rapid range expansion of fire ants from Alabama to eastern Texas appears to have affected the diversity of ground-dwelling species vulnerable to the ants (B. Vinson in Revkin 1989).

Theoretically, an ideal strategy for protection of a representative sample of biological diversity within a state would include a series of interconnected areas arranged along gradients of expected climate change (Graham 1988; Peters 1989; Noss 1991). In this manner, species could move at their own rate along the gradient. Where this is not possible, restoration technology may aid in artificially moving those species most vulnerable to extinction as threshold conditions shift along the climate gradient.

Complex Interaction of Microclimatic Factors

The data do not currently exist to predict exactly what ecological changes will occur with global warming. For example, global warming is certain to change precipitation patterns, but the regional effects are open to some dispute depending on whether scientists consult global climate models, anomalies in weather patterns, or the paleontological record. As discussed for agricultural plants (see Chap. 7), key limiting factors for native plants may involve an interaction of precipitation, temperature, evaporation, soil moisture retention, soil chemistry, and stimulation by carbon dioxide.

Seasonality of rainfall relative to the growing season of plants can have an important impact. For example, studies of vegetational changes in the Chihuahuan Desert of New Mexico suggest that the vegetation is shifting from grasses to shrubs as a result of changes in the seasonality of drought (Neilson 1986). Wetter winters favor growth of shrubs, and drier springs reduce proliferation of grasses. Shrubs can take advantage of rainfall during the winter and endure the droughts of summer. However, grasses do not grow during winter (despite rainfall) and are susceptible to dry conditions in the spring and summer.

For many native species of plants, the extremes of temperature or rainfall have more of an influence on survival than the annual mean (Merrill and Young 1959). Also, stresses due to climatic factors near the threshold of tolerance may make individual species more susceptible to diseases or other pathogens. Each species has a unique set of tolerance ranges to physical factors, and such tolerances change during the lifetime of the individual. Some species are dependent on other species for modification of microclimates and soils (Perry et al. 1990). For example, in the Chisos Basin of Big Bend National Park, tree seedlings are less frequent on the denuded soils downhill from trails than uphill (Whitson 1974). The removal of vegetation downhill results in changes in soil microorganisms, temperature, nutrients, and moisture, all of which are important factors influencing seed sprouting and seedling survival.

Uncertainty Regarding Projections

JANE PACKARD

Although decision makers want clear-cut projections about the potential effects of climate change on biodiversity, the best scientists will be very careful about the statements they make, because ecological systems are more sensitive to the frequency and duration of climatic extremes than to the mean temperature. So far, global climate models do not claim to display the precision needed to predict the duration, frequency, or seasonality of droughts. Therefore, ecologists do not have the information they need to make accurate predictions.

For Texas, projections regarding summer rainfall are highly variable among the models of global climate change (Kellogg 1990). Two out of five models actually project an increase in summer rains for the southern portion of Texas. However, since three of the five models predict a decrease in summer rains, that is the projection accepted as a working hypothesis for the region.

We do not yet have adequate projections of how global warming would affect seasonality of precipitation in West Texas. Even regional weather models are still primitive in their abilities to predict actual seasonal changes (Dickinson et al. 1989). In contrast to the predicted decline in spring/summer rain due to increasing CO_2, weather anomalies such as warm Arctic springs (Jager and Kellogg 1983) and El Niño conditions (Risser 1990) tend to increase spring precipitation carried by weather systems from the West and Gulf coasts. Such an increase in spring/summer precipitation could counteract predictions based solely on temperature (Trenberth et al. 1988).

Furthermore, it is difficult to distinguish the potential influence of global warming from other interacting factors. The shift of grasses to shrubs in the Chihuahuan Desert may also be explained by overgrazing, which reduces soil coverage (Schlesinger et al. 1990) and increases shrub seed dispersal (Archer 1990). In addition, as explained in Chapter 7, C3 plants will have a relative growth advantage under conditions of enhanced CO_2. This may, for instance, enable shrubs to compete more effectively with grasses, independent of changes in the seasonality of precipitation (Risser 1990). The relative competitive abilities of other native plant species that differ in photosynthetic pathways (C3 vs. C4) may be facilitated by warmer temperature, and such interactions remain to be investigated for native vegetation (Vitousek 1989).

The current shift in the philosophical metaphors underlying the science of ecology (Botkin 1990) further complicates the degree to which scientists will agree on projected changes in biological communities due to climate change. Previously, ecological communities were seen as coevolved units with feedback loops that resisted change in abiotic factors and species composition. According to this mechanistic viewpoint, communities are likely to shift in distribution but not in composition. Currently, each species is viewed much more as an individual entity, responding to changes in the set of factors that limit its distribution. According to this view of "discordant harmony," community composition is likely to change as individual species shift in distribution at different rates and in different directions. Although the latter view may be more realistic for most (but not necessarily all) communities, it presents a tremendous challenge to derive predictions about the landscape level based on extrapolations from the individual and population levels. Given current technologies, some scientists express great confidence in being able to meet this challenge (Vitousek 1989; Botkin 1990).

Much more refinement of regional models of global climate change will be necessary before it is possible to refine predictions of the most likely ecological changes in Texas. Nevertheless, having made such disclaimers about our predictive abilities given current information, it is possible to identify the salient questions that need to be asked regarding potential changes in each of the natural regions of Texas.

Potential Changes in Natural Regions of Texas

Vegetation in each natural region of Texas is likely to respond differently, as determined by gradients of temperature and rainfall, which cross distinctive geological features (Figure 6.5). The probabilities of freezes and droughts change inversely in a northwest/southeast gradient (Thomas 1975; Owen and Schmidly 1986). Overlaid on this is an east/west gradient of precipitation influencing soil moisture retention and the distribution of tree species. In the following subsections, the climatic characteristics and vegetation of each natural region will be described, and primary questions regarding potential changes in biodiversity will be identified for each region.

Pineywoods—East Texas

Historically, pines and oaks blanketed the rolling hills of the Pineywoods (Thomas 1975), while tall hardwoods filled the seasonally flooded bottomlands (Graham 1992). Even today,

JANE PACKARD

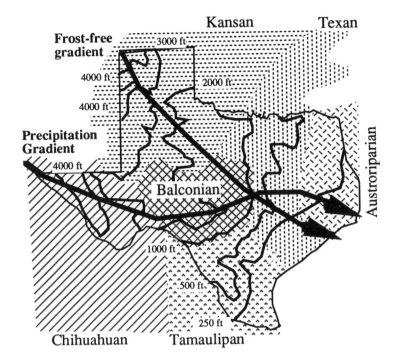

Figure 6.5.
The six biomes of
Texas (shaded) are
larger units classi-
fying vegetation
types in the region
(Blair 1950); they
are a function of
gradients of pre-
cipitation (thick
arrow), annual
frost-free period
(thick arrow), and
underlying geolog-
ical features (eleva-
tion represented
by medium-width
solid lines)
(Thomas 1975).

flowering dogwoods and other shrubs provide scenic beauty in the spring.

Known by scientists as the Austroriparian biotic province (Blair 1950), which extends into Louisiana, Arkansas, and Oklahoma, the Pineywoods of eastern Texas represent Texas' most important forest resource. The climate in this area is cooler and wetter than other portions of Texas, representing the type of climatic conditions known as humid subtropical (Norwine 1978).

The original vegetation in much of this region has become fragmented as a result of forest plantations and agriculture. Game species such as turkey and deer flourish in a mosaic of vegetation patches that include an understory of diverse species. Rare species with specialized requirements, such as the endangered red-cockaded woodpecker, are dependent on fragments of old-growth forests with hollow trees suitable for nesting. Remnant fragments of bottomland hardwoods along waterways are rich in biological diversity and provide potential travel corridors for wildlife. Replacing the native vegetation with homogenous pine plantations would eliminate much of this diversity.

BIODIVERSITY

According to one theory, the boundaries of this forested area would be likely to move toward the northeast due to changes in soil moisture retention. This would represent an interaction of the general northward contraction of the forests of the eastern United States (Davis and Zabinski 1991) and the projected eastward movement of the zone of soil moisture retention adequate to support an oak/hickory/pine forest in Texas.

Alternatively, species composition of the forest communities might change. Species differ in their response to the combined effects of CO_2 and water stress (Tolley and Strain 1984; Sionit et al. 1985; Williams et al. 1986). Will certain species gain a competitive advantage over others? How will successional patterns be changed?

Theoretically, fragments of bottomland hardwoods along rivers would show less change than upland forests, presuming there are no human related changes in flooding patterns of rivers. If water control structures are built, or pressure increases to harvest bottomland hardwoods, this community might be affected indirectly by human response to climate change.

Grassland/Forest Transition—Central Texas

Located west of the Pineywoods is a grassland/forest transition zone known as the Texan biotic province (Blair 1950). The diversity of vegetation and geological features within this transition zone include oak woodland, cross timbers, bottomland forests, and prairies (Figure 6.1). Historically, the growth of trees in this region was probably controlled by fires (Strength and Harcombe 1982). The climate in this region is humid subtropical to subtropical subhumid, a little drier than the Pineywoods to the east and cooler than the plains to the south (Norwine 1978).

Natural prairie vegetation has become fragmented where the rich black soils are cultivated. The natural patches of oaks remain interspersed with meadows in regions predominately used as cattle pasture. Strips of oak woodland and prairie run in a southwest/northeast direction in concert with geologic features and parallel to the predicted gradient of change in soil moisture retention. More information is needed to understand the connectivity of these remaining fragments, but it is likely that fragmentation is more extreme in the prairies than in the cross timbers and the oak woodlands.

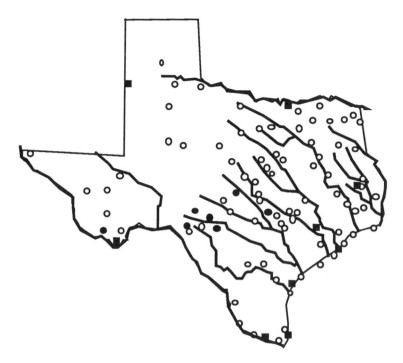

Figure 6.6.
The river drainages providing potential dispersal corridors connecting habitat fragments in Texas are in the same direction as the frost-free gradient and perpendicular to the precipitation gradient. The symbols represent state parks and wildlife management areas (circles); state natural areas (dots); and national parks, preserves, and wildlife refuges (squares). The thick lines represent rivers, and thin lines represent state boundaries.

Several alternative hypotheses might be posed regarding vegetation changes in this region. Those tree species limited by soil moisture retention might be expected to retreat along gradients to the northeast, resulting in a decline of woodlots. If the expansion of brush species from the south was previously limited by severe freezes, species more typical of the South Texas Plains might be expected to invade. Alternatively, if the differences in carbon pathways are important in moderating the response to climate change, shrubs and trees might replace grasses under conditions of CO_2 enrichment.

The geological features of Texas are dominated by the southeasterly recession of the coastline and the southeasterly direction of river flows (Figure 6.6). Thus, the rivers run in a direction perpendicular to the bands of geologically uniform terrain and could act as barriers to movement along the predicted gradient of soil moisture retention.

Gulf Coast

Barrier islands stretching along the coast, salt-grass marshes surrounding bays and estuaries, and inland prairies and bottomland hardwoods flanking some rivers all contribute to the diversity of the coastal region. The shoreline runs parallel to the gradient of rainfall, and climatic variation is primarily influenced by storms from the Gulf.

The Gulf Coast region is widely known for its importance as an overwintering region for waterfowl (Reid and Trexler 1991) and shorebirds from the Central Flyway extending into the Canadian Arctic. The barrier islands and estuaries are important for shorebirds. Ducks move between feeding areas in the estuaries and inland freshwater ponds. Geese feed and loaf in the mosaic of salt marshes, rice fields, and inland wetlands.

Human influences on the landscape include conversion of the coastal prairies to agricultural use and extensive urbanization around bays with deep water ports. Development of tourism and leisure activities have greatly modified certain portions of the barrier islands. The Attwater's prairie chicken is currently endangered because of the wide separation of suitable fragments of prairie habitat. The decline of the endangered whooping crane has been arrested with protection of the winter feeding grounds on bays and islands. The Houston toad is endangered by urban development of its habitat. Kemp's Ridley sea turtle is an example of a highly specialized species, nesting only on specific stretches of beach on barrier islands.

The predicted effects of climate change on increasing salinity of estuaries and flooding of salt marshes are discussed in Chapter 5. In general, coastal systems are stressed by multiple changes and are not likely to be resilient to the additional consequences of climate change (Ibid.). A more specific analysis of Texas' coastal region is needed to determine the extent of predicted changes in coastal wetlands and the implications for migratory waterfowl.

South Texas Plains

South Texas brushlands constitute the Tamaulipan biotic province, which extends almost to the Tropic of Cancer, where distinctively tropical vegetation begins (Blair 1950). This subtropical, subhumid "desert jungle" is unique. Influenced by storms from the Gulf, it nevertheless receives sporadic rainfall and is susceptible to droughts. This semiarid climate is characterized by warm neotropical temperatures and higher humidity than the arid western portion of the state (Norwine 1978).

Distinctive differences in plant communities exist within

JANE PACKARD

this region along rivers, on the flat plains, and along the coast. The Coastal Sand Plains of the King Ranch are well known as good wildlife habitat and extensive cattle range. Exotic species such as the nilgai antelope have been introduced to this region. Desertification induced by prolonged over-grazing of grass on the flat plains has resulted in mixed brush species dominated by mesquite (Bogusch 1952). Much of this region is excellent habitat for deer and is easily managed for quail hunts. Denser brush along drainages provides good habitat for javelina, also a game species. The native pecan woods that used to flank rivers (Inglis 1964) have been reduced to small fragments, providing habitat for diverse species of birds.

Most of the brush has been cleared from the rich Rio Grande Valley, the delta, and the banks of the lower Rio Grande. This loss of habitat for wildlife has critically threatened endangered species such as the ocelot and jagaroundi, which are limited to thick stands of subtropical/tropical brush and are found nowhere else in the United States. Although increased agriculture initially boosted the numbers of white-winged doves, a popular game bird, recent declines in the flocks are thought to be due to reduction in the stands of trees that provide suitable nesting habitat. Vegetation in this subtropical region appears to be important as a staging area for neotropical migratory songbirds, and a wide diversity of bird species are sighted in the region because of the overlap in ranges of bird species from temperate and tropical regions. Specific locations, such as the shallow waters in the salt pans of Sal del Rey, attract a high diversity of shorebirds.

Habitat restoration has been initiated along the Rio Grande (Jahrsdoerfer and Leslie 1988). This project is directed toward increasing the corridors linking existing patches of brush and involves planting of native brush species (Hayes et al. 1987).

Theoretically, a change in temperature would have little effect on the plant communities in this region, since most are adapted to the warm climate. However, sites dependent on shallow water, such as Sal del Rey, would most likely be affected because of greater rates of evaporation.

The uncertainty regarding projected changes in rainfall in this region makes predictions difficult. If rainfall increases, species typical of more tropical regions of the Tamaulipan biotic province might be expected to migrate northward. If rainfall decreases, or droughts become more prolonged, those species more sensitive to extended dryness will be expected to decline. Under drought conditions, some encroachment of creosote bush might be expected from the west. To the extent that herbaceous and other woody plant productivity is reduced by the volatile compounds from creosote, the quality of wildlife habitat might be reduced by this invasion.

Hill Country—Edwards Plateau

The scenic Edwards Plateau is well known for the meadows interspersed with oak/juniper woodlands that grow on limestone soils and escarpments, providing the unique features characterizing the Balconian biotic province (Blair 1950). The climate, slightly cooler than the south and drier than the east, is known as subtropical steppe (Norwine 1978).

The former native plant communities of this region, substantially changed by domestic livestock grazing, provide a good example of how biodiversity can be reduced as the native species within a region decline. Grass cover that previously limited establishment of woody plants has been reduced where sheep overgrazed, and, with the resulting loss of soil, dense juniper stands became established at the expense of grasses, particularly where fire was suppressed. Subsequently, closed canopies of juniper shaded out the diverse communities of broad-leafed plants that produce showy wildflowers in the spring. Elimination of predators favored an increase in white-tailed deer, which together with sheep and cattle graze on the broad-leafed plants. Goats compete with deer for the leaves and twigs of shrubs and leave a distinctive browse-line in some pastures.

Specialized habitats in the Balcones Canyonlands are home to nine species currently under protection as endangered or threatened and another six species that are under consideration for protection (BAT 1990). For example, the black-capped vireo is endangered and the golden cheeked warbler is threatened because of reductions in nesting habitat. The vireo requires a mosaic of oak/juniper woodlands interspersed with meadows, and the warbler requires oak-dominated forests in deep canyons. These habitats are directly threatened by urban development around Austin and are now part of a Regional Habitat Conservation Plan designed to redirect development to less-sensitive areas (BAT 1990). Furthermore, the black-capped vireo is endangered by the invasion of brown-headed cowbirds that lay their eggs in vireo nests and reduce nestling survival. Cowbird populations have increased with cattle operations and illustrate the detrimental impacts of a widely distributed generalist species invading the habitat of a specialized native species with limited distribution.

The limestone karst in this region has numerous caves, sinkholes, and fissures where water has dissolved the limestone. This karst provides limited habitat for unique invertebrates, including a pseudoscorpion, two beetles, and two spiders that are endangered (BAT 1990). Disturbance of the vegetation and pollution of water from urban runoff are considered the major threats in the recharge zones that maintain the microclimates of the karst habitat. In addition, global warming could increase demand for irrigation and municipal water pumped from the Edwards aquifer, further reducing water flow in Comal and San Marcos springs, unique habitats for a blind catfish and two endangered salamanders.

Again, a simple change in mean temperature theoretically would have little effect on native communities in this region, where most species are adapted to moderate temperatures and dry conditions. The edges of this region are more bounded by soil and geological features than by gradual gradients in temperature and soil moisture retention.

Several hypotheses can be postulated to account for changes in community composition due to the interaction of other factors associated with global warming. If the frequency of severe winter freezes were reduced, species such as blackbrush might expand in range northward into the plateau. A reduction in rainfall appears more likely than an increase in this region. In the past, occasional droughts in this area have caused mortality in live oak and shin oak (Merrill and Young 1959). If precipitation declined or droughts became more frequent, would moisture-sensitive shrubs be reduced in density and distribution? Would a reduction in oak be detrimental to the endangered black-crowned vireo and yellow-cheeked warbler as well as to deer that feed upon acorns? Would a reduction in rainfall affect recharge of the aquifer and the specific conditions required by endangered karst invertebrates? How would different plant species respond to CO_2 enrichment, and would this positively affect establishment of new patches of oaks?

Rolling Plains and High Plains—Panhandle

Historically, the grasses of the flat plains in the Panhandle used to be the southernmost extension of the vast prairies known as the Kansan biotic province (Blair 1950). This biome includes two natural regions, Rolling Plains and High Plains (Figure 6.1). The flat, high plains supported immense herds of buffalo, pronghorn, and vast prairie-dog towns (Graham 1992). In the canyons, cut by the headwaters of rivers draining from the Rolling Plains toward the Gulf, are remnants of the pinyon/juniper/oak biota that used to extend to the Rocky Mountains during a cooler epoch (Wells 1965). Current climatic conditions in the Panhandle are characterized as middle-latitude steppe, indicating more freezing days than southern regions (Norwine 1978).

Native vegetation in the High Plains has been almost eliminated due to agricultural development. Only small fragments of prairie remain, and playa lakes provide important habitat for waterfowl in a mosaic dominated by agricultural lands. Geological breaks, such as the Palo Duro Canyon, provide habitat for introduced, nonnative barbary sheep (aoudad). The effect of grazing by these exotic sheep on native plant diversity has not been assessed.

Habitat restoration has been initiated in the Rolling Plains (Hayes et al. 1987). Specific seed mixtures appropriate to the microenvironments required by native prairie plants were used successfully in restoring native vegetation in Copper Breaks State Park, Caprock Canyons State Park, and Lake Colorado City State Recreation Area.

Theoretically, a simple change in temperature would have little influence, because species in this region are adapted to winter freezes. However, without additional rainfall, playa lakes might shrink in size and dry up more quickly on a seasonal basis. The Palo Duro Canyon represents a unique geographical feature, and it is difficult to predict how its microclimate would respond to global warming.

Scenarios predicting changes in rainfall for this region differ between the High Plains and Rolling Plains (Chapter 7). The High Plains is more likely to receive the same or less rainfall, whereas the Rolling Plains is likely to receive an increase in rainfall. How will differences in C_3 and C_4 photosynthesis influence the competition among species in adjusting to potentially greater water loss on the High Plains and better growing conditions (higher temperature and rainfall) on the Rolling Plains? Will increased grass vitality in prairie fragments on the Rolling Plains reduce the probability of shrub establishment at the same time adult shrubs benefit from CO_2 enrichment?

JANE PACKARD

The wide-open panoramas, short brush, arid hills, and mountains of west Texas represent the northeastern extent of the Chihuahuan biotic province (Blair 1950; Schmidt 1983). Warm and dry climatic conditions are typical of this subtropical desert (Norwine 1978), located between two mountain masses. The Chihuahuan Desert is influenced by humid weather systems from the Gulf of Mexico during the summer, and during the winter it receives precipitation transported sporadically by cyclones in the Pacific (Schmidt 1983).

The mountains and scattered hills in this desert region provide much variation in terrain and vegetation (Henrickson and Johnston 1983). Pines, oaks, pinyons, and junipers grow on permeable soils at higher altitudes, with sotol/lechugwe at intermediate elevations, grasslands on fine, moisture-retaining soils, and desert scrub/woodlands on low-elevation permeable soils. The taller Davis and Guadalupe mountains in the northern portion of this region are more closely affiliated with the southern end of the Rocky Mountain range, whereas the biota of the Chisos Mountains in the south is more closely associated with the northern tip of the Sierra del Carmen range that extends into Mexico.

Due to the nature of the terrain, these mountains represent stepping-stones of habitat fragments within the desert lowlands (Wauer 1983). Distinctively different flora and fauna are found in the habitats of high and low altitudes. For example, white-tailed deer typically have sedentary home ranges in the pine/oak woods at higher elevations, whereas mule deer aggregate in patchy, transient areas of good forage at lower elevations. Home ranges of mountain lions and javelina are larger at lower elevations, where they find less food per area than at higher elevations. Frosts at higher elevations limit the distribution of some cactus; other plants are limited by dry conditions in the lower flats.

Two rivers in this region represent a distinctive habitat type that contributes to the diversity of the biota. The Rio Grande cuts a west/east transect, and the Pecos River has a southeasterly course to its junction with the Rio Grande.

Theoretically, the greatest changes in vegetation likely to occur with warming of this region would be movement of vegetational zones upward in altitude. For mountains of low altitude such as the Chisos, this may mean additional stress on existing pine/oak woods. Will pine/oak woods persist at

BIODIVERSITY

139

the tops of the taller Davis Mountains and disappear from the Chisos? Rare plants adapted to medium altitudes may undergo habitat fragmentation as suitable conditions disappear from the valleys and are limited to isolated hills.

Questions Raised in Projecting Ecological Changes

Imagine a cross superimposed on the map of Texas (Figure 6.5). The horizontal bar is the freeze line, and the vertical bar is the tree line (threshold of soil moisture retention for trees). Now, move that cross to the northeast and you have a simplistic image of what is projected to occur in Texas with an increase in temperature, assuming (1) no change in precipitation, (2) biotic communities move as a unit, and (3) no complications due to soil requirements and no potential barriers such as rivers and escarpments. Now consider the questions that are raised if we consider geographical features such as bands of soil, rivers, canyons, mountains, and escarpments.

If freezes become less frequent in the south, the control of brush species vulnerable to freezes might be reduced, resulting in the invasion of southern brushland into the escarpment of the Edwards Plateau. The vegetation of the High Plains and Rolling Plains could in turn be displaced by that from the Edwards Plateau, unless the distribution of these species is restricted to areas with limestone soils. Would the vegetation in canyons in the High Plains remain the same? To what extent would we expect the vegetation zones in west Texas to move upward in altitude and northward along the mountain range?

If the zone of adequate soil-moisture retention and humidity moves along the gradient toward the east, the following vegetational changes might be expected. The distribution of current hardwood/pine forests could be reduced in eastern Texas. The post-oak scrub in the central region might move northeast within the zone of suitable soils, with species from the South Texas Plains invading from the south. Would creosote invade South Texas Plains from the west?

The fine tuning of how the composition of communities would change poses another set of questions. Different species will respond differently to scenarios of more or less rain. The seasonality of rainfall or duration of drought could be critical for some species. Would sustained drought limit vulnerable oak species in the Edwards Plateau, and how would this affect species listed as endangered and threatened?

JANE PACKARD

Differences in photosynthetic pathways will influence responses to variability in rainfall and CO_2 enrichment; will oaks in the central region increase, while grasses in the Rolling Plains inhibit establishment of woody species?

It quickly becomes apparent that an in-depth analysis of the landscapes in each region needs to be completed to clarify the projected effects of climate change on biodiversity in Texas. This is particularly true if the projected changes in agricultural practices and urban development are to be taken into account.

Implications for Protected Areas and Species

What are the implications of potential changes in native ecosystems for the decision makers of today? The state of Texas is committed to maintaining its natural heritage of flora and fauna via a system of protected areas and regulations designed to protect species vulnerable to extinction. The policy of the Natural Resource Protection Branch of the Texas Parks and Wildlife Department incorporates an ecosystem perspective (Hayes et al. 1987), which typifies an excellent progressive approach to the issue. This policy requires extensive coordination with private organizations (Nature Conservancy) and federal agencies (Environmental Protection Agency, Fish and Wildlife Service, National Park Service).

Generalizations

The protected sites most vulnerable to global climate change will be those that are smallest and most isolated from other natural areas, e.g., prairie vegetation in the Rolling Plains. Areas that are connected by patterns of land use that encourage movement of native species between fragments of habitat will be less vulnerable, e.g., extensive cattle ranching in the South Texas Plains.

The protected species most vulnerable to extinction will be those that are adapted to specific microclimates likely to disappear with global warming and those that are unable to move long distances between suitable habitat fragments, e.g., karst invertebrates in the Balcones Canyonlands. As populations of protected species become isolated in small fragments of habitat, they are more likely to become extinct, e.g., Attwater's prairie chicken. Alternatively, those that live together in large areas transfigured by human land-uses may become more susceptible to the combined stresses that they encounter as a result of global warming, e.g., the Gulf Coast region.

Beyond these generalizations, it is difficult at this time to predict what changes will occur, because each ecosystem and species has its unique set of adaptations and interrelations with the physical world (Vitousek 1989). However, one factor that decision makers should examine carefully is whether the basic structure of protected areas will facilitate the transition to a changing climate.

Regional Mosaics of Protected Areas

The analysis required to determine whether there is sufficient habitat protection to sustain viable populations of native species is complex and requires a regional approach (Scott et al. 1991). This type of analysis is known from model programs in other states as "GAP analysis." It goes beyond just identifying areas protected for scenic and recreational values, examining the values of landscapes for maintaining sets of native species with complementary habitat requirements (Brown 1991, pp. 66–71).

An example of this regional approach is the proposed bioreserve, which would protect habitat for endangered species and recharge zones for the Edwards aquifer in the Hill Country (BAT 1992; Stevens 1992). In this pioneering project, the stated goal is to respect and understand the needs of private, municipal, county, state, and federal landowners in the region and to find win-win solutions as alternatives to the strict preservationist approaches used in the past. The need to comply with regulations of the Endangered Species Act was the incentive for diverse groups to come to the table and address the difficult issues involved. Although communication has been problematic in this project, it is only through trials of this sort that private and governmental organizations will learn to work better together on resolving the issues of the future.

Because of the regional diversity in Texas, the following questions need to be asked for each region. The first question is whether representative fragments of habitat currently are protected on private and public lands in each of the natural regions (Figure 6.1). The second is whether there are sufficient linkages among protected areas within a region for recolonization to occur as climatic conditions shift. The third is whether there are routes of colonization extending across regions along the expected gradients of climatic change.

Restoration Technology

Restoration technology may factor more predominantly in resolving regional conflicts in the future. Among some ecologists, there has been resistance to this concept of tampering with nature. However, the techniques are gathering wider acceptance in view of the realities of how natural systems have already been substantially altered by human activities. Wetland restoration is now an accepted technique in mitigation proceedings. Why not harness technology to the benefit of maintaining viable populations of native species?

The mechanistic way of thinking resulting from the industrial revolution has locked many managers into thinking that native communities in an area need to be protected and maintained in the same state as encountered by European pioneers in the 19th century (Botkin 1990). This way of thinking may also be the basis of preservationist policy of some agencies, which comes in direct conflict with the development policy of other agencies. An analysis of the potential changes in native communities due to climate change presents a fundamental challenge to the mechanistic way of thinking. It illustrates how communities have changed over geologic time and may be expected to change in distribution and species composition in the future.

Perhaps the greatest reservation expressed by ecologists with respect to mitigation proceedings is the humbling realization of how little humans know about the requirements of native species. Restoration technology needs to be adapted to rescue operations designed to move vulnerable species between otherwise inaccessible fragments of habitat as climatic conditions move along gradients. Global climate change may require the ultimate in habitat mitigation procedures.

This effort will need to be supported by sufficient human, technological, and economic resources if it is to succeed. However, it may offer viable alternatives to resolve current conflicts among private, local government, state, and federal interests.

Policy Alternatives

Governments have been encouraged to take anticipatory rather than reactive measures in adapting to climate change and to address the regulations protecting endangered species. Once a species is extinct, reactive measures will not revive it.

In evaluating alternative options for anticipatory actions, Smith et al. (1991) recommend using the criteria of flexibility, economic efficiency, feasibility, and consideration of associated benefits. They identify several policy options with regard to natural systems: (1) strengthen and enlarge existing protected areas, (2) establish migration pathways between existing protected areas, (3) protect areas that may become suitable habitat for threatened and endangered species in the future, (4) increase restrictions on zoning and management around reserves, (5) avoid permanent alterations to rivers and streams, which may be important migratory pathways under changing climate, (6) evaluate species stocking and introduction strategies, (7) reduce destruction and pollution of habitats in general, and (8) adjust species preservation programs to more broadly protect habitat and ecosystems.

These policies are all very appropriate from the biological standpoint; however, they need to be adapted to be workable in the sociopolitical context of each region. For example, in some cultural groups, zoning restrictions around reserves are seen as an infringement on private property rights and abuse of government power. Most of the land in Texas is under private ownership; therefore, viable populations of native species are not likely to be maintained solely on public lands. Workable, mutually beneficial solutions need to be further developed to compensate private landowners who protect native species. For example, changes in the inheritance tax could provide incentives for ranchers around Attwater's Prairie Chicken National Wildlife Refuge to adopt agricultural practices beneficial to prairie chickens occupying their lands (S. E. Labuda, pers. comm.). Currently available incentives often involve aspects of tax regulations. Given a tight economic climate, a thorough review of existing tax incentives and implementation of additional incentives would be very sound policy.

Conclusions and Recommendations

A proactive approach to managing Texas' natural heritage in the context of climate change will be more cost-effective than reactive measures. Texas possesses one of the richest natural heritages in North America, because of its location at the intersection of several biomes. Considerable effort has been invested in protecting this resource for the enjoyment of present and future generations. The quality of this investment needs to be protected in the future.

The ability of landscapes to withstand and respond to global climate warming will depend on the degree to which protected fragments of habitat are linked by corridors along the gradients of climate change. Each natural region needs to be examined in more detail to determine the likely shifts in distribution of native species within the mosaic of agricultural, urban, and natural areas.

The existing collaborative efforts of private, state, and federal agencies to conduct systematic analyses of land use in each region (GAP analysis) should be supported and even accelerated to provide a sound basis of information for planned development. More information is needed on the potential influences of global climate change on native species, as well as the indirect effects of changing agricultural practices and urban development. Multidisciplinary teams, including biologists, economists, sociologists, and planners, are needed to address issues that involve conflict resolution. Development of economic incentives for landowners to protect the natural heritage of their lands could be used as effective alternatives to land acquisition.

Restoration technology needs to be amplified and adapted to artificial movement of vulnerable native species. As climatic conditions shift from old fragments to new, some species may not be able to move naturally due to human land-use that functions as a barrier between suitable fragments. In all cases of planned introductions, the action should be taken with full consideration of social, economic, and political realities.

Acknowledgments

I am very grateful to the following people who provided invaluable input at various stages in the preparation of the manuscript: Steve Archer, James Carrico, Terry L. Cook, Fred Gehlbach, Gary L. Graham, Craig A. McMahan, James Norwine, David H. Riskind, and R. Douglas Slack. Any errors or oversights are my own; the abovementioned individuals are not to be held accountable.

References

Archer, S., 1990. Development and Stability of Grass/Woody Mosaics in a Subtropical Savanna Parkland, Texas, U.S.A. *Journal of Biogeography* 17:453–462.

Biological Advisory Team (BAT), 1990. *Comprehensive Report of the Biological Advisory Team.* Austin Regional Habitat Conservation Plan.

Blair, W., 1950. The Biotic Provinces of Texas. *Texas Journal of Science* 2:93–117.

Bogusch, E., 1952. Brush Invasion of the Rio Grande Plains of Texas. *Texas Journal of Science* 4:85–91.

Botkin, D. B., 1990. *Discordant Harmonies.* Oxford University Press, New York.

Brothers, T. S., and A. Spingarn, 1992. Forest Fragmentation and Alien Plant Invasion of Central Indiana Old-Growth Forests. *Conservation Biology* 6:91–100.

Brown, B. A., 1991. Landscape Protection and the Nature Conservancy. In: *Landscape Linkages and Biodiversity,* W. E. Hudson (ed.). Island Press, Washington, D.C.

Davis, M. B., and C. Zabinski, 1991. Changes in Geographical Range Resulting from Greenhouse Warming: Effects on Biodiversity in Forests. In: *Consequences of the Greenhouse Effect for Biological Diversity,* R. L. Peters (ed.). Yale University Press, New Haven.

Dickinson, R., R. Errico, F. Giorgi, and G. Bates, 1989. A Regional Climate Model for the Western United States. *Climatic Change* 15:383–422.

Emanuel, W., H. Shugart, and M. Stevenson, 1985. Climatic Change and the Broad-Scale Distribution of Terrestrial Ecosystem Complexes. *Climate Change* 7:29–43.

Graham, R. W., 1988. The Role of Climate Change in the Design of Biological Reserves: The Paleoecological Perspective. *Conservation Biology* 2:392.

Graham, G. L., 1992. *Texas Wildlife Viewing Guide.* Falcon Press, Helena, Mont.

Hayes, T. D., D. H. Riskind, and W. L. Pace, III, 1987. Patch-within-Patch Restoration of Man-Modified Landscapes within Texas State Parks. In: *Landscape Heterogeneity and Disturbance,* M. G. Turner (ed.). Springer-Verlag, New York.

Henrickson, J., and M. C. Johnston, 1983. Vegetation and Community Types of the Chihuahuan Desert. In: Invited papers from *The Second Symposium on Resources of the Chihuahuan Desert Region, United States and Mexico,* J. C. Barlow, A. M. Powell, and B. N. Timmermann (eds.). Chihuahuan Desert Research Institute, Alpine, Tex.

Inglis, J., 1964. *A History of Vegetation on the Rio Grande Plains.* Texas Parks and Wildlife Department, Austin.

Jager, J., and W. Kellogg, 1983. Anomalies in Temperature and Rainfall during Warm Arctic Seasons. *Climatic Change* 5:39–60.

Jahrsdoerfer, S. E., and D. M. Leslie, Jr., 1988. *Tamaulipan Brush-*

land of the Lower Rio Grande Valley of South Texas: Description, Human Impacts and Management Options. U.S. Fish and Wildlife Service, Biological Report No. 88(36), Washington, D.C.

Kellogg, W. W., 1990. Climate Change Expressed in Human Terms. In: *The Rio Grande Basin: Global Climate Change Scenarios*, W. Stone, M. Minnis, and E. Trotter (eds.). Water Resource Research Institute, Albuquerque, N.M.

Merrill, L., and V. Young, 1959. Effect of Drought on Woody Plants. *Texas Agricultural Progress* 5:9–10.

Neilson, R., 1986. High-Resolution Climatic Analysis and Southwest Biogeography. *Science* 232:27–34.

Norwine, J., 1978. Twentieth-Century Semi-Arid Climates and Climatic Fluctuations in Texas and Northeastern Mexico. *Journal of Arid Environments* 1:313–325.

Noss, R. F., 1991. Landscape Connectivity: Different Functions at Different Scales. In: *Landscape Linkages and Biodiversity*, W. E. Hudson (ed.). Island Press, Washington, D.C.

Owen, J., and D. Schmidly, 1986. Environmental Variables of Biological Importance in Texas. *Texas Journal of Science* 38:99–119.

Perry, D., J. Borchers, S. Borchers, and M. Amaranthus, 1990. Species Migrations and Ecosystem Stability During Climate Change: The Below Ground Connection. *Conservation Biology* 4:266–274.

Peters, R., and J. Darling, 1985. The Greenhouse Effect and Natural Reserves. *BioScience* 35:707–717.

Peters, R. L., 1989. Threats to Biological Diversity As the Earth Warms. In: *Global Change and Our Common Future: Papers from a Forum*, R. S. DeFries and T. F. Malone (eds.). National Academy Press, Washington, D.C.

Reid, W. V., and M. C. Trexler, 1991. *Drowning the National Heritage: Climate Change and U.S. Coastal Biodiversity.* World Resources Institute, Washington, D.C.

Revkin, A. C., 1989. March of the Fire Ants. *Discover* (March): 71–76.

Risser, P., 1990. Impacts of Climate Change and Variability on Ecological Systems. In: *The Rio Grande Basin: Global Climate Change Scenarios*, W. Stone, M. Minnis, and E. Trotter (eds.). Water Resource Research Institute, Albuquerque, N.M.

Saunders, D., and C. de Rebeira, 1991. Values of Corridors to Avian Populations in a Fragmented Landscape. In: *The Role of Corridors in Nature Conservation*, D. Saunders and R. Hobbs (eds.). Surrey Beatty and Sons, Chipping Norton, Aust.

Schlesinger, W. H., J. F. Reynolds, G. L. Cunningham, L. F. Huenneke, W. M. Jarrell, R. A. Virginia, and W. G. Whitford, 1990.

Biological Feedbacks in Global Desertification. *Science* 247: 1043–1048.

Schmidt, R. H., Jr., 1983. Chihuahuan Climate. In: Invited papers from *The Second Symposium on Resources of the Chihuahuan Desert Region, United States and Mexico*, J. C. Barlow, A. M. Powell, and B. N. Timmermann (eds.). Chihuahuan Desert Research Institute, Alpine, Tex.

Scott, J. M., B. Csuti, and S. Caicco, 1991. Gap Analysis: Assessing Protection Needs. In: *Landscape Linkages and Biodiversity*, W. E. Hudson (ed.). Island Press, Washington, D.C.

Sionit, A., B. R. Strain, N. Hellmers, G. H. Riechers, and C. N. Jaeger, 1985. Long-Term Atmospheric CO_2 Enrichment Effects and the Growth and Development of *Liquidambar styraciflua* and *Pinus taeda* Seedlings. *Can. J. For. Res.* 15:468–471.

Smith, J., A. Silbiger, R. Benioff, J. Titus, D. Hinckley, and L. Kalkstein, 1991. *Adapting to Climate Change: What Governments Can Do*. U.S. Environmental Protection Agency, Climate Change Adaptation Branch.

Soulé, M., D. Bolger, A. Alberts, J. Wright, M. Sorice, and S. Hill, 1988. Reconstructed Dynamics of Rapid Extinctions of Chaparral-Requiring Birds in Urban Habitat Islands. *Conservation Biology* 2:75–92.

Stevens, W. K., 1992. Novel Strategy Puts People at Heart of Texas Preserve. *New York Times*, March 31 issue.

Strength, D., and P. Harcombe, 1982. Why Don't East Texas Savannahs Grow Up to Forest? *The American Midland Naturalist* 108: 278–294.

Thomas, G. W., 1975. Texas Plants—An Ecological Summary. In: *Texas Plants: A Checklist and Ecological Summary*, F. Gould (ed.). Texas Agricultural Experiment Station, College Station.

Tolley, L. C., and B. R. Strain, 1984. Effects of Atmospheric CO_2 Enrichment and Water Stress on Growth of *Liquidambar styraciflua* and *Pinus taeda* Seedlings. *Can. J. Bot.* 62:2135–2139.

Trenberth, K., G. Branstator, and P. Arkin, 1988. Origins of the 1988 North American Drought. *Science* 242:1640–1645.

Van Devender, T. R., 1983. Pleistocene climates and endemism in the Chihuahuan Desert Flora. In: Invited papers from *The Second Symposium on Resources of the Chihuahuan Desert Region, United States and Mexico*, J. C. Barlow, A. M. Powell, and B. N. Timmermann (eds.). Chihuahuan Desert Research Institute, Alpine, Tex.

Vitousek, P. M., 1989. Terrestrial Ecosystems. In: *Global Change and Our Common Future: Papers from a Forum*, R. S. DeFries and T. F. Malone (eds.). National Academy Press, Washington, D.C.

Wauer, R. H., 1983. Parks and Other Reserves As Islands of Protection with Special Reference to the Chihuahuan Desert. In: Invited papers from *The Second Symposium on Resources of the Chihuahuan Desert Region, United States and Mexico,* J. C. Barlow, A. M. Powell, and B. N. Timmermann (eds.). Chihuahuan Desert Research Institute, Alpine, Tex.

Webb, T., III, 1987. The Appearance and Disappearance of Major Vegetational Assemblages: Long-Term Vegetational Dynamics in Eastern North America. *Vegetation* 69:177–187.

Wells, P., 1965. Scarp Woodlands, Transported Grassland Soils, and Concept of Grassland Climate in the Great Plains Region. *Science* 148:246–249.

Whitson, P. D., 1974. *The Impact of Human Use upon the Chisos Basin and Adjacent Lands.* Scientific Monograph Series 4, National Park Service, Washington, D.C.

Williams, W. E., K. Garbutt, F. A. Bazzaz, and P. M. Vitansek, 1986. The Response of Plants to Elevated CO_2 IV. Two Deciduous-Forest Tree Communities. *Oecologia* 69:454–459.

BRUCE McCARL, WESLEY ROSENTHAL,
CHING-CHENG CHANG, AND RICHARD M. ADAMS

7. Agriculture

Agriculture is a significant sector within the Texas economy. It uses about 19 million acres for crops, of which 4 million are irrigated, as well as 114 million acres for livestock. It also consumes 58 percent of the state's water. Agriculture's economic contribution includes about $12.5 billion of total gross sales in the state. Primary production and agribusiness/processing create employment for more than 20 percent of the state's work force.

Prosperity in agriculture is dependent upon climatic conditions. Changes in temperature, precipitation, and atmospheric chemical content have implications for plant growth and water supply, as well as for soil characteristics, pests, and diseases. Thus, this industry may be at risk given the possible incidence of global warming. This chapter examines the vulnerability of agriculture in Texas to global warming.

Estimating the effects of climatic change on agriculture is difficult. Basically, there are three methods that could be used to make such an estimate. The first, based on observation, would entail waiting for climate change conditions to occur either globally or in representative regions. This approach is not practical for the combination of CO_2 and climatic effects, if the intention is to predict change in a timely manner so that appropriate responses can be developed. The second would involve experiments in which agricultural production systems are subjected to climatic change scenarios and the production implications observed. This, however, is also not feasible, as the sites and systems to be investigated would render such an undertaking quite expensive and, even if completed, the results would not reveal the effects on crop mix, markets, international trade, livestock herd size, etc. Thus, we turn to a third, simulative-based approach, where models are used to simulate crop yields, crop mix choice, and market processes. This simulation requires the adoption of scenarios including both climate effects and agricultural production/consumption conditions. The climate scenarios adopted are those resulting from the GISS and GFDL global circulation models, as well as one of the scenarios posed in Chap. 2. Because future rates of technological progress and consumption growth cannot be predicted, the model scenarios use 1990 conditions. Prior experience has shown that the model variations introduced by making assumptions about future technological progress, demand, export, etc., are far larger than the implications of most phenomena such as global warming.

The first part of the chapter discusses how global warming might influence agricultural processes. Subsequently, results are presented from an assessment of the influence of global warming on crop yields and the agricultural economy under 1990 conditions. Although the results show that agriculture in the United States and Texas is sensitive to climate change with respect to land and water usage, as well as crop and livestock production, global warming does not appear to have a significant effect on the state's or nation's agriculturally based economic welfare. There are, however, negative implications for crop producers in some regions.

Factors Determining the Sensitivity of Agriculture to Climate

Agricultural production is influenced by climate in numerous ways. These include temperature and water based influences, such as plant water demand, environmental/plant/livestock interactions, soil fertility, pest and disease incidence, and available water supply.

Plant Water Demand

Climatic conditions significantly affect plant water usage. For maximum rates of photosynthesis, plants need to keep leaf temperature within a specific range. This is achieved by transpiring water. Temperature, wind, solar radiation, and humidity all have a direct effect on the rate of plant transpiration (Blaney and Morin 1942; Thornthwaite 1948; Jensen and Haise 1963). A warmer climate would cause an increase in plant water demand. Assuming constant available moisture, this increased demand would cause increased water stress. Reductions in harvestable yield due to water stress would depend on the timing of the stress. For most crops, the critical time is near anthesis or flowering and during seed filling (Denmead and Shaw 1960; Louwerse 1980). Such stress would either decrease yield or cause farmers to initiate different practices to escape dry conditions. For example, planting date, crop mix, crop rotation, cropping frequency, or livestock stocking rate may change (Imeson et al. 1987). In addition, irrigation may increase in areas where adequate water supplies are available.

Thus, from the water demand standpoint, agriculture is vulnerable to global warming, because a warmer environment would increase water requirements to maintain current production practices and/or necessitate different farming practices or land-use patterns.

Water Availability

Climatic change can influence soil moisture conditions and irrigation water supply. Soil moisture is a key factor in supporting dryland crop growth and determining irrigation requirements. A temperature increase, without compensating precipitation increases, would reduce soil moisture, particularly for shallow soils. Assuming cropping season precipitation remains the same, reduced soil moisture would increase plant water stress for dryland production, with an accompanying reduction in yields. Under irrigated conditions the result would be increased water requirements.

Increased regional precipitation, which may occur under global warming, could compensate for the effect of temperature on the soil moisture content. However, there is a nonlinear relationship between evaporation and temperature, thus a larger percentage increase in precipitation than in temperature would be required to maintain constant soil moisture conditions. In the absence of irrigation increases or compensating precipitation, drier soil moisture conditions would move northerly and easterly in Texas, with an associated shift in regional vegetation mix (see Chap. 6).

Climatic change would also influence irrigation water availability. Within Texas, major water uses include agriculture, urban populations, manufacturing, and electric generation. Agriculture currently uses 58 percent of the water used in the state (TWDB 1990). However, with the Texas population expected to increase by 25 percent in the next 30 years, urban and industrial water use is projected to increase. Non-

BRUCE MCCARL,
WESLEY ROSENTHAL,
CHING-CHENG CHANG,
AND
RICHARD M. ADAMS

agricultural demand is expected to increase if current practices are to be maintained under warmer conditions and future growth requirements are to be met. This implies reduced water availability to agriculture, especially in areas that now face water scarcity such as the Edwards Plateau, the Rio Grande basin, and the Colorado River basin. Water runoff may also decrease, as warming implies an increase in water use by watershed vegetative cover, thereby decreasing flows into surface water systems and infiltration into aquifers. Increased temperature would also increase evaporative losses from surface water.

Consequently, agriculture will face increased competition for, in all likelihood, a smaller supply of water. It appears that agriculture will have less water to use with or without climate change. Agricultural responses to reduced supplies include increased dryland acreage, introduction of alternative crops or more drought tolerant cultivators, and larger investments in water conservation practices.

Environment/Crop/Livestock Interactions

Climatic change and atmospheric CO_2 concentrations can also alter temperature and the length of the growing season. Plant growth is sensitive to both. Temperatures above or below the optimum range result in lower crop yields (Lowry 1969; Squire and Unsworth 1988).

Longer growing seasons may be the result of increased temperature (Williams et al. 1988) and thus would have a direct impact on a number of crops in Texas. For example, the citrus industry in the Rio Grande Valley has recently encountered freezes that caused a significant reduction in acreage. Global warming might reduce the possibility of freezes, allowing acreage expansion. Similar effects may occur in the winter vegetable industry.

Increases in CO_2 concentration have a direct influence on total biomass production. Previous research under controlled conditions indicates that production is increased with higher CO_2 concentrations (Kimball 1983; Kimball and Idso 1983; Cure and Acock 1986). Plants fall into two families, C3 and C4, based on the photosynthetic pathway used to fix CO_2 from the atmosphere. C3 plants include barley, wheat, cotton, rice, and soybeans. They have been found to have a 20–40 percent increase in growth rate with a doubling of CO_2 concentration. C4 plants such as sugarcane, sorghum, and corn also benefit, although the increase is significantly less. Overall, increases in CO_2 concentration could be beneficial; however, weed growth would also be stimulated.

Livestock production could also be affected by temperature increases. There would be a need to alter intensive confinement operations, adopt new breeds, and create more shade. In general, weight gain is inhibited by higher temperatures, and more heat-tolerant breeds tend to produce less meat per unit of input. Thus, warming could well reduce livestock production.

Soil Fertility

No comprehensive study has been published dealing with the effects of climate change and global warming on soils. Higher temperature could increase the rate of microbial decomposition of organic matter, thus affecting soil fertility (Hillel and Rosenzweig 1989). Higher temperatures could also increase root biomass production, thereby offsetting the effect of higher rates of decomposition through enhanced cycling and N_2 fixation. Each of these changes could be affected by changes in precipitation patterns and soil moisture concentration.

Wind erosion may also be enhanced under climatic change. Drier conditions resulting in lessened soil moisture would increase wind erosion. Estimates indicate that a temperature increase of 3.5°C with no change in precipitation would increase wind erosion by 24–29 percent (Williams et al. 1988).

Pests and Diseases

Studies suggest that higher temperatures may extend the geographic range of specific pests and diseases. A recent study by Parry (1990) demonstrated that the European corn borer would move northward 165–200 km with a 1°C increase in temperature. Similar results are possible for pests within Texas. For example, the geographic extent and population density of sorghum midge and corn earworm would likely increase in a warmer climate. As a result, climatic changes could enhance pest outbreaks and reduce yields. Besides insects, fungal and bacterial diseases could increase in severity in areas where precipitation increased. Such a

BRUCE MCCARL,
WESLEY ROSENTHAL,
CHING-CHENG CHANG,
AND
RICHARD M. ADAMS

scenario is possible in the more humid areas of east Texas (Beresford and Fullerton 1989).

Analysis of the Sensitivity of Texas Agriculture to Climate Change

An analysis of the sensitivity of Texas agriculture to climate change cannot be done in isolation, because Texas agriculture is a component of U.S. and world agriculture. Consequently, the effects of climate change on Texas agriculture were analyzed in the context of the U.S. agriculture sector, taking into account international trade.

The analysis proceeds in four stages: (1) the selection of climate scenarios; (2) the use of the Erosion Productivity Impact Calculator (EPIC) crop-growth simulation model to generate information on the sensitivity of crop yield and irrigation water use to climate change; (3) adaptation of assumptions from other studies on water availability; and (4) economic analysis using a model of the U.S. agricultural economy. Each of these study phases will be discussed below.

Climate Change Scenarios

Three climate change scenarios were chosen for evaluation. Two are GCM-driven scenarios used in the 1989 EPA climate change effects study: the first of these was generated with the Goddard Institute for Space Sciences (GISS) general circulation model; the second is from the Princeton Geophysical Fluid Dynamics Laboratory (GFDL) general circulation model. The third scenario (CTEMP) assumed a 1°C temperature increase plus a 20 percent reduction in precipitation. The effects of the climatic changes were examined for 63 regions in the U.S., including 8 regions in Texas (Figure 7.1). The GISS and GFDL climatic projections for each of the Texas regions are given in Table 7.1, while the assumptions for the rest of the country appear in Adams et al. (1990). Note that both the GISS and GFDL scenarios contain approximately equivalent temperature change, but that the GISS scenario implies a greater increase in precipitation than the GFDL scenario. In particular, the GFDL scenario gives the greatest reduction in precipitation (to 87 percent) in the Trans-Pecos and High Plains, whereas GISS predicts a slight increase for these regions.

BRUCE MCCARL,
WESLEY ROSENTHAL,
CHING-CHENG CHANG,
AND
RICHARD M. ADAMS

Figure 7.1.
The eight Texas regions used in the U.S. agricultural sector model (ASM).

Simulation of Texas Crop Yields and Crop Water Use Requirements

Biophysical simulation was employed to generate estimates of the consequences of climate change on crop yields and water requirements. The weather data in Table 7.1 were used in the EPIC model to simulate crop yields (Sharpley and Williams 1990).

Before presenting the results, a few words on the development and properties of EPIC are in order. EPIC is a highly flexible model developed by the Agricultural Research, Soil Conservation, and Economic Research Services of the U.S. Department of Agriculture. It accommodates parameters descriptive of weather, crop phenology and physiology, physical and chemical conditions of soil, farming practices—including tillage, irrigation, and pest control—and farm economics. EPIC simulates biomass production and yield, evaporation, irrigation requirements, and the number of days on which growth is constrained by temperature, moisture, or nutrient stress.

EPIC is a model that has been validated for a wide range of

Table 7.1. Average Annual Deviations in Temperature (°C) and Precipitation (P, relative change) Used in the Analysis

	GISS		GFDL	
	T	P	T	P
Trans-Pecos	4.9	1.01[a]	4.8	0.87
High Plains	4.6	1.03	4.8	0.87
Rolling Plains	3.9	1.12	4.2	1.11
Blacklands	4.3	0.93	3.8	0.97
East Texas	4.3	0.93	3.8	0.97
Edwards Plateau	4.6	1.03	3.8	0.97
Coastal Bend	5.2	1.09	3.8	0.97
South Texas	4.3	0.93	3.8	0.97

[a]Precipitation is 1% above current levels.

soil and climate conditions. For this study, soil and climate data bases were developed for all 63 U.S. regions for cotton, wheat, corn, and sorghum, where those crops were predominant in the regions. In addition, the EPIC version used incorporates changes in the efficiency of water use and the rate of photosynthesis as the CO_2 concentration changes. Thus, the simulations presented here involve yields under a base case with no temperature increase and 330 ppm (parts per million) CO_2, compared with scenarios with climate change and 550 ppm CO_2. For the second case, photosynthesis rates were increased by 35, 25, and 10 percent for soybean, wheat, and corn, respectively.

EPIC is used for this study, as it was not possible to conduct crop growth chamber experiments on a sufficiently wide scale to simulate the crop yield consequences of increased carbon dioxide concentrations, as well as changes in the temperature and precipitation regimes. EPIC results were simulated for corn, cotton, wheat, and sorghum. The reader should note that the results depend critically on the validity of the EPIC simulation results.

Table 7.2 shows an example of the data generated for the wheat crop in Texas. It is evident that the different climate change scenarios have implications for crop yields. This is particularly true for irrigated wheat yields and appears in part to be due to limitations in water availability, at least in the High Plains region.

Table 7.2. Change in Yield and Water Requirements for Wheat with Climate Change (Percent)

	Irrigated Wheat Yield			Dryland Wheat Yield			Irrigated Water Use		
	GISS	GFDL	CTEMP	GISS	GFDL	CTEMP	GISS	GFDL	CTEMP
Trans-Pecos	-11	14	36	12	-15	3	37	13	-2
High Plains	-55	7	30	-42	-10	18	-60	6	7
Rolling Plns				4	-3	10			
Blackland	-31	12	17	1	14	-73	15	37	2
East Texas	-31	12	17	44	13	15	15	37	2
Edwards Plat				12	-17	4			
Coastal Bend	-31	12	17	-40	11	13	15	37	2
South Texas	17	11	7	-30	-21	-11	-37	-26	-5

Hydrological Impacts on Water Availability

The hydrological impacts on water availability for the GISS and GFDL scenarios are the same as those used in Adams et al. (1990). A simple hydrologic mass-balance approach was used to derive water resource availability in the face of GISS and GFDL model forecasts for evaporation, rainfall, and temperature.

Considerable variation between the climate forecasts was evident for availability of irrigation water in the United States. For example, an increase of 16 percent was projected by GFDL for the southeast, whereas GISS predicted a decrease of 9 percent. For the Southern Plains, which includes Texas, GFDL predicted a decrease of 3 percent, and GISS gave a decrease of 2 percent. A decrease of 22 percent was assumed for the CTEMP scenario for all regions of the country.

Economic Analysis

The analysis was done using the U.S. agricultural sector model (ASM). The model has been documented in a number of places, most recently in Chang et al. (1992) and Chang and McCarl (1992). It was also used in an earlier global climate change assessment (Adams et al. 1989a; 1990). The analytical procedure of this study is similar to those of the above mentioned studies, and readers in need of elaboration should refer to those reports. Briefly, the forecasts of crop yield and water use obtained from EPIC were imposed on the ASM, along with the water supply changes.[1] ASM was then run with and without these changes to generate the economic implications of global warming. The ASM base model is set up for 1990 conditions, without any of the changes in demand, factor supply, and international conditions that will likely occur between now and the time global warming is expected. This assumption is used because the errors in forecasting the future world would be far larger than the anticipated global warming effect.

The ASM represents production and consumption of 24 primary agricultural commodities, including both crop and livestock products in 63 U.S. regions. Processing of agricultural products into 36 secondary commodities is also in-

---

[1] In the study by Adams et al. (1989a) crop yields were generated using the CERES family of crop simulation models.

cluded. Water resources are disaggregated in the model into surface water and groundwater available in each of the 63 regions. Surface water is available for a constant price up to a prespecified quantity, but pumped groundwater is provided according to a supply schedule, in which the unit price increases with increasing rates of withdrawal. The model assumes that a large number of individuals make up both production and consumption sectors, each operating under competitive market conditions, thereby maximizing the area under the demand curves less the area under the supply curves. This area is a measure of economic welfare or net social benefit. Both domestic and foreign consumption (exports) are considered. This model structure allows projection of the effects of global warming on (1) the regional agricultural economies across the United States; (2) irrigated versus dryland cropping trade-offs in response to regional water demand and availability; and (3) producer welfare at the regional and national levels, as well as consumption effects for both domestic and foreign consumers.

Because the only crops simulated in the EPIC model were cotton, wheat, sorghum, and corn, average yield and water use changes for these crops were applied to other, nonsimulated crops. Thus, changes in crop yield for a region came from either the simulated change for that particular crop or the average value for simulated crops in that region. Different adjustments were developed for irrigated and dryland crops. In addition, pasture and grazing land availability for livestock production was adjusted by the same factor as that determined for dryland crops.

Another methodological feature that differs from the predecessor study (i.e., Adams et al. 1989a) is that here all results incorporate CO_2 growth-enhancing effects. Thus, the comparison described here is between base 1990 conditions with 1990 weather and CO_2 levels (330 ppm) and scenarios incorporating GCM weather predictions and 550 ppm of CO_2.

Results of the Economic Analysis

BRUCE MCCARL,
WESLEY ROSENTHAL,
CHING-CHENG CHANG,
AND
RICHARD M. ADAMS

A total of four ASM model runs were performed: a base without climate change, and one for each climate change scenario. The overall societal welfare results of this analysis are shown in Figure 7.2. These results show total societal welfare increases of about one-third percent under the CTEMP scenario and about one-half percent under the GFDL scenario, with a basically unchanged level of welfare under the

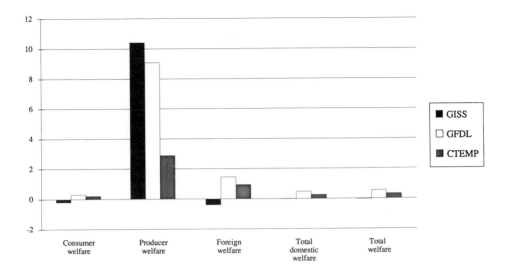

Figure 7.2.
National economic
effects of climate
change (% change
in $U.S.).

GISS scenario. In addition, producers benefit under all scenarios, gaining between 3 and 10 percent in terms of farm
income, whereas consumer welfare shows gains under the
GFDL and CTEMP scenarios, but exhibits a slight loss (0.2
percent) under the GISS scenario. Similarly, foreign welfare
shows roughly the same patterns of change as consumer welfare. These results suggest that national agricultural sensitivity to global climate change is small. Apparently, the EPIC
growth-stimulating effects of CO_2, coupled with cropping
pattern substitution, overcomes the negative effects of water
supply and yield.

When model projections regarding commodity prices and
production are reviewed, price decreases for cotton, soybeans, wheat, sorghum, rice, hay, silage, sugarcane, sugar
beets, potatoes, nonfed beef, and milk are observed across
all scenarios, and these price decreases are matched by increased production levels. The results also indicate livestock
feed substitution, with less reliance on grain-intensive systems and more roughage-intensive and nonfed grazing systems. Other commodity price and production changes show
greater variation between scenarios.

Figures 7.3a and 7.3b provide a breakdown of changes in
selected crop and livestock production for Texas and the
United States. In Texas, more cotton, hay, and cattle are projected, while production of wheat, sorghum, rice, and potatoes falls.

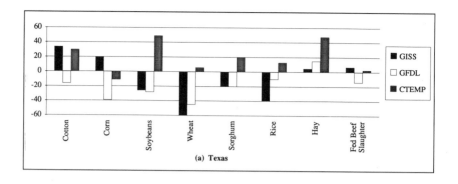

(a) Texas

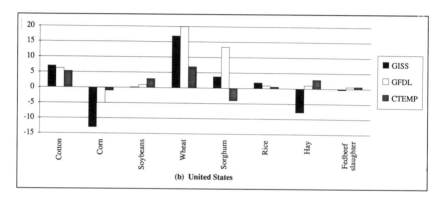

(b) United States

BRUCE MCCARL,
WESLEY ROSENTHAL,
CHING-CHENG CHANG,
AND
RICHARD M. ADAMS

Figure 7.3.
Percentage change
in crop harvested
acreage and
livestock
production for
(a) Texas and
(b) the United
States.

Figure 7.4 summarizes resource use nationally under these conditions. Several results are observable in these data: (1) there is less cropland acreage utilization and less dryland usage under all scenarios; (2) agricultural labor use and irrigated acreage increase under all scenarios; and (3) pasture land, animal months of grazing (AUMS), and water use show mixed results. In addition, average water use per acre declines in the GFDL and CTEMP scenarios, indicating a trend toward greater water-use efficiency. The reduction in water use is even more apparent when the data for Texas are examined (Figure 7.5a).

Considerable variation is also apparent from region to region within the United States. The most significant changes occur in the Southern Plains area (including Texas and Oklahoma), where cropland is reduced. The Lake States, Cornbelt, and Delta regions also show a consistent reduction in cropland, whereas Northeast, Northern Plains, and Appalachian regions show cropland increases. This indicates a northward shift in crop acreage. However, this trend is not

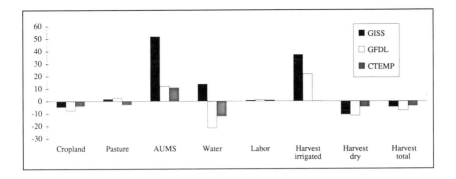

uniform. Figures 7.5a and 7.5b summarize some of the major changes in input use for Texas and the United States.

While national producer profits increase, there are regional differences. Namely, regional producers' profits increase in all regions but the Cornbelt, which loses under all scenarios. Farmers in the Northeast, Northern Plains, and Pacific regions benefit the most under climate change, although this is not necessarily consistent from one scenario to the next. However, in the scenarios where a positive effect is evident, this also corresponds to an increase in cropland acreage and suggests that these regions would benefit from a northward movement of crop zones. The Southern Plains region also benefits, despite losses in crop acreage and reductions in water use, largely because of changes in commodity prices.

For Texas the results are mixed, with farm profits increasing 19 percent under the GISS scenario and decreasing approximately 5 percent under GFDL and CTEMP. This discrepancy between the models is largely due to differences in regional crop yield and water availability projections. For instance, data from the GISS and CTEMP scenarios result in large increases in the amount of pasture in the High Plains and Rolling Plains, whereas small declines are predicted using data from GFDL.

At least part of the reason these results vary stems from differences in water supply availability, which have a direct impact on land-use patterns, particularly the amount of irrigated acreage. For the Rolling Plains, an increase in water use is predicted using CTEMP data, and a very large decrease is projected under the GFDL scenario. Overall, water use is predicted to decline in Texas, with the exception of South Texas, where increases ranging from 14 to 44 percent are evident.

Figure 7.4.
Changes in input use with climate change (% change in use).

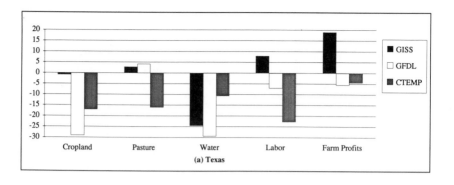

(a) Texas

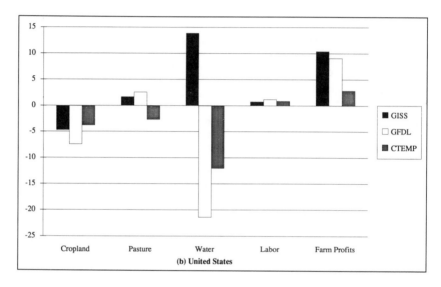

(b) United States

Figure 7.5.
Changes in input use and farm profits (% change with global warming) for (a) Texas and (b) the United States.

BRUCE MCCARL,
WESLEY ROSENTHAL,
CHING-CHENG CHANG,
AND
RICHARD M. ADAMS

The largest decline in water use occurs in the Central Blacklands, East Texas, and the Trans-Pecos. However, estimates of the predicted change vary by as much as a factor of 3.

The results may also be examined in terms of regional Texas implications. Farm profits by Texas subregion are shown in Figure 7.6. However, the characteristics of ASM tend to render such results less reliable than the national results. It appears that East Texas loses under all scenarios, with results for the High Plains, Trans-Pecos, Central Blacklands, and Coastal Bend depending on the scenario. Rolling Plains, Edwards Plateau, and South Texas show gains under all of the scenarios. The gains and losses evident in each region correspond to specific changes in input usage. For example, net income losses in East Texas are matched by reductions in crop acreage, pasture land, and water use. Rolling

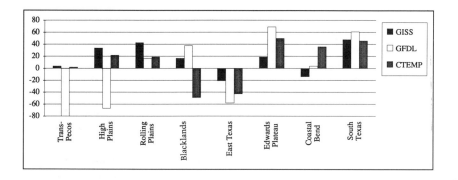

Plains producers gain as a result of increases in pasture and AUMS, and more labor-intensive livestock production.

Figure 7.6.
Percentage changes
in subregional farm
profits.

Conclusions

A quantitative examination of the agricultural effects of global warming was carried out in a nationwide context. Generally, the results show that, under 1990 agricultural conditions, agriculture in the United States and Texas is sensitive in terms of land and water usages, as well as crop and livestock production. However, in terms of agricultural-based economic welfare, the simulated effects of global warming are not great. There will be regional displacements, with the most vulnerable Texas region being East Texas. There is also uncertainty for crop producers' profits in some of the subregions, and Texas crop acreage will decline in general.

The nature of these results, particularly the overall resilience of agriculture to global warming, is not entirely unexpected. The pattern is similar to the results of earlier studies when CO_2 enrichment is considered (Adams et al. 1989a; 1990). Furthermore, one should note that the predicted changes are small and relatively more favorable than those obtained with similar assessment methodologies involving the agricultural implications of farm program revisions (Chang et al. 1992) and ozone concentration reductions (Adams et al. 1989b).

References

Adams, R. M., J. D. Glyer, and B. A. McCarl, 1989a. The Economic Effects of Climate Change on U.S. Agriculture: A Preliminary Assessment. In: *The Potential Effects of Global Climate Change* on the United States. U.S. Environmental Protection Agency, Report to Congress.

Adams, R. M., J. D. Glyer, S. L. Johnson, and B. A. McCarl, 1989b. A Reassessment of the Economic Effects of Ozone on U.S. Agriculture. *Journal of Air Pollution Control Association* 39:960–968.

Adams, R. M., C. Rosenzweig, R. M. Peart, J. T. Ritchie, B. A. McCarl, J. D. Glyer, R. B. Carry, J. W. Jones, K. J. Boote, and L. H. Allen, 1990. Global Climate Change and U.S. Agriculture. *Nature* 345:219–224.

Beresford, R. M., and R. A. Fullerton, 1989. Effects of Climate Change on Plant Diseases. DSIR Plant Div. Submission to Climate Change Impacts Working Group, Wellington, N.Z.

Blaney, H. F., and K. V. Morin, 1942. Evapotranspiration and Consumptive Use of Water Empirical Formulas. *Trans. Amer. Geophys. Union* 23:76–83.

Chang, C. C., B. A. McCarl, J. W. Mjelde, and J. W. Richardson, 1992. Sectoral Implications of Farm Program Modifications. *Amer. J. of Agric. Econ.* 74:39–49.

Chang, C. C., and B. A. McCarl, 1992. Scope of ASM: The U.S. Agricultural Sector Model. Working Draft, Texas Agricultural Experiment Station.

Cure, J. D., and B. Acock, 1986. Crop Responses to Carbon Dioxide Doubling: A Literature Survey. *Agric. and Forestry Metocol.* 38: 127–145.

Environmental Protection Agency (EPA), 1989. *The Potential Effect of Global Climate Change on the United States*. Draft Report to Congress, U.S. Environmental Protection Agency.

Denmead, O. T. and R. H. Shaw, 1960, 1962. Availability of Soil Water to Plants as Affected by Soil Moisture Content and Meteorological Conditions. *Agron. J.* 45:385–390.

Hillel, D., and C. Rosenzweig, 1989. The Greenhouse Effect and Its Implications Regarding Global Agriculture. Mass. Agric. Expt. Stn., Research Bulletin No. 724, Amherst, Mass.

Imeson, A., H. Dumont, and S. Sekliziotis, 1987. Impact Analysis of Climatic Change in the Mediterranean Region, Vol. F. European Workshop on Interrelated Bioclimatic and Land Use Changes. Noordwijkerhout, Neth.

Jensen, M. E., and H. R. Haise, 1963. Estimating Evapotranspiration from Solar Radiation. *J. Irrig. Drain. Div.* ASCE 89:15–41.

Kimball, B. A., 1983. Carbon Dioxide and Agricultural Yield: An Assemblage and Analysis of 430 Prior Observations. *Agron. J.* 75: 779–788.

Kimball, B. A., and S. B. Idso, 1983. Increasing Atmospheric CO_2: Effects on Crop Yield, Water Use and Climate. *Agric. Water Mgt.* 7:55–72.

BRUCE MCCARL,
WESLEY ROSENTHAL,
CHING-CHENG CHANG,
AND
RICHARD M. ADAMS

166

Louwerse, W., 1980. Effect of CO_2 Concentration and Irradiance on Stomatal Behavior of Maize, Barley and Sunflower Plants in the Field. *Plant Cell Environ.* 3:391–398.

Lowry, W. P., 1969. *Weather and Life: An Introduction to Biometeorology.* Academic Press, New York.

Parry, M., 1990. *Climate Change and World Agriculture.* Earthscan, London, U.K.

Sharpley, A. N., and J. R. Williams (eds.), 1990. EPIC—Erosion/Productivity Impact Calculator: 1. Model Documentation. USDA, Agricultural Research Service, Technical Bulletin No. 1768.

Squire, G. R., and M. H. Unsworth, 1988. Effects of CO_2 and Climatic Change on Agriculture. Contract Report to the Dept. of Environment, Dept. of Physiology and Environ. Sci., University of Nottingham, Sulton Bonington, U.K.

Texas Water Development Board (TWDB), 1990. *Water for Texas — Today and Tomorrow.* TWDB, Document No. GP-5-1, Austin.

Thornthwaite, C. W., 1948. An Approach Toward a Rational Classification of Climate. *Geogr. Rev.* 38:55–94.

Williams, G. D. V., R. A. Fautley, K. H. Jones, R. B. Stewart, and E. E. Wheaton, 1988. Estimating Effects of Climatic Change on Agriculture in Saskatchewan, Canada. In: *The Impact of Climatic Variations on Agriculture,* Vol. I, Assessments in Cool Temperatures and Cold Regions, M. L. Parry, T. R. Carter, and N. T. Konijn (eds.). Kiuwer. Dordrecht, Neth.

JUDITH CLARKSON, JOHN D. WILSON,
AND WOLFGANG ROESELER

8. Urban Areas

Global climate models have been used to anticipate climate change over the next half-century or so as a result of a doubling of CO_2 and other gases in the atmosphere. A temperature rise of about $2-4°C$ is anticipated worldwide by international research institutes, and Texas can expect a similar warming trend. In addition to predicted changes in mean temperature, precipitation, and sea level, an increased frequency of extreme events such as floods and droughts is also forecast. For Texas, an area prone to such events, this could have a more immediate impact. So far in this volume we have focused on the effects of climate change on natural ecosystems, with particular attention to water resources and estuarine environments. Here we shift our attention to urban areas.

Climate change is unlikely to have a dramatic effect on the quality of life in most Texas cities. With the exception of low-lying coastal cities that may struggle against a gradual rise in sea level and an increase in major storms, cities will be able to adapt to the changing circumstances. In some respects, cities are less vulnerable to climate change than other parts of the state, because the urban environment has evolved to insulate people from their environment. Our work places and homes are usually air conditioned, the transportation system remains useful in all but the worst storms, and the resources cities depend upon will continue to be available, although perhaps at a higher price.

Changes in the urban economy will most likely come in the form of higher prices, especially for agricultural products, water, and energy. Although some research has suggested that climate change might lead to higher agricultural output in specific regions (see Chapter 7; Achanta 1992), most studies suggest that world agricultural production is likely to fall, resulting in higher prices for agricultural products. This will significantly affect those cities dependent on industries involved in food processing, forest and paper products, textiles, and clothing. These industries represent approximately 5 percent of Texas' employment and earnings (*Dallas Morning News* 1987, pp. 428–429).

However, the greatest impacts for Texas cities will probably come from higher energy prices and new challenges in water resource management. Although many water projects have focused on an extreme event or condition and have consequently been overdesigned, "almost as if anticipating climate change," the magnitude of future climate change could well produce alterations in the hydrologic cycle that overwhelm safety margins of existing systems (Frederick and Gleick 1988, p. 135). Managing future water problems through traditional methods may be especially difficult, because most of the best reservoir and dam sites in Texas have already been developed.

Increasing demand for energy as a result of higher temperatures is likely to result in higher costs. In addition, strategies designed to limit greenhouse gas emissions could have a direct impact on energy production and costs. One such strategy might be to increase the taxes paid by consumers for energy, and it has been proposed, as a direct response to the perceived threat of global warming, that this tax be based on the carbon content of the fuel. Thus, response strategies themselves could also be considered an impact of climate change.

In this chapter we consider the potential impacts of climate change on urban areas from three perspectives:

1. the difficulties associated with managing more limited water resources under conditions where the frequency of extreme events is expected to increase;

2. the direct impacts of rising temperatures on energy demand, air pollution, public health, and urban ecosystems;

3. the potential problems associated with managing urban areas as a result of climate change.

Management of Water Resources

Water management policies in Texas have focused on meeting the state's water demands and providing flood protection through the construction of surface water reservoirs. This focus logically stemmed from the periodic cycles of severe drought and floods that affect nearly every region of the state. Because the majority of the reservoir capacity is committed through permits and contracts over the next 30 years, the existing infrastructure may have inadequate capacity to satisfy future growth. Yet the population in the state continues to grow, and municipal water demand alone will increase by 75–100 percent over current levels by the year 2040 (TWDB 1990, p. 3-2).

The present infrastructure will be stressed further under a global warming scenario. Global warming is expected to result in a reduction in available surface water supplies. The combination of decreased rainfall and higher average temperatures will have the synergistic effect of stressing water supplies, and this could be exacerbated if accompanied by an increased frequency of tropical storms. With increasing demand for water, river authorities are under constant pressure to increase the amount of stored water in reservoirs. Such an increase is inevitably at the expense of the flood pool and is in direct conflict with the authorities' concurrent responsibility for flood control.

Increases in Frequency and Severity of Flooding

Evidence suggests that a changing climate will not introduce new phenomena to the regions of Texas, but merely intensify already existing conditions. The Houston-Galveston urban region, with its high groundwater table, subsidence, and long history of severe flooding along its coastline and bayous, will be particularly vulnerable and could experience permanent loss of urban land in sensitive areas, necessitating extensive relocation programs.

In addition, a rise in sea level would enable salt water to penetrate farther inland and upstream into rivers, bays, wetlands, and aquifers (Smith and Tirpak 1989, p. 127). Water managers in New Orleans, when asked what components of their system were most vulnerable to climate change, replied that the water intake locations were sensitive to salinity. Were sea level to rise, water intake facilities would have to be relocated far upstream at great expense (Schwarz and Dillard 1990, p. 346). Coastal cities, such as those in Fort Bend County that withdraw their water directly from rivers, could be affected and may have to relocate their intake structures to a point farther upstream. The city of Corpus Christi, which withdraws water from the river following its release

JUDITH CLARKSON,
JOHN D. WILSON,
AND
WOLFGANG ROESELER

from Lake Corpus Christi, had to build a saltwater barrier to protect its intake structure from salt water at high tides. An additional impact of sea-level rise could be saltwater intrusion of coastal aquifers, particularly in areas where extensive withdrawal of groundwater has taken place in the past. Thus, in many different ways, the water supplies of coastal cities may be vulnerable to sea-level rise.

Along the Texas coast, the Houston-Galveston area is particularly vulnerable because of subsidence caused by groundwater withdrawal. Subsidence has exceeded 1.5 feet (0.5 m) in a bowl-shaped region more than 70 miles (110 km) across (Gabrysch 1984), and a few isolated spots have subsided nearly 10 feet (3 m). The cities of Beaumont, Port Arthur, Orange, Freeport, and Corpus Christi subsided 0.2–1.0 feet (0.1–0.3 m) between 1906 and 1974 (Brown et al. 1974).

Subsidence developed into an even more serious problem in the 1950's after the opening of the Houston ship channel. The resulting development led to an increase in demand for water, which was supplied by pumping fresh water from two aquifers found under Harris and Galveston counties. The subsidence that followed led to loss of property, estimated at $100–113 million. Many structures, such as roadways and ferry landings, had to be rebuilt, and docking facilities at the ship channel were abandoned because the lower elevations made the facilities obsolete (Gulf Coast Waste Disposal Authority 1975).

In many ways the impacts of subsidence are analogous to those of sea-level rise. For this reason, a study of the effects of subsidence over the last 30–40 years provides some insight into probable consequences of climate change for coastal regions. In addition, subsidence will be an exacerbating factor and, with increasing water demands, could become more critical if groundwater withdrawals are not reduced in these areas.

Another factor increasing the vulnerability of the area to flooding is coastal erosion, which is also exacerbated by subsidence. The Gulf Coast states have the highest average annual coastal erosion rate in the nation, exceeding 5 feet per year (Leatherman 1989). Coastal erosion is primarily a natural process and has long been attributed to tidal action, particularly that brought on by severe storms. Of the 370 miles (600 km) of Texas Gulf shoreline, approximately 60 percent is eroding at rates between 1 and 50 feet (1–15 m) per year (Texas General Land Office 1990). The most extreme case of beach erosion is found at Sargent Beach, where the shoreline is eroding at least 33 feet (10 m) per year and has retreated 1,000 feet (300 m) since 1956. This has not only led to the loss of real estate, including homes, but has also begun to place the Gulf Intracoastal Waterway in danger of being breached.

The Galveston seawall was built in the early 1900's to protect the island of Galveston from flooding. At one time there was a 300-foot beach in front of the seawall, but by 1940 the beach was entirely lost to erosion. Since then, the sand level has continued to drop in front of the seawall, and rocks have been placed farther seaward for protection during storms. The continued sand depletion, however, has caused these rocks to sink, so a "second line" of rocks, even farther seaward, has been put into place. In this case, structures were built to protect other structures, and this expensive process will, in all likelihood, have to proceed even more quickly under accelerated sea-level rise conditions. Moreover, with an increase in storm intensity and storm surges under conditions of global warming, the seawall may no longer offer adequate protection for the island. Studies by the U.S. Army Corps of Engineers show that for every extra foot of water during a storm, the damage to buildings increases by about 10 percent (Leatherman 1990).

Some climatologists have speculated that global warming will increase both the number and intensity of tropical storms in the future. Historically, hurricanes strike the Texas coast every 5 years, and the potential for devastating damage already exists, particularly from storm surges. In Galveston, storm surges of 15–18 feet (5–6 m) accompanied the great storm of 1900; in 1989, Hurricane Hugo brought a storm surge of 20–25 feet (6–8 m). These numbers illustrate the risk to high-density development along the coast. Even without sea-level rise, the danger from tropical storms will continue to grow with increasing coastal development. Moreover, large population centers place greater demands on the existing coastal roads and bridges. These access points are easily flooded, increasing the likelihood that people may be trapped on the immediate coast.

The EPA has identified four reasons why flooding would be expected to increase with rising sea level:

1. A higher sea level provides a higher base for storm surges to build upon. A 1-meter sea-level rise would enable a 15-

JUDITH CLARKSON,
JOHN D. WILSON,
AND
WOLFGANG ROESELER

Table 8.1. Potential Impacts and Responses to Sea-Level Rise in Urban Areas

Impacts
- Greater vulnerability to flooding
- Loss of waterfront property
- Higher water table
- Coastal protection costs of $2–20 billion
- Salinization of surface and ground water

Exacerbating Factors
- Subsidence
- Coastal erosion

Policy Responses
- Advanced planning for future storms
- Construction of salinity dams
- Moving water intake structures
- Construction and enlargement of groins and seawalls
- Development restrictions in coastal and flood-prone areas
- Injection wells to prevent salinization of groundwater sources

year storm to flood many areas that today are flooded only by a 100-year storm.

2. Beach erosion would leave oceanfront properties more vulnerable to storm waves.

3. Higher water levels would reduce coastal drainage, thereby increasing flooding attributable to rainstorms.

4. A rise in sea level would raise water tables, flooding basements and perhaps raising groundwater above the surface (Smith and Tirpak 1989, p. 127).

A summary of the potential impacts of sea level rise is given in Table 8.1.

In 1990, the Intergovernmental Panel on Climate Change predicted a 1.5 foot (44 cm) rise in sea level by 2070. Another source suggests that sea level may increase by 6–9 inches (14–24 cm) by the year 2030 (Warrick and Barrow 1990). Some earlier predictions suggested that sea level could increase as much as 6 feet (2 m), but estimates have been revised downward in the past few years. A 3-foot (1 m) rise in sea level by the year 2100 (significantly larger than current predictions but still a possibility) is projected to require protection of developed areas by building bulkheads and levees, pumping sand, and raising barrier islands. Nationwide, this could cost $73–111 billion (cumulative capital costs in 1985 dollars); $50–75 billion of this would be spent to protect barrier islands (Smith and Tirpak 1989, p. 123).

In a study by Leatherman (1984), the cost of protecting recreational beaches and barrier islands was based on the cost of pumping sand. Eighty percent of the nation's beaches were included in the study. For a 3-foot rise by the year 2100, cumulative costs (in 1986 dollars) were $26.7 billion. Twothirds of these costs would by borne by Texas, Louisiana, Florida, and South Carolina, with Texas' share amounting to $8.5 billion. This compares with anticipated costs in Texas through the year 2100 of $350 million under current conditions. Even adjusting for recent, less severe predictions of sea-level rise, Texas coastal cities should expect costs to increase fivefold or more during the next 50 years—total costs are likely to exceed several billion dollars, but to be less than several tens of billions.

Except in severe cases, advance, comprehensive, and site-specific planning could make adaptation to sea-level rise a manageable task. In a study of the economic impacts of sea-level rise in Charleston, South Carolina, a rise of about 3 feet by 2075 would cause damages amounting to approximately 17 percent of the total economic activity in the area; with planning, however, this figure could be reduced to about 4 percent (Titus 1984). If Texas cities avail themselves of similar opportunities to limit future expense, the rough economic analysis above suggests that the potential savings are in the billions of dollars.

As with the problems of erosion and wetland loss, global warming and sea-level rise will only aggravate existing storm vulnerability. Sea-level rise will enlarge the areas vulnerable to flooding if defense structures such as dunes and wetlands are lost. Although it may be impossible to mitigate these losses, being prepared for storm events may be the best policy option at this time. The recent (August 1992) devastation from Hurricane Andrew to the Florida and Louisiana coasts reinforced the need for advanced planning to help alleviate some of the impacts, such as loss of life, associated with severe storms in vulnerable areas.

JUDITH CLARKSON,
JOHN D. WILSON,
AND
WOLFGANG ROESELER

Texas experienced a devastating drought in the 1950's. Given the major population growth since that time, a repeat of such climatic conditions could be very serious for many of the state's major metropolitan areas. Even under current conditions, some metropolitan areas will have difficulty meeting future water needs (assuming continued population growth), despite the fact that municipal demand would have priority of use.

Allocation of surface water in Texas is determined by the doctrine of prior appropriation. Under this doctrine, the party that first puts a source of water to beneficial use obtains the right to use that water. However, rights to water that were obtained after 1931 (except for those from the Rio Grande) are subject to the Wagstaff Act, which specifies that an appropriation "for any purpose other than domestic or municipal use is subject to the right of any city or town to make further appropriations of the water for domestic or municipal use without paying for the water" (Texas Water Code, S. 11.028). In contrast, no such regulation of groundwater usage exists, and landowners own all of the water they can capture below their land and put to reasonable use. Thus, cities that depend upon groundwater have no legal recourse during periods of high demand.

Potential water-supply problems were documented in a recent study of global warming in Texas (Schmandt and Ward 1991). The study used water budgets based on the drought of record for the state of Texas in the years 1951–1960. A global warming scenario based on an average temperature increase of 3.5°F and a precipitation reduction of 5 percent was added to the 2030 demand scenario. The study determined that the municipal reservoir volume of Zone 1 of the Trinity River would decline to below 20 percent of capacity in the seventh year of a severe drought. The Rio Grande would be fully depleted by the seventh year—even under demand predictions for the year 2000, *without* additional global warming or precipitation change. In fact, under current conditions, the Rio Grande is seriously vulnerable in a severe drought. The study also projected that municipal reservoir volume in Zone 2 of the Colorado River would fall as low as 30 percent of capacity in the seventh year of the model drought. Thus, three important sources of surface water, which serve a major portion of the state's urban population, including Dallas and Austin,

URBAN
AREAS

175

are at risk if climate change increases the frequency, duration, and/or severity of droughts.

Texas relies heavily on its reservoirs for dependable supplies of water. In the past, building an additional reservoir was the preferred method for increasing supplies. Now, however, there are few cost-effective sites available for building reservoirs, and the majority of rivers in the state are already fully or over appropriated. Few experts are advocating structural solutions to the problem of water shortages. Some opportunity may exist for interbasin transfers of water, although the ambitious schemes of the past for transporting vast quantities of water to west Texas were not considered cost-effective. Currently, consideration is being given to transferring water from Toledo Bend Reservoir in east Texas to Houston as an alternative to the construction of Wallisville Reservoir. This may be the first stage in a scheme to transport water to coastal cities like Corpus Christi that are located in more arid river basins.

Other cities are vulnerable because they are dependent on declining groundwater resources. In El Paso, the primary sources of municipal and industrial supply are the Hueco Bolson deposits, which are being inundated with saline water from adjacent saline water bearing sands as fresh water is depleted. Because there is no unappropriated surface water available to the city, devising methods for stretching existing supplies is critical for continued economic growth in the area.

El Paso is developing water conservation plans and methods for reusing wastewater. Its Fred Hervey Water Reclamation Plant is capable of receiving 10 million gallons of wastewater every day. The potable water produced here has a chemical purity superior to that found at the untreated, natural freshwater source. It provides up to 6,700 acre-feet per year for recharge to the aquifer and subsequent reuse. This amount could increase to 35,000 acre-feet in the future (1990, p. 3-93). Although the technology exists to install reclamation systems in individual households, economies of scale seem to favor community reclamation systems.

San Antonio is completely dependent on the Edwards aquifer for its supplies, and in 1990 it was within 1 day of instituting mandatory water rationing. Because withdrawal of water from the aquifer is currently unregulated, the city competes with local irrigators for limited supplies. Conflicts between user groups are likely to intensify with global climate change, as demand for water increases and recharge of

JUDITH CLARKSON,
JOHN D. WILSON,
AND
WOLFGANG ROESELER

176

the aquifer from surface water sources declines. Better management of the region's water supplies is in everybody's interest. If local entities cannot agree on a plan, there is little doubt that one will be imposed on the region by some higher level of government. As a last resort, the federal government may be forced to intervene, perhaps under the Endangered Species Act, to protect species dependent upon the spring flows at San Marcos.

Another closely related issue is water quality. Because of large surface water withdrawals, river flow below both El Paso and Dallas is reduced to a trickle in summer months and consists primarily of treated effluent from municipal wastewater treatment plants. Increasingly saline municipal and agricultural return flows and highly saline inflows from tributaries have resulted in high salinity levels in much of the Rio Grande. The water in Falcon Reservoir, the major source of supply for the Lower Rio Grande Valley, has an average value for total dissolved solids of 600 mg/l. This is more than double that found in the majority of drinking water supplies in the United States as a whole. Surface water supplies in the area are limited, and groundwater also has high levels of total dissolved salts.

Desalination technology has been applied for years in arid regions in the Middle East, North America, and elsewhere, converting, on a large scale, sea water, water of saline aquifers, and brackish surface and groundwater into potable water. While distillation remains the principal system in desalination, other methods have gained recognition. They include electrodialysis, reverse osmosis, and freezing processes. The most appropriate technology depends upon the specific chemical properties of the water to be treated, with distillation being cost-effective only for sea water.

In Texas, the most common method is reverse osmosis for brackish groundwater and surface water sources with less than 5,000 mg/l dissolved salts. Typically, the water is split streamed, with a portion of it being treated and then blended back with the main stream to desired quality. The goal is to reduce the salinity to an acceptable level at the least cost. This method is currently being used for water supplies from Lake Granbury and Robinson Reservoir in the Brazos River basin. However, if limitations in freshwater availability make the use of increasingly brackish water a necessity, this will increase the cost of supplying municipalities with drinking water.

Thus, whether through water transfer schemes, increased

demand for recycled wastewater and conservation, or desalination, meeting municipal water needs will become more expensive and uncertain in the future, and better management of existing supplies will therefore become increasingly important and cost-effective (Roeseler 1982).

Direct Impacts of Higher Temperatures

Energy Demand

While global warming may result in warmer winters and reduce demand for heating in northern regions, it most likely will increase the demand for cooling in the summer in southern states. In Dallas, for instance, a 4–5°C increase in temperature will increase the number of days with highs above 100°F from 19 to 78 per year (Hansen et al. 1987, p. 45). Many studies suggest that a number of climate-related factors, including increased energy use for air conditioning, will lead to relatively higher energy prices. One study, which should be considered speculative, suggests that climate change–induced energy generation will increase by 7–33 percent in Texas (Smith and Tirpak 1989, pp. 194, 374). However, as discussed in Chapter 9, a 10–15 percent increase may be a more realistic figure for an average rise in temperature of 2°C. This increase in demand will naturally place an upward pressure on energy prices.

Another factor that could result in higher energy prices is a reduction in the use of coal as a source of electrical power. Coal has been a cheap source of power, but environmental considerations, including the fact that it produces the highest levels of CO_2 per unit of energy, may make it a less desirable option in the future. As a result of amendments to the Clean Air Act that require reductions in sulfur dioxide emissions, the capital cost of building and retrofitting coal plants has increased dramatically. Similar requirements to control CO_2 emissions and/or a carbon tax on energy sources could make coal uncompetitive with other fuels.

In general, demand for energy has stabilized in industrialized countries since the oil crisis of 1973. Improvements in energy efficiency have offset increases in economic activity, and there is every indication that this trend will continue. In some parts of the United States, there is excess electric-generating capacity, because plants built in the 1980's were designed in the 1970's, when energy consumption was increasing at a significant annual rate. However, in some parts

JUDITH CLARKSON,
JOHN D. WILSON,
AND
WOLFGANG ROESELER

of the country, new generating capacity will be required before the end of the century. With nearly a decade needed to plan and build a large power plant, these capacity decisions can no longer be delayed.

Based on experience over the last 10 years, the recent trend has been to wait as long as possible before committing to a new plant. This approach favors gas-fired plants, which have shorter construction lead times and lower capital costs; persistent low gas prices have also contributed to this trend. However, this appears to be an interim strategy. Although known reserves of gas are thought to be adequate for at least 25 years, based on current consumption patterns, a significant increase in gas prices will be necessary to encourage more exploration and development (Energy Ventures Analysis, Inc. 1990, p. 3-16). A longer-term strategy for meeting electricity demand is needed, if only to replace existing plants as they are retired.

An alternative option is nuclear power. However, the two nuclear power projects in Texas have proved to be very expensive sources of power, and it will be a long time before another nuclear power plant is built. Moreover, there are outstanding safety and nuclear-waste disposal issues that have to be resolved before nuclear power becomes a viable alternative in Texas and elsewhere. Nevertheless, since nuclear power emits few air pollution or climate-related gases, it will remain a viable option for growth of the electric power industry. The various methods of nuclear energy production continue to be under intensive research and development.

In the short run, the abundant supply of natural gas provides an important opportunity. Natural gas is a "greenhouse efficient" fossil fuel. Less carbon dioxide per unit of energy is emitted than for oil or coal. If the United States moves to natural gas as a primary energy resource, Texas cities will benefit from the change. Greater demands for natural gas drilling and pipeline equipment will support industries in cities like Houston and Beaumont. In the long run, however, the world is likely to turn to renewables such as wind and solar energy. Although Texas is not likely to become a major exporter of electricity derived from renewables, this region could become as important in the renewable energy business as it has been in the fossil fuel energy business, by becoming a major manufacturer of renewable energy technology. Currently, the petrochemical industry employs 5 percent of all Texas' workers directly in processing, and at least as many more in mining, pipeline construction, and management.

However, there is at present little indication of an emerging renewable energy industry (*Dallas Morning News* 1987, pp. 428–429).

Local Air Pollution

The temperature increase that may be associated with climate change in Texas could also exacerbate ozone formation in urban regions. Ozone in cities is the result of chemical reactions involving oxygen, nitrogen oxides (NOx), volatile organic compounds (VOCs) such as petrochemical gases, and ultraviolet radiation. In general, ozone formation increases at higher temperatures. One study suggests that a 4°C (7.2°F) temperature increase would lead to a 10 percent increase in peak ozone concentration (Smith and Tirpak 1989, p. 214). Another source attributes a 10 percent increase in smog events to each 5°F increase in temperature (Akbari et al. 1992, p. xix).

However, the relationship between temperature and ozone formation depends on a number of independent factors. The highly detailed studies needed to answer these questions have not yet been attempted in any Texas city. In fact, such detailed airshed modeling has only been completed in a few cities throughout the world. In each case, local conditions continue to dominate global factors under any likely scenario (Ibid.). In Texas' urban regions, although the temperature increase due to climate change is likely to make air pollution control more difficult, other factors will probably be far more important (DOE 1990, p. 101).

Air pollution may, in fact, be lessened as a by-product of climate change related policies. Although past efforts have been moderately successful at reducing pollution from stationary sources, progress has been slower with respect to mobile sources. Within Texas, the cities of Houston, Dallas, El Paso, and Beaumont are still not in compliance with the requirements of the Clean Air Act. California has taken more aggressive steps to control vehicle emissions, by adopting more stringent emission levels and mandating the use of alternative fuels for fleet vehicles.

In the future, both local air pollution reduction efforts and climate change policies are likely to depend on similar strategies—taxes on fossil fuels and programs to reduce driving. A strategy that could have beneficial impacts for the Texas economy would encourage the use of natural gas. Recent legislation requiring the conversion of fleet vehicles to

JUDITH CLARKSON,
JOHN D. WILSON,
AND
WOLFGANG ROESELER

compressed natural gas will have the twofold benefit of reducing air emissions, including CO_2, and stimulating natural gas demand (Roeseler 1981).

Public Health

Delivery of public health and emergency services, even under the best of circumstances, is a complex and resource intensive effort, to a point where health care in America and demands for reform have emerged as major political issues. Under stress of disasters, such as hurricanes and major floods, or in the face of epidemics and heretofore uncommon diseases, available services may be stretched to their limits. This is particularly true for small, rural jurisdictions, where deficiencies are not uncommon. One such area is the Lower Rio Grande Valley, where high infant-mortality rates and poor sanitation will make the area particularly vulnerable, especially if an increase in tropical diseases occurs.

Public officials are confident that the medical expertise exists to cope with such an eventuality, and Texas has some of the country's major medical centers. It is important that adequate health care is available to those most in need, and that health care personnel are trained in a timely manner to anticipate changing geographic distributions of diseases. In particular, vector-borne diseases could change their geographical distribution. For instance, while Texas may benefit from a northward movement of ticks, which transmit Rocky Mountain spotted fever, mosquito-borne diseases such as malaria could increase. However, these predictions are hard to make because of the importance of a number of other factors, such as the amount of standing water, the extent and effectiveness of vector control programs, and whether immigrants become a source of infectious agents (Smith and Tirpak 1989, pp. 226–231).

Ecosystems in Urban Regions

Despite continued development, ecosystems continue to play an important role in the urban environment. For city dwellers, trees are the most visible manifestation of the environment: their shade contributes to cooling buildings, their beauty provides the focal point of many parks and avenues.

The EPA's *Potential Effects of Climate Change in the United States* projects serious threats to forests throughout the United States. With warming, the climate zones for many forests could migrate northward. Within 30–80 years it is possible that forests will lose diversity of species as well as diminish in size. If the climate stabilizes at some point, forests should be able to recover, but the process will be measured in centuries. The EPA report also suggests that indirect impacts of climate change, such as drier soils, may contribute to a loss of forested area (Ibid., pp. 71–92).

In an urban region the impacts should be somewhat different. Two types of trees predominate in the urban environment: planted or transplanted trees and small forests. Planted trees are generally selected for appearance and other factors. If they die as a result of climate changes, it is a simple and relatively inexpensive matter to replace them. Small urban forests, however, may not be as easily replaced. Their loss would contribute to the ongoing problem of reduction in ecosystem diversity.

Though less visible to most urban residents than tree dieback, a loss of coastal wetlands due to sea-level rise could be the most important impact on urban ecosystems. A 3-foot rise in sea level threatens 25–80 percent of U.S. coastal wetlands (Ibid., p. 123). Inundation of coastal wetlands could greatly decrease the vitality of ecosystems in urban regions that depend on those wetlands. In the Houston-Galveston region, more than half of 14 endangered and threatened species are dependent on wetland habitat, including Armand Bayou, which is severely threatened as a result of saltwater intrusion resulting from subsidence. Loss of wetlands due to sea-level rise could interact with a change in climate to drastically reduce or eliminate many different ecosystems in urban regions, thereby reducing biodiversity. Such a loss would deprive urban residents of many recreational opportunities, including hunting, fishing, and bird-watching.

Managing the Impacts of Climate Change

It is likely that some of the more significant consequences of climate change for urban areas will result from indirect impacts. Water quality, for example, is not directly related to climate change. Yet, as climate change increases demand for water, increases the variability of surface water supplies, and decreases water purification by wetlands, the task of maintaining safe drinking water could be made just that much more difficult.

Short-term water pollution problems may be directly ex-

JUDITH CLARKSON,
JOHN D. WILSON,
AND
WOLFGANG ROESELER

acerbated (or mitigated) by local manifestations of climate change. An increase in the frequency of short, intense rainfalls will tax many storm sewer systems and increase the runoff from roads and yards into streams and rivers, without the diluting effects that result from sustained rainfall. It is doubtful, however, that climatic modeling will be able to predict whether climate change will reduce or increase the frequency of this type of storm in the near future.

As already discussed, higher temperatures may exacerbate ozone air pollution in cities. A further point is that *changing* temperatures may make strategies developed under one climate less effective than expected under another. The risk of climate change will simply make the task of projecting the impact of various air pollution strategies more complex and the decisions more difficult.

Again, this uncertainty will play an important role in wetlands management. Several wetlands restoration projects are underway in Texas, particularly in the Galveston Bay region. Sea-level rise may make these projects more difficult to design, implement, and manage. The additional uncertainty will make these projects that much more complex.

Climate change could also lead to increased frequency of hurricanes, thunderstorms, tornadoes, and other extreme weather events throughout Texas. In urban regions, this may mean that existing infrastructure and buildings are not designed to accommodate such climate conditions. Given that the replacement time for the more massive buildings and public works is long compared with the expected rate of climate change, these buildings may not be replaced with more durable structures quickly enough to keep up with the changing climate, resulting in higher maintenance costs. Efforts to maintain barrier islands may become more difficult if major portions of the islands are destroyed during severe storms, and rising sea level will compound these effects. Without these barrier islands, the coastal urban regions will be far more vulnerable to these storms.

This increased frequency in extreme events is likely to lead to higher insurance rates. To date, however, annual losses due to adverse weather and climate in the United States represent only about 2 percent of gross revenue of any economic sector, except agriculture. Even if climate change doubled or tripled the losses in every economic sector, weather- and climate-related losses would remain below 1 percent in most sectors. In commercial aviation (vulnerable to airport closings and flight hazards), losses only amount to 1 percent of gross revenue (Maunder and Ausubel 1985).

In the construction sector, losses due to adverse climate are also only 1 percent (Ibid.), but changing climate conditions will affect the design and construction of buildings and other structures. Rainfall is responsible for most delays in construction, but wind, snow, humidity, fog, frost, and heat also affect construction. Many "weather-design" values for the construction industry are based on calculated return-periods of extreme weather. For large, modern buildings, climatic change is unlikely to affect safety, because buildings are generally built to very low levels of risk. However, most housing may not have as great a safety margin (Parry and Read 1988, pp. 27–32).

While not investigated in Texas, it is possible that increased summer temperatures could cause direct damage to urban infrastructure, buckling roads and damaging pipes. A reduction in the number of construction days due to a higher frequency of peak temperature days is a possibility. Yet the cumulative effect of these factors in most Texas cities is likely to be insignificant. Only in the most vulnerable coastal cities will climate change have important direct effects on urban infrastructure. In fact, for the more northern Texas cities, milder winters might be of moderate economic benefit due to reduced heating costs and fewer blizzards and road icings.

On balance, this survey suggests that providing adequate services in urban areas will become an increasingly complex task, particularly as a result of climate change. In some cases, especially if winter weather is less severe, there will be benefits. However, the increase in extreme events and the problems associated with sea-level rise will pose long-term problems for public officials in most coastal, semiarid, and arid regions.

The urban issues and potential phenomena we have reviewed here with respect to global climate change exist now and have to some extent occurred throughout history in one form or another. Global climate change may take several decades before its full impacts are evident, and there is no certainty that these potential changes will actually come to pass. However, we should remember from these analyses that floods and droughts, air pollution and ozone destruction, are of immediate concern, and many technically feasible solutions exist. Addressing these issues now will allow for an

JUDITH CLARKSON,
JOHN D. WILSON,
AND
WOLFGANG ROESELER

orderly transition in the way we manage our environmental resources; dealing with problems in a time of crisis will not produce optimum solutions.

References

Achanta, A. N., 1992. Potential Impact of Global Warming on Indian Rice Production. Association of Mitchell Prize Laureates, *1991 Young Scholars Research Papers*. Center for Global Studies, Houston Advanced Research Center.

Akbari, H., S. Davis, S. Dorsano, J. Huang, and S. Winnett, 1992. *Cooling Our Communities: A Guidebook on Tree Planting and Light-Colored Surfacing*. U.S. Environmental Protection Agency.

Brown, L. F., R. A. Morton, J. H. McGoven, C. W. Kreitler, and W. L. Fisher, 1974. Natural Hazards of the Texas Coastal Zone. Bureau of Economic Geology, University of Texas at Austin.

Dallas Morning News, 1987. *1988–1989 Texas Almanac and State Industrial Guide*. Texas Monthly Press, Austin.

Department of Energy Multi-Laboratory Climate Change Committee (DOE), 1990. *Energy and Climate Change*. Lewis Publishers, Chelsea, Mich.

Energy Ventures Analysis, Inc., 1990. *Evaluation of the Prospects for Long-term Competitive Pricing for Natural Gas*. Prepared for the City of Austin.

Frederick, K. D., and P. H. Gleick, 1988. Water Resources and Climate Change. In: *Greenhouse Warming: Abatement and Adaptation*, N. J. Rosenberg et al. (eds.) Proceedings of a Resources for the Future workshop held in Washington, D.C., June 14–15, 1988.

Gabrysch, R. K., 1984. Case History no. 9.12: The Houston-Galveston Region, Texas. In: *Guidebook to Studies of Land Subsidence due to Groundwater Withdrawal*. UNESCO Studies and Reports in Hydrology 40.

Gulf Coast Waste Disposal Authority, 1975. *Land Subsidence in the Houston Gulf Coast Area*. Report to the 64th session of the Texas State Legislature.

Hansen, J., I. Fung, A. Lucis, S. Lebedeff, D. Rind, R. Ruedy, G. Russell, and P. Stone, 1987. Prediction of Near-term Climate Evolution: What Can We Tell Decision-makers Now? In: *Preparing for Climate Change, Proceedings of the First North American Conference on Preparing for Climate Change: A Cooperative Approach*. Proceedings of a conference held in Washington, D.C., October 27–29.

Leatherman, S. P., 1984. Coastal Geomorphic Responses to Sea Level Rise: Galveston Bay, Texas. In: *Greenhouse Effect and Sea*

Level Rise: A Challenge for this Generation, M. C. Barth, and J. G. Titus (eds.). Van Nostrand Reinhold, New York.

Leatherman, S. P., 1989. *Impact of Accelerated Sea Level Rise on Beaches and Coastal Wetlands.* Elsevier, Amsterdam, Neth.

——, 1990. Global Warming, Sea Level Rise and Coastal Impact, Proceedings of the 6th Terminal Operators Conference, Amsterdam.

Maunder, W., and J. Ausubel, 1985. Identifying Climate Sensitivity. In: *Climate Assessment: Studies of the Interaction of Climate and Society*, R. Kates, J. Ausubel, and M. Berberian (eds.). John Wiley and Sons, New York.

Parry, M. L., and N. J. Read, 1988. *The Impact of Climatic Variability on U.K. Industry.* Atmospheric Impacts Research Group Report 1, University of Birmingham, U.K.

Roeseler, W. G., 1981. Synthetic Fuels and Other Petroleum Substitutes. Institute of Transportation Engineers 6Y26.

Roeseler, W. G., 1982. *Successful American Urban Plans.* Lexington Books, Lexington, Mass.

Schmandt, J., and G. Ward, 1991. *Texas and Global Warming: Water Supply and Demand in Four Hydrological Regions.* Lyndon B. Johnson School of Public Affairs, University of Texas at Austin.

Schwarz, H. E. and L. A. Dillard, 1990. Urban Water, In: *Climate Change and U.S. Water Resources*, P. E. Waggoner (ed.). Wiley, New York.

Smith, J. B., and D. Tirpak, 1989. *The Potential Effects of Global Climate Change on the United States.* U.S. Environmental Protection Agency, Report to Congress.

Texas General Land Office, 1990. Draft: *Texas Coastal Management Plan.* Austin.

Texas Water Development Board (TWDB), 1990. *Water for Texas — Today and Tomorrow*, TWDB, Austin.

Titus, J., 1984. Can Coastal Communities Adapt to a Rise in Sea Level? In: *The Greenhouse Effect: Policy Implications of Global Warming*, D. Abrahamson and P. Ciborowsiki (eds.). Proceedings of a symposium held in Minneapolis, Minn., May 29–31, University of Minnesota, Publication No. CURA 88-8.

Warrick, R. A. and E. M. Barrow, 1990. Climate and Sea Level Change: A Perspective, *Outlook on Agriculture* 19:7.

JUDITH CLARKSON,
JOHN D. WILSON,
AND
WOLFGANG ROESELER

9. Economy

P hysical and scientific evidence presented in previous chapters seems to show that it is virtually certain that both greenhouse gases (GHGs) and temperatures have been and are increasing. The instrument recordings shown in Chapter 1 leave little doubt that the Earth has been warming for the last 150 years or so. Recordings also show a steady rise in greenhouse gases, primarily as a result of fossil fuel burning in industrial processes, motorized vehicles, and utility generators.

Figure 1.6 shows that, despite some fluctuations in the trend, there has been an overall increase in temperature in the northern hemisphere since the beginning of the century. The causes and effects of this phenomenon are still not known with certainty, and the magnitude of the temperature fluctuations cannot be predicted. Thus, it is impossible to know what the impacts on the environment will be and at what point mitigating action will be necessary. On these questions, most scientists agree that we can only be certain that we are still uncertain.

This fact merely compounds the problem of making economic forecasts which, even when all historical facts are known, are among the most variable and inconclusive of all sciences. In addition, the interrelationship between the environment and the economy is not well understood, and this uncertainty becomes an integral part of any consideration of policies that might be adopted to reduce the rate of global warming.

For our economic impact discussion, the predicted 2°C (3.6°F) increase in temperature over the next 50 years is accepted as the most likely climatic outcome if past trends continue. Moreover, we accept the most widely identified *cause* of the temperature rise: the relative increase in carbon dioxide, CFCs, methane, and other greenhouse gases. Since these are associated with industrial activity and the burning of fossil fuels, any action to halt, slow, or postpone warming by reducing greenhouse gases will likely require public action directed toward the segments of the economy that produce such pollutants.[1]

In this chapter, we will focus on two potential consequences of our predicted global warming scenario. First, let us assume that global warming continues as predicted and without major public policies toward abatement of greenhouse gases. Hence, over a 50-year planning horizon we assume that temperature will rise 2°C. It is then possible to make some very general statements about the possible future effects of this phenomenon on the growth in employment and/or gross domestic product of each of the major components of Texas' economy. We can also make some predictions about the cost of adaptation or mitigation of expected impacts.

Second, let us assume that political action is attempted, now or in the near future, to stop the process of global warming. This action will also have implications for the future growth and development of the Texas economy, including effects on investment and operating costs of individual businesses. Hence, we recognize that not only does global warming hold potential impacts for the economy, but political action to halt the process also has a set of impacts that must be considered.

While a complete analysis of such impacts is beyond the scope of this text, we can examine the feasibility and economic efficiency of unilateral action on the part of Texas within the context of the global problem of reducing the production of greenhouse gases. Is it rational for the people of Texas to enact rules and/or restrictions that may reduce the state's production of GHGs but may also increase costs of production of goods and services, alter the terms of trade with Texas' trading partners, and affect employment and personal income within the state? As its name implies, global

LONNIE L. JONES
AND
TEOFILO OZUNA

188

[1] Many will argue that the connection between atmospheric warming and these causes has not been proved, and it is true that no scientific experimentation has demonstrated the cause and effect of the observed phenomenon. In this, we have what I will call the "Surgeon General's problem." That is, the best we can do is to build statistical data and tests to show correlation between the two events. If this correlation is high enough, a conclusion may be warranted, just as it was in the linking of smoking to lung cancer.

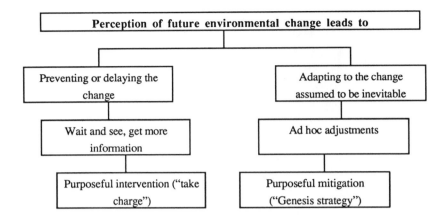

Perception of future environmental change leads to	
Preventing or delaying the change	Adapting to the change assumed to be inevitable
Wait and see, get more information	Ad hoc adjustments
Purposeful intervention ("take charge")	Purposeful mitigation ("Genesis strategy")

climate change is a problem involving all countries of the world. The focus of this text is on one state in one of those countries. Hence, considerations of changing the way we do business in Texas must be viewed in light of changes in the rest of the world.

The alternative courses of action available were suggested for Australia by Henderson-Sellers and Blong (1989), in a simple decision tree (Figure 9.1). A comparison of the expected results of these choices provides at least an ordinal criterion from the standpoint of economic impact.

Figure 9.1. Alternative choices of action based on perception of future environmental change.

The Evolution of the Texas Economy

The Texas economy is complex and ever evolving. Historically, Texas has depended primarily on agricultural and mineral (oil and gas) production as the base of its economy. These are still important sectors. In recent decades, however, these two mainstays have declined in relative importance, giving way to the more rapidly growing industrial, service, and trade sectors.

Figure 9.2 indicates the relative importance of the major sectors of the economy in terms of employment. Services, including both personal and business services, provided almost 24 percent of all jobs in Texas in 1991. Wholesale and retail trade businesses account for over 23 percent of total employment, and government ranks third, with almost 18 percent. The traditional sectors of agriculture and mining together accounted for less than 10 percent of all jobs in the economy in 1991.

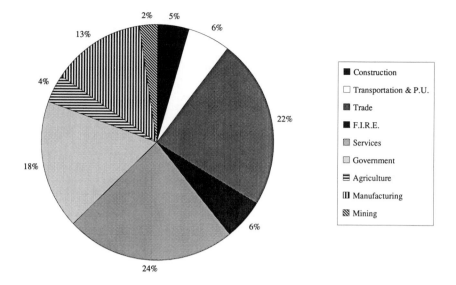

Figure 9.2.
Employment in
Texas by sector,
1991.

Changing Economic Structure

For several years, the most rapid employment growth in the Texas economy has been in the services and government sectors, including federal, state, and local governments. This trend is expected to continue into the foreseeable future. Figure 9.3 shows a comparison of employment by sector in 1991 with a projection of employment by sector in 2011. All sectors of the economy are expected to grow, with the exception of agriculture and mining, which are projected to maintain the same employment levels as in 1991. Significant increases in employment are expected in services, trade, government, transportation, and public utilities. Somewhat slower growth is projected for manufacturing and construction.

The projected structure of the Texas economy into the next century reflects underlying trends that are already underway. It is expected to evolve toward a service oriented economy, becoming less dependent on its traditional sectors. By 2011, the services sector will provide almost 30 percent of the jobs, and transportation and utilities will provide about 7 percent (Figure 9.4). All other sectors of the economy are projected to maintain about the same relative position in 2011 as in 1991.

LONNIE L. JONES
AND
TEOFILO OZUNA

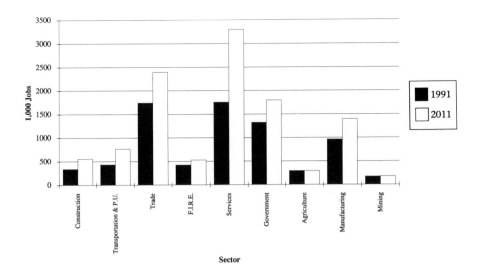

Figure 9.3.
Texas employment
by sector, 1991 and
2011 projected.

Projected Gross State Product

Gross state product (GSP) is a widely used measure of the growth of a state's economy. Like gross domestic product (GDP) for the nation, it is a measure of the total value of goods and services produced in 1 year within Texas. Sometimes referred to as *value added*, it measures the economic returns to all employed factors of production—land, labor, capital, and management. Figure 9.5 shows Texas' GSP for the historical period from 1970 through 1990, and projected GSP from 1995 through 2015. The annual dollar values shown in Figure 9.5 are nominal and include the effects of inflation. For the projected years, an inflation rate of approximately 4.5 percent is assumed.

Gross state product in Texas is projected to grow to $2,000 billion by the year 2015. This compares to a value of $365 billion in 1990, and just over $54 billion in 1970. In part, this rapid growth reflects the compounding effect of inflation. However, it also reflects the fact that Texas continues to enjoy one of the most rapidly growing economies in the United States. This growth is projected to continue well into the next century.

The service-producing sectors of the economy are projected to grow significantly faster than the goods-producing sectors (see Figure 9.5). This is a continuation of a well-established trend in Texas. The service-producing sectors are

ECONOMY

191

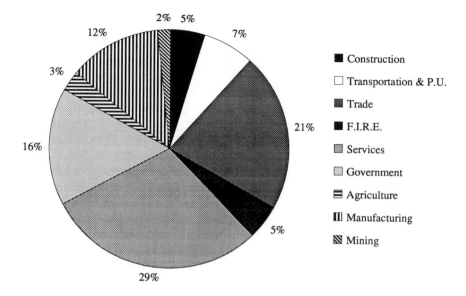

2% 5%

12%

7%

3%

21%

16%

5%

29%

■ Construction

☐ Transportation & P.U.

▨ Trade

■ F.I.R.E.

▨ Services

▨ Government

☰ Agriculture

Ⅲ Manufacturing

▨ Mining

Figure 9.4.
Projected
employment for
Texas by sector,
2011.

made up of a wide variety of business establishments, including both personal and business services. An important phenomenon in Texas'· economic growth in recent years, and expected for the future, is the growth in high-technology service enterprises. While many service jobs pay relatively low wages, high-technology service enterprises are attractive because they are high income producers, have significant spinoff economic effects, and emit very few by-products that affect the environment.

Economic Growth and GHG Emissions

Figure 9.6 presents a comparison between GSP in nominal and real dollars. Real-dollar projections take out the influence of inflation by expressing the projected quantity of goods and services produced in constant 1982 dollars. This expression is important when making comparisons through time of GSP growth with greenhouse gas emissions or other pollutants measured in physical units.

For a given level of technology, there exists a direct relationship between the amount of economic growth and environmental pollution, including GHG emissions. More people, more economic activity, more travel, and more demand increase the pressure on all environmental and natural resources.

LONNIE L. JONES
AND
TEOFILO OZUNA

192

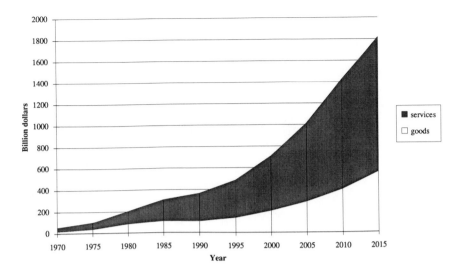

As indicated in earlier chapters, the primary contributors to GHG emissions in Texas are manufacturing, utilities, oil and gas production, and transportation (Schmandt et al. 1992). Those sectors of the economy that contribute the least amount of GHGs are the services industries other than transportation. It is significant, therefore, that the sectors of the economy in Texas that are growing the fastest contribute the least to GHG emissions, as well as to other forms of air and water pollution.

This means that the Texas economy can be expected to become a relatively cleaner economy in the future. This potential is borne out by the projections of real GSP and emissions of CO_2 equivalents, as shown in Table 9.1. CO_2 equivalents include carbon dioxide, methane, and CFC gas emissions; real GSP is expressed in constant 1982 dollars.

CO_2 equivalent emissions per million dollars of GSP trend downward significantly from 3,910 tons per million in 1980 to 1,920 tons per million in 2010. This 50 percent drop in emissions per million dollars of GSP reflects the rather stable annual emissions of GHGs during this period and a steadily growing GSP. Therefore, while Texas' contribution to total GHG emissions is projected to remain significant and slowly increasing, its future economy is projected to become relatively cleaner due to a shift to cleaner industries and services as the primary sources of GSP.

These projections suggest that continued emphasis on

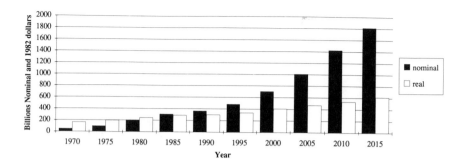

Figure 9.6.
Nominal versus
real gross state
product (GSP).

growth in the service sectors of economy in Texas can do much to reduce the state's relative contribution to total GHG emissions. Economic development efforts by state agencies and local communities might place greater emphasis on attracting and encouraging those businesses that can achieve a low ratio of GHG emissions per dollar of contribution to GSP. While service-providing businesses meet this goal, it might also be feasible to attract manufacturing, utility, and transportation enterprises that employ the newest technologies in pollution control and have a record of sensitivity to future environmental needs. In the past, most economic development efforts have focused on a single objective—the creation of jobs and personal income. Future development programs that recognize multiple objectives, including both economic and environmental objectives, will be needed to provide Texans with a satisfactory standard of living, while simultaneously protecting the environmental amenities of the state.

Implications of Climate Change on the Economy of Texas

The continued rise in global temperature may be expected to have several effects on the growth and development of the Texas economy. The primary industries affected by climate are those closely tied to natural resources, such as agriculture, forestry, and commercial fishing. The impacts of climate change on these industries are covered in other chapters of this book. Here, we wish to address the impacts on sectors of the economy further removed from dependence on natural resources, such as manufacturing, services, utilities, retail and wholesale trade, and construction. As shown in the

LONNIE L. JONES
AND
TEOFILO OZUNA

Table 9.1. CO₂ Equivalent Emissions per Million Dollars of GSP

Year	CO_2 Equivalents[a] (million tons)	GSP[b] ($billion)	Emissions per $million (tons)
1980	965	247	3910
1990	967	300	3226
2000	696	408	2376
2010	1028	535	1920

[a] All GHGs expressed in CO_2 equivalents based on a 500-year integration time horizon (see Schmandt et al. 1992).

[b] Real GSP in 1982 dollars. Projections by the Texas Comptroller of Public Accounts.

previous sections, these sectors make up the largest part of the Texas economy in terms of employment and GSP. The impact of temperature increase on these sectors is expected to be less direct than and of a different nature from that of natural resource–based industries.

At least two major impacts are anticipated in these sectors of the economy. First, a rising temperature will necessitate an increase in capacity and output of the utilities sector, primarily electricity. Second, a rise in sea level is expected to accompany rising global temperatures. Since much of Texas' population and economy is concentrated along the coastal region stretching from Beaumont–Port Arthur on the northeast coast to Brownsville on the southwest coast, a sea-level rise may significantly impact municipalities and industries within this region. The primary economic impact is likely to be the cost of mitigating the effects of higher tides.

Impact on Electricity Demand

In 1992, Texas utility companies had a total installed generating capacity of 60,394 megawatts (MW), and total sales of 252,777,203 megawatt hours (MWH). Statewide, installed generating capacity has been growing at about 680 MW per year, while demand has been growing at 1,300 MW per year. Thus, the current excess capacity of about 5,000–6,000 MW is steadily declining, at an average rate of about 600 MW per year (Adib 1992). By the year 2000, it is expected that the excess capacity will be eliminated and that future increases in demand will be met solely by newly constructed generating facilities.

Texas, like most southern states, uses more electricity for space cooling than for heating. Because capacity must be constructed to match summer peak demand for electricity, peak demand for cooling is highly sensitive to temperature increases. An increase in average temperature is likely to necessitate large increases in generating capacity, unless a greater effort is made to promote conservation through rate restructuring and improvements in energy efficiency of buildings.

Linder *et al.* (1987) studied the potential impacts of long-term global warming–associated temperature changes on regional electricity demands and utility investment and operating plans. Linder found that temperature increases significantly increase annual and peak demands and could require construction of new generating capacity. The study also shows that this increase in demand for electricity would be greatest in the southern region of the United States, where most of the electricity is used for cooling. Linder estimates that for the region including Texas, the climate-induced increase in electricity generation would rise by 10–15 percent above baseline growth in 2055. As a result, to meet peak demand, Linder estimates that generating capacity would need to increase 20–30 percent above that needed to meet baseline, or normal, growth (Smith and Tirpak 1990, pp. 579–596).

Table 9.2 presents estimates of baseline and global warming–induced capacity requirements for Texas for 1992 and 2050. In the absence of climate change, demand for electricity can be related to the general growth in the economy as measured by gross state product (GSP). Hence, baseline electricity capacity requirements are assumed to grow at the same rate as GSP. Since the GSP growth rate may be variable, two projections are made. The low GSP estimate in Table 9.2 assumes a relatively slow annual growth rate of 1.2 percent per year, whereas the high GSP estimate assumes a growth rate of 2.5 percent per year. This latter assumption corresponds closely to the projected economic growth rate made by the Texas Comptroller of Public Accounts (Plaut 1992). The additional impacts of climate change on capacity needs in Texas are estimated by using Linder's estimate of a 20–30 percent increase in capacity above the baseline for the south-

Table 9.2. Potential Impacts of Climate Change
on Electric Utility Capacity

| | 1992 | 2050 | |
		Low GSP	High GSP
Baseline Capacity (MW)	60,394	121,327	229,681
Baseline plus Global Warming (MW)	60,394	151,659	287,101
Global Warming Requirements (MW)		30,332	57,420
Cumulative Cost for Additional Capacity ($billions)[a]		35.6	67.5

[a]Dollar values are expressed at constant 1991 levels.

ern region of the United States. A midpoint of 25 percent is used for the estimates in Table 9.2.

Baseline generating capacity in Texas is estimated to grow to 121,327 MW in the low GSP scenario and 229,681 MW in the high GSP scenario. These requirements include no allowance for climatic change. With a 25 percent increase above baseline in response to a 2°C (3.6°F) increase in temperature, capacity requirements increase to 151,659 and 287,101 MW in the low and high GSP cases, respectively. The capacity requirements due to global warming are estimated to be from 30,332 MW to 57,420 MW by 2050. This is the additional capacity, above normal growth, needed to meet higher demands for electricity due to a 2°C rise in temperature. Under the high GSP growth scenario, the additional capacity required as a result of global warming is almost equal to the total installed capacity of the state in 1992 (60,394 MW).

It is estimated that the cumulative cost of construction of the additional, climate-induced generating capacity needed between the years 2000 and 2050 will range from $35.6 billion to $67.5 billion under the alternative scenarios. These construction costs are in constant 1991 dollars, and therefore do not include the effects of inflation. Construction costs per kilowatt of capacity were estimated at $1,175. This is a weighted cost of a generating unit made up of a composite fuel source consisting of 55 percent gas/oil, 15 percent coal, 15 percent lignite, 10 percent nuclear, and 5 percent hydro and cogeneration (Adib 1992).

As a matter of perspective, if the baseline demand did not grow between 1992 and 2050, the cost to construct electric generating capacity in response to a 2°C temperature rise would be $18 billion, or about 4.5 percent of current GSP. Hence, under global warming conditions, and assuming that Texas generates all its own electricity, we can expect the electric utilities sector to undergo above-average growth and become an increasingly significant part of the Texas economy.

Linder estimates electric utility annual cost of operations to be about 20 percent of cumulative capacity cost. Using this estimate, Texas' utility sector operating costs in response to global warming could range near $13 billion per year to cover variable costs, depreciation, and other fixed costs. Generating capacity is required to meet peak—i.e., summer—demand. Thus, a warmer summer accompanied by a warmer winter will have the effect of increasing the excess capacity during nonpeak periods. This increase in excess capacity and change in the distribution of seasonal demand during the year adds to the cost of operation.

It may be feasible under these conditions to plan for regionally integrated electrical systems with interregional bulk power exchanges and capacity sales over time and as climate changes. If implemented, this system could enable Texas to purchase electricity needed for peak (cooling) periods from other regions rather than constructing high-capital, low-fuel cost generating plants that would be fully utilized for only a relatively short period of time annually. Such an interregional system could reduce costs and provide a more optimal use of constructed generating capacity. It could also mean that the need to construct capacity within the state would be less than indicated in Table 9.2.

Other factors also may modify the need for increased generating capacity in Texas. The first is the effect of higher utility rates on electricity demand. All of the above projections follow Linder's assumption of a continuation of current levels of electricity consumption per dollar of GSP. As capacity expands and operating costs rise in response to higher temperatures, utility rates will, by necessity, also rise. Higher prices may mean consumption per capita or per dollar of GSP would be reduced, as consumers attempt to save money by changing consumption patterns.

Typically, price increases have acted as incentives for the development of more advanced technologies, such as more efficient generating and transmission systems. Improved in-

LONNIE L. JONES
AND
TEOFILO OZUNA

sulation, more efficient air conditioners, alternative construction designs, and other methods of reducing cooling costs may also be stimulated by rising temperatures and electricity costs. As outlined in Chapter 3, many of these conservation strategies are cost-effective today; further increases in energy costs will add to the attractiveness of increasing energy-use efficiency.

Sea-Level Rise

A second major impact of global warming on the economy of Texas is the associated rise in sea level, predicted to be approximately 1 meter. This change would be especially problematic along the Texas coastal zone for two reasons. First, the Texas coast is relatively flat, low lying for many miles inland, and in the process of sinking. Hence, the relative sea-level rise is greater than the absolute rise, and as a consequence, the danger to coastal land and property is increased. The second economic concern is that of the heavy concentration of industrial, municipal, recreational, and other economic activity along areas that would be affected by a rise in sea level.

Previous research (Barth 1984) indicates that the relative sea-level rise will be greatest along the coasts of Louisiana and Texas because of the combined effects of land subsidence and a rising sea. A rise in sea level would inundate wetlands and lowlands, accelerate coastal erosion, exacerbate coastal flooding, threaten coastal structures, raise water tables, and increase salinity of rivers, bays, and aquifers (Barth and Titus 1984). No study has been conducted of the economic losses and costs that may be associated with a general sea-level rise along the Texas coast. However, previous studies have addressed similar situations in specific regions of the coast.

The expected effects of sea-level rise along the coast of Texas are similar in nature to those related to land subsidence found by Jones et al. (1976) in the Houston-Galveston area. Because of excessive groundwater pumping, land in this area had subsided by as much as 9 feet between 1943 and 1974. Subsidence along the immediate coastline was generally less than 1 foot. Nevertheless, the area was found to suffer from property damage and value loss in residential, industrial, commercial, and public properties as a result of temporary or permanent flooding. These losses, together with the cost of structures to prevent flooding and sea water encroachment, amounted to $73 million ($215 million in

1992 dollars) over a 5-year period, from 1969 to 1973. The damages and property value loss estimates did not include catastrophic damages from tidal surge, hurricanes, etc.

Another potential impact is loss of wetlands and the productivity of bays and estuaries that support major economic enterprises of commercial and sport fishing and other coastal-related recreational activities. Ozuna and Jones (1991) estimated the impact of these activities on the regional and state economies in 1987: The combined economic activity supported by commercial fishing and recreation along the coast was $1,625 million on the coastal economy and $2,564 million on the Texas economy as a whole. Use of the bays and estuaries also created almost 49,000 jobs and $675 million of personal income in Texas.

As mentioned above, much of Texas' economy and population is concentrated along the coast. The Gulf Coast economy continues to be the fastest growing in the state; in 1991, this region added more jobs than any other in Texas. Since the state's recovery in the late 1980's, Houston has dominated Texas' recent expansion, creating more than 40 percent of all new jobs in the state since 1989 (Sharp 1991). Other coastal metropolitan areas are also experiencing economic growth, including Beaumont–Port Arthur, Galveston–Texas City, Brazoria, Corpus Christi, and Brownsville. Leading the economic growth of this area are the petrochemical industry, makers of oil-field machinery, steel, plastics, high-tech electronics, and various instruments.

This region may be expected to continue to grow in employment and population, even in the face of global warming. Climate is a factor in industrial location decisions by business leaders, but is generally less significant than other factors, such as proximity to markets, availability of natural resources, availability of labor, transportation systems, and other elements that affect the cost of doing business. With the coastal shipping facilities giving access to export markets, and other favorable location factors, it is not expected that the projected temperature increase between now and 2050 will have much effect upon manufacturers' tendency to choose the Texas Gulf Coast as a place to locate. Hence, the major impact on the industrial economy of the region is expected to be that of increased construction and other mitigating actions, as industry and municipalities become affected by the rising sea level.

Many of the necessary measures to hold back the sea in developed areas, such as rebuilding ports, constructing

LONNIE L. JONES
AND
TEOFILO OZUNA

levees, or rebuilding beaches, can be postponed until flooding and/or inundation are imminent. On the other hand, sea-level rise could become a part of the current planning process for future economic growth, including land use decisions. Some experts have argued that this would be more efficient than not responding until the rise occurs (Smith and Tirpak 1990).

In large measure, the efficiency of allowing for future sea-level rise in current development planning depends upon the certainty with which the event is expected. If we are certain, it may well be that engineering and land use plans that avoid future damages and losses would be less costly than making repairs at some future date. However, if plans are laid in anticipation of sea-level rises that do not occur within the planning horizon, the decision may be less efficient and could lead to a misallocation of resources. The certainty of sea-level rise will, no doubt, be a topic of discussion in development planning circles in the future.

Mitigating Strategies for Texas

Most of the literature dealing with the economic trade-off between global warming costs and the benefits of reducing greenhouse gas emissions has taken a global view. That is, the analysis treats the entire globe as one economy. Then, the calculus involves finding the optimum level of emission reduction by comparing the marginal costs and marginal benefits for the global economy over a range of reduction strategies. For example, Nordhaus (1991) estimates optimum percentage reductions in global greenhouse gases under several scenarios of global warming damage. For the medium damage case, he estimates the global optimal reduction to be 11 percent below current levels. This is the reduction level at which the marginal cost of reduction is just equal to marginal damages for all nations as a whole. At this level, almost all emission reduction comes from reduction in use of CFCs, the most immediate and least costly GHG reduction alternative.

Such global analyses are quite valuable in understanding the cost-benefit trade-offs that must be considered in deliberating political actions for the global warming phenomenon. However, they fall short of providing information needed for evaluating political actions at the subglobal level, such as for a nation or a state. Actions of the subglobal entity must be considered not only in terms of the direct pros and cons of those actions, but also in terms of the actions of all other entities that contribute to and share in the problem.

Responding to global warming over the long run will require reducing emissions of greenhouse gases. However, global warming is a phenomenon that depends on global, aggregate emissions. This international dimension of the global warming problem is a source of substantial interdependence among nations (and, within the United States, among states). Each country receives an economic benefit from using the environment as a receptacle for emissions, and at the same time each country is damaged by the environmental problems these emissions cause. However, such benefits and damages differ significantly among countries. Hence Texas, in evaluating alternative strategies for ameliorating its emission of greenhouse gases, must take both international and domestic perspectives into account.

Theoretically, global warming can be seen in two ways: as a problem of managing a common property resource, or as a problem dealing with the voluntary provision of a public good. In the first case, the atmosphere can be defined as a common resource whereby (1) it is sufficiently large that it is costly to exclude potential beneficiaries from obtaining benefits from its use, or (2) property rights to the resource are such that potential beneficiaries cannot be legally excluded. With respect to greenhouse gas emissions, some countries (or states) benefit from using the atmosphere as a receptacle for its emissions, and since the atmosphere is sufficiently large, it is costly to prohibit them from doing so. Alternatively, because property rights to the atmosphere are not well defined, countries cannot be legally excluded from using the atmosphere as a greenhouse gas emission receptacle. While the benefits for any country (or state) are primarily related to domestic emissions alone, the damage inflicted is linked to both domestic and foreign emissions, thus creating a problem of externalities.

The end result is that individual countries using the atmosphere for greenhouse gas emissions face a tragic situation in which their individual rationality leads to an outcome that is not rational from the perspective of the world. Since no institution possesses supranational powers for solving this greenhouse gas emission externality problem, standard solutions for environmental externalities are not available. The protection of the atmosphere is left to voluntary agreements among sovereign countries (or, within the

LONNIE L. JONES
AND
TEOFILO OZUNA

United States, among the states). However, as with most international agreements, problems of enforcement and monitoring generally arise, and these undercut the agreement.[2]

An alternative viewpoint is to see global warming not as a problem of greenhouse gas emissions but as one of decreasing the Earth's capacity to recycle carbon dioxide. Since carbon dioxide is recycled by plants and vegetation, a decrease in their stock will result in the increased retention of carbon dioxide by the atmosphere. In this respect, deforestation and soil destruction add to the global warming problem. Thus, countries that have already deforested much of their land, or countries like Brazil who have ongoing deforestation policies, have contributed or currently contribute to the global warming problem.

In the case of Brazil, which is a major repository of plants and vegetation (i.e., the Amazon Rain Forest), simple economics tells us that the private cost to Brazil of pursuing a forest depletion policy, as it relates to carbon dioxide, will be far less than the global social costs. Why is this so? Brazil does not take into account damages incurred by the rest of the world. Hence, one would expect Brazil (and other countries, including the United States) to deplete its forests at a faster pace than is globally warranted and thus exacerbate the global warming problem, as is presently the case.

As can be observed from the above arguments, confronting the problem of global warming—whether through reductions in GHG emissions, reductions in the loss of plants and vegetation, or both—requires government action at the international, national, and state levels. However, governments realize that they cannot undertake unilateral policy actions to mitigate the problem of global warming and still maintain their economic competitiveness. For example, any government instituting a tax on the carbon content of specific fuels used to produce products will most likely increase the costs of the finished products, and this will decrease its

---

[2] The limited success of the Organization of Petroleum Exporting Countries (OPEC) in controlling oil price by limiting production is an example of the difficulty of maintaining an international coalition in which each country must subvert its own economic goals to that of the larger group. OPEC's ability to significantly restrict oil production lasted less than 1 decade and included fewer than a dozen countries.

economic competitiveness with economies that have not in-stituted such a tax. Similar results could be expected from the setting of standards on the fuel efficiency of motor ve-hicles or the energy efficiency of household appliances. In most cases, this loss of competitiveness causes governments to be hesitant or to behave strategically with respect to enacting policies that will reduce the problem of global warming.

Mitigating Policy Options for Texas

Given that international and federal government action will most likely be necessary in solving the global warming prob-lem, the overriding question is, Should Texas enact policies or strategies that mitigate the emission of its own green-house gases? Before addressing this question, however, one should also ask, What is Texas doing *now* to mitigate the global warming problem? Currently, Texas does not have an official policy regarding global warming. However, it does have in place a number of initiatives that have an effect on the level of GHG emissions, namely, the Natural Gas Ini-tiative, recycling programs, and the Texas Clean Air Act (Schmandt et al. 1992). Each of these initiatives, although not designed to address the global warming problem directly, contributes to mitigating GHG emissions.

Any new policy initiative implemented by Texas to re-lieve the global warming problem should be commensurate with the continued growth of the Texas economy. The poli-cies enacted should consider not only the impact on GHG emissions but also the cost of these policies to the state and its citizens. In this respect, "coincidental policies" that re-duce not only GHG emissions but also production or trans-portation costs should be advanced. Such policies would in-crease Texas' competitive position in domestic as well as international markets. Examples of these policies include encouraging multiple occupancy of vehicles, improving the energy efficiency of existing public buildings and residential homes, and encouraging use of natural gas. Overall, the goal should be to enact policies that are cost-effective in the short run, while increasing our ability to deal with the potential threat of global warming.

LONNIE L. JONES
AND
TEOFILO OZUNA

Conclusions

As discussed throughout this book, global warming could have serious implications for Texas. In this chapter we have considered some of the likely economic impacts. With higher temperatures and the possibility of new programs to limit greenhouse gas emissions, energy demand and costs are likely to increase. Meeting the challenge of controlling this rate of growth in demand through conservation measures, while addressing the need for increased generation capacity, will require an integrated approach to energy policy if costs are to be contained so that Texas can remain competitive in world markets. In addition, rising sea level, an existing problem that will be exacerbated by global warming, could result in economic hardship for coastal communities and affect industries that depend on coastal resources. This could have implications for the economy of the state as a whole. Again, effective planning could mitigate some of these impacts by, for instance, restricting development in flood-prone areas.

Whether Texas should embark on a program for reducing greenhouse gas emissions is more questionable. It is likely that unilateral action would result in a reduction in the competitiveness of Texas' industries if, for example, a tax were imposed on energy consumption. However, an aggressive program to encourage energy conservation could be beneficial by controlling emissions while at the same time reducing production costs. Thus, it appears that adaptive strategies will have the greatest economic benefit at the state level. However, that is not to say that measures to reduce greenhouse gas emissions should not be considered, provided that the economic consequences are carefully weighed.

References

Adib, P., 1992. Resource Place for Texas Utilities (unpublished projections). Texas Public Utilities Commission, Austin.

Barth, M. C., and J. G. Titus (eds.), 1984. *Greenhouse Effect and Sea Level Rise: A Challenge for this Generation.* Van Nostrand Reinhold, New York.

Henderson-Sellers, A., and R. Blong, 1989. *The Greenhouse Effect: Living in a Warmer Australia.* New South Wales University Press, Kensington.

Jones, L. L., and J. P. Warren, 1976. Land Subsidence Costs in the Houston-Baytown Area of Texas. *Management and Operations,* 597–599.

Linder, K. P., M. J. Gibbs, and M. R. Inglis, 1987. Potential Impacts of Climate Change on Electric Utilities. New York State Energy Research and Development Authority, Report 88-2, ICF Incorporated, Washington, D.C.

Nordhaus, W. D., 1991. To Slow or Not to Slow: The Economics of the Greenhouse Effect. Coulves Foundation for Research in Economics, Paper No. 791, Yale University, New Haven.

Ozuna, T., and L. L. Jones, 1991. Economic Impacts of Sport Fishing, Other Recreational Activity, and Commercial Fishing in the Texas Gulf Coast. Paper presented at the Annual Meetings of the International Association of Impact Assessment, Urbana-Champaign, Ill.

Plaut, T. 1992. Conditions of the Texas Economy. Unpublished report to the Comptroller's Panel of Economic Advisors, Austin.

Schmandt, J., S. Hadden, and G. Ward, 1992. *Texas and Global Warming: Emissions, Surface Water Supplies and Sea Level Rise.* Lyndon B. Johnson School of Public Affairs, University of Texas at Austin.

Sharp, J. 1991. Fiscal 1991: A Look Back, Sidestepping the Slowdown. *Fiscal Notes* 11 (Nov.): 1–16.

Smith, J. B., and D. A. Tirpak, 1990. *The Potential Effects of Global Climate Change in the United States.* Hemisphere, New York.

LONNIE L. JONES
AND
TEOFILO OZUNA

JUDITH CLARKSON AND JURGEN SCHMANDT

10. Policy Options for Addressing the Impacts of Global Warming on Texas

Although there is uncertainty as to the actual timing, magnitude, and regional effects of global warming, the scientific community agrees that it poses a considerable and certain threat to some ecosystems and may have adverse consequences for social and economic systems. The Intergovernmental Panel on Climate Change (1990), in its authoritative summary of information on global warming, puts it this way: "We are certain [that] . . . emissions from human activities will enhance the greenhouse effect, resulting on average in an additional warming of the Earth's surface." It is also likely that the Earth will experience warming at a rate much faster than at any other time in its history. In 1989, the Environmental Protection Agency reported to Congress that the *rate* of global warming, rather than the *amount* of warming, may be the most important factor affecting both natural and managed systems. The faster the warming, the harder it will be to adapt. The ability of natural ecosystems (forests, wetlands, barrier islands, national parks) to adapt to a rapidly warming climate is limited. The range and population size of many species could decrease; many may face extinction. For managed systems the threat is somewhat less, if strategies designed to adapt to global warming are implemented.

Thus, two types of strategies for addressing the problem of global warming are emerging. The first involves a range of mitigative strategies that would reduce the rate of accumulation of greenhouse gases. The second consists of adaptive strategies that would address the consequences of a warmer climate. In proposing a role for Texas, it is clear that adaptive strategies are more easily implemented at the regional level.

Therefore, it is in Texas' best interests to determine the magnitude of the threat and act accordingly. Because it is difficult for governments to act on long-term risks—significant impacts from global warming will not be felt until 2030—strategies that address both current and future needs will provide the greatest immediate benefit and be the easiest to implement. For example, improved management of water resources can help in coping with current increases in demand as well as conditions expected as a result of global warming.

With regard to mitigation, we need to recognize that Texas is as large a producer of greenhouse gases as countries like the United Kingdom and Italy. Therefore, it can also be argued that Texas would be well advised to provide a leadership role among U.S. states in developing strategies for reducing the emissions of greenhouse gases. One advantage of this strategy would be that when, and if, greenhouse gas reductions are required by the federal government, Texas would be in a position to influence the types of restrictions to be implemented. For example, a significant portion of Texas' greenhouse gas emissions result from the processing of petrochemicals that are later exported to other states. It would make a difference for Texas whether production or consumption of petrochemicals were taxed.

Another argument stems from the tenet in the field of pollution control that "the polluter pays" for the cleanup of its pollution. In cases where it is clear-cut that a given pollutant has resulted in specific damage, such as a point-source discharge of industrial waste, this is a relatively straight-forward and achievable goal. However, in the case of greenhouse gas production, where the linkages between emissions and climate change are a matter of significant debate and uncertainty, more scientific evidence may be necessary to advance this claim. Lacking a compelling linkage between the production of such gases and impacts at a local level, it is unlikely that extensive new state legislation will be forthcoming. It is essential that other, more short-term benefits be identified, if a reduction in greenhouse gas emissions is to be accomplished.

In this chapter we focus on adaptive strategies. Because the timing and magnitude of the impacts of global warming are so uncertain, many claim that it is premature to spend precious public funds on mitigation policies. However, many of the potential impacts will exacerbate existing trends, particularly those related to limitations in water supplies, coastal erosion, and energy efficiency. Thus, a reasonable ap-

JUDITH CLARKSON
AND
JURGEN SCHMANDT

proach would be to focus on those strategies that would have immediate benefit, while also preparing us for the possibility of a warmer climate. In general, the policies that are consistent with this philosophy increase the sustainability of economic development and reduce vulnerability to catastrophic events.

Sustainable Development and Vulnerability to Climate Change

Much has been written on sustainable development in recent years. The international Brundtland Commission concluded in its report that sustainable development was the most urgent task facing mankind (World Commission on Environment and Development 1987). The commission defined *sustainable* development as "meeting the needs of the present without compromising the ability of future generations to meet their own needs." This concept is still not generally accepted among policymakers, because they see no urgency to change the type of high-input economy that has created wealth in the modern world. However, as we face the possibility of an economy limited in its growth potential by the availability of energy and water, an orderly transition to more sustainable, less–input intensive practices is called for.

In Texas one of the greatest threats to continued growth is likely to be limited water supplies. San Antonio has been rejected by at least one company looking for a relocation site because of potential water shortages and lack of a drought management plan. Drought conditions have occurred periodically in Texas' past, and the possibility of such events occurring in the future is likely to increase under global climate change. In general, predictions about climate change include an increasing frequency of extreme events: where flooding is a problem now, it is likely to get worse in the future; where drought conditions prevail, water availability will most likely become an increasing problem; and where hurricanes pose a hazard to coastal communities, their frequency and severity is likely to increase.

Identifying existing vulnerabilities is a first step in planning for the possibility of adapting to greater adversity. Planning for limitations in water supplies is consistent with the current need to serve an ever-increasing population with little opportunity for increases in supply. Coastal vulnerabilities to sea-level rise already exist as a result of subsidence and coastal erosion. Addressing these problems through better land use management is a cost-effective approach to potential storm events. The remainder of this chapter addresses some of the problem areas for Texas. With an ever-increasing population, it is certain that greater demands will be made on our resources. This is a compelling argument for the adoption of policy options that are more consistent with sustainable development.

Increasing the Sustainability of Agriculture

Although model results presented in Chapter 7 suggest that the consequences of global warming in Texas may not be very serious for the agricultural sector, these results do not take into account other changes that are likely to occur over the next 50 years, including increasing population pressure on land and water resources and further declines in groundwater tables. In addition, it is likely that our dependence on a few genetically uniform varieties of food stocks will make us vulnerable to changes in climate and pests.

In fact, the high-input type of agriculture practiced in the Western world is likely to be ill-suited to dealing with changing climatic conditions. While the intensive use of fertilizers and pesticides has greatly enhanced the short-term output of farms, their long-term output has been put at risk because these chemicals have weakened the system of natural predators that could otherwise provide protection against invasions of new varieties of pests. These practices have created additional long-term problems by polluting water supplies, overdrafting aquifers, and increasing soil erosion. More sustainable forms of agriculture are needed if we are to meet future needs for food, particularly under changing climatic conditions.

A greater commitment by government to help in the development and adoption of more sustainable practices is called for. In Texas, improvements in water use efficiency are a priority, and financial incentives in the form of low-interest loans have been made available. More efficient irrigation systems developed by Texas A&M University have improved water use efficiency and cut energy use by 30–50 percent. Integrated management practices developed for rice have increased yields by 44 percent and reduced water use by 25 percent and nitrogen fertilizer and pesticide requirements by 35–50 percent (Texas A&M University 1988).

Currently, the agricultural assistance programs administered by the federal government encourage overproduction

JUDITH CLARKSON
AND
JURGEN SCHMANDT

and require the intensive use of fertilizers and pesticides. Because these programs have such a dramatic impact on farming practices, it is difficult to make predictions about future farming practices and crop production. The predictions presented in Chapter 7 assume that climate change and increases in CO_2 are superimposed on current conditions. However, a change in federal policies could have a much greater impact on agricultural productivity than the changes that were used as the basis for the model predictions.

An important component of reducing vulnerability to climate change is maintaining genetic diversity. Currently, 95 percent of our food is produced by 30 different kinds of plants, each of which is dominated by a few genetically uniform varieties. Maintaining stocks of genetically diverse varieties will be critical for adapting to changing conditions (Kellogg and Schware 1981, pp. 68–69). Two approaches, both requiring a significant commitment by governmental agencies, are required to ensure success. One involves storing, under laboratory conditions, stocks of as many different kinds of seeds that have potential food value as possible. This approach could be supplemented, using genetic engineering, so that varieties with increased resistance to disease and drought are developed in a timely manner in anticipation of changing conditions. Such a strategy would involve a very small investment of resources and have a potentially very large payoff.

A second approach would protect natural ecosystems. It is entirely possible that hybridization of existing food stocks with wild plants will be necessary to increase their resistance to disease and drought conditions. Maintaining genetic diversity by protecting as many species as possible is another way of ensuring continued agricultural productivity. Over the last few decades, species have been disappearing at an alarming rate, primarily through habitat loss. As described in Chapter 6, Texas does have a number of protected park and wildlife areas that represent at least some of the diversity of natural areas within the state. However, with climate change it is entirely possible that areas set aside to protect specific species will no longer be within the species' range as temperatures increase or water supplies dwindle. Under these circumstances, it will be impossible for land acquisition programs to keep up with the demand for habitat protection; more innovative approaches will be needed. Currently, the Texas Parks and Wildlife Department is initiating a number of programs to increase its effectiveness in protecting a vari-

POLICY OPTIONS
FOR ADDRESSING
THE IMPACTS OF
GLOBAL WARMING
ON TEXAS

211

ety of species. One of these programs involves working with landowners to provide habitats on private land. Another program is designed to create dispersal corridors that would allow animals and plants to migrate between limited areas of suitable habitat.

Vulnerability as It Relates to Wealth: The Case of the Lower Rio Grande Valley

It is generally accepted that impoverished areas will be the most vulnerable to climate change. Inevitably, those areas of the world that have the most assets, including capital, infrastructure, and natural resources, will be in the best position to adapt to climate change. The healthiest populations will be most able to deal with disease epidemics, and those with emergency equipment will cope the best with unexpected disasters.

Within Texas, the Lower Rio Grande Valley (LRGV), a four-county area in the most southerly part of Texas, will be especially vulnerable to climate change. This stems from several sources: poverty, illiteracy, disease, limited water supplies, and lack of infrastructure. All of these conditions interact to limit opportunities for economic development in the valley (Schmandt and Ward 1991; Schmandt and Mu 1992).

The LRGV is semiarid, prone to drought, and economically dependent on its agricultural base. The area consists of a rich alluvial basin, most of which is cultivated. While some of the acreage is restricted to rain-fed cotton and grain sorghum, 40–50 percent of the land is irrigated, enabling the production of high-value crops such as fruit and vegetables. Because of the widespread use of irrigation, agriculture accounts for more than 85 percent of water demand in the LRGV. Even so, the demand for water is so much greater than the supply that only in the wettest years are all of the agricultural needs met. In addition, with high birthrates and continuing immigration, municipal demand for water is expected to increase 2–3-fold by the year 2040. Because municipal use has a higher priority than agricultural use, this will be at the expense of agricultural users.

As discussed in the next section, current problems of water availability will be exacerbated by global climate change. An increase in the severity and frequency of floods and droughts will diminish the firm yield of the reservoir system,

JUDITH CLARKSON
AND
JURGEN SCHMANDT

while higher temperatures will increase the demand for irrigation water. Because so much of the economy currently depends both directly and indirectly on agriculture, a comprehensive approach to economic development in the LRGV is needed; the development of a less water-intensive industrial economic base for the region is called for.

Currently, the largest manufacturing sector in the LRGV is the textile and apparel industry, which employs significant numbers of low-paid workers. However, with the North American Free Trade Agreement it will become increasingly difficult for these plants to compete with those in Mexico. Ideally, industries that manufacture equipment and electronics should be encouraged to relocate to the valley. This would require a large investment in the infrastructure of the region, including increasing the educational level of the work force.

Overcrowding, contaminated drinking water, inadequate sewage treatment, and poor nutrition are all associated with a variety of infectious and parasitic diseases. The majority of residents have no health insurance, and many depend on socialized health services available in Mexico. All of these factors contribute to absence from and substandard performance at school. In addition, many students see no compelling reason to finish high school, when all that is available is a minimum-wage job.

The interrelationship between poor education, inadequate health care, and lack of opportunity perpetuates the economic depression. Thus, the economic and natural resource limitations of the LRGV make it particularly vulnerable to climate change. Structural changes in its economic base are needed if it is to support a growing population under increasingly limited water supplies.

Improving Water Management

Addressing water management issues is a good example of a strategy that has the potential for immediate, beneficial impacts, in addition to anticipating the responses dictated by a climate change scenario. Because much of Texas is hot and arid, it will be difficult to meet the water demands of its growing population, even without climate change. Thus, increases in temperature, accompanied by reductions in precipitation, will pose a considerable challenge. The severe drought of the 1950's resulted in a reduction in stream flow to approximately half of average levels. A repeat of these con-

POLICY OPTIONS
FOR ADDRESSING
THE IMPACTS OF
GLOBAL WARMING
ON TEXAS

213

ditions would require considerably more sophisticated management techniques than those currently in place, given the population growth that has occurred since that time.

Our study of water supply and demand under drought of record conditions shows shortages in all of the river basins examined—Trinity, Colorado, and Rio Grande, as well as the Edwards aquifer. Shortages would be more severe if drought conditions were combined with an increase in temperature of 2°C and a 5 percent decrease in precipitation (Schmandt and Ward 1991). In either case, greater controls would have to be imposed on municipal users, and agricultural users would have to be severely curtailed. This could result in permanent changes in cropping practices, particularly if hotter conditions increase the water requirements of existing crops.

The management of water resources in Texas currently stresses a largely local or regional approach. This is due, in part, to the widely different climatic and hydrologic conditions across the state. As water becomes more scarce, however, there is a growing recognition that regional management may be insufficient to handle all of the state's water management needs. Moreover, there is a growing realization that regional responses directly affect the state as a whole. For instance, recent efforts have highlighted the need to ensure minimum flows of fresh water to bays and estuaries. If, as predicted in Chapter 4, stream-flows into the Gulf of Mexico are reduced by 35 percent as a result of global warming, this objective will be harder to meet. In addition, as coastal areas attempt to combat subsidence through the restriction of groundwater withdrawal, new sources of surface water will be needed to meet coastal water needs.

Projected Demand

The dependable firm surface water supply is the uniform yield that can be withdrawn annually from total storage through long drought periods, dependable run-of-the-river supplies, and dependable supplies from those reservoirs that are not run in a firm yield mode. In total, this amounts to about 11.4 million acre-feet (maf). Current demand amounts to approximately 14.8 maf, of which 6.7 are supplied from groundwater. With statewide demand projected to increase to 19 maf by 2040, and a small decline in groundwater use, an additional 2 maf of supply will be needed. The Texas Water Development Board (TWDB) estimates that by the year 2040 new surface water reservoirs could account for 1.4 maf,

JUDITH CLARKSON
AND
JURGEN SCHMANDT

while use of return flows and expanded water reuse could provide an additional 0.63 maf of total supplies (TWDB 1990, p. 3-2).

Although total water use requirements in Texas are expected to increase over a 50-year planning horizon from 1990 to 2040, this rate is slower than that previously predicted by the TWDB in their 1984 water plan. The December 1990 TWDB Water Plan cites the changing demographic and economic trends of the 1980's as the reason for this change, which in the case of the agricultural sector represents a decline in total water use. The primary factors underlying this trend include (1) a reduction in irrigated acreage and increased water use efficiency; (2) a lower base population and inferior economic conditions; and (3) lower than expected population and economic growth rates in the 1980's.

Historically, water used for irrigation has accounted for the largest portion of Texas' water use. However, irrigation water use peaked in 1979 when it reached 13 maf. Projected declines in the irrigation portion of the statewide water budget are reflective of the substantial reduction in water requirements resulting from water conservation and increased use efficiencies, projected to total 1.6 maf in savings annually by 2020. According to the high-case forecast, total demand for irrigation water is expected to decrease from 8.5 maf per year estimated for 1990 to 6.6 maf annually by 2040. This constitutes a decrease of about 22 percent over current levels of use (Ibid., p. 3-2).

Thus, water use practices can and do change over a relatively short time interval. Not surprisingly, this decline in agricultural water use is driven by economic factors, including increases in the cost of water, opportunities in the Lower Rio Grande Valley to sell water rights to municipalities, and economic incentives to reduce irrigated acreage under the Department of Agriculture's Land Bank Program. As a result, opportunities do exist to encourage more efficient use of existing supplies and provide economic incentives to ensure that water is put to its highest-value use.

Policy Options

Two general approaches may be taken to respond to the problem of decreased water availability in the state: resource expansion and resource management. Resource expansion is accomplished through structural solutions that involve either the construction of additional reservoirs to capture more water or interbasin transfers of existing supplies. These options face serious financial and environmental obstacles. An alternative approach is to better manage existing supplies through conservation, water pricing, and enforcing the existing structure for allocation of supplies. Each of these options could be utilized to improve upon the present management system and may enable the state to better cope with the widely varying regional effects of global warming. Although we have analyzed each of these alternatives as separate policy options, it is important to note that they are not mutually exclusive. Indeed, conservation efforts and marginal pricing could enhance the current system of water allocation.

Structural Solutions

The Texas Water Development Board reports that 14 major new reservoirs are proposed to meet future demand over the next 50 years. Additionally, the TWDB estimates that 29 water conveyance projects will be required to carry water from new and existing reservoirs to areas of greatest demand (Ibid., p. 1). These estimates assume water savings of 20 percent through conservation efforts and do not take the effects of climate change into account. The magnitude and number of these projected structures raise serious concerns about the feasibility of this approach.

The construction of additional reservoirs faces four major obstacles: (1) the most favorable sites for reservoir construction in the state have already been developed; (2) reservoir construction often entails a 30-year lead time; (3) projects of this magnitude raise serious environmental concerns; and (4) federal funding for such projects has decreased dramatically in recent years. Similar problems face projects for interbasin transfers of water. Not the least of these is the huge costs associated with the construction of a large number of reservoirs and conveyance projects, which would severely strain the financial resources of the state. The TWDB estimates these costs to be approximately $4.81 billion, with the requisite water and wastewater treatment plants estimated to cost $32.19 billion over the next 50 years (Ibid., p. 2). With an average decline in state revenues of 4.8 percent per year (adjusted for consumer price increases and population growth) over the past 9 years, questions concerning funding for these projects will certainly arise (Texas Legislative Budget Office, 1991, p. 15).

A legal restriction on interbasin transfers represents another obstacle to such a response. The Texas Water Code mandates that interbasin transfers of surface water may only be considered for water that exceeds the 50-year water requirements of the originating basin. This restriction minimizes flexible water planning and represents a failure to recognize the disparate availability of water throughout the state. Among the TWDB's "priority policy recommendations" is the removal of this restriction (TWDB 1990, pp. 4-7-4-8).

Given the huge costs associated with resource expansion, the legal constraints concerning water transfers, and the real decline in state revenue, the feasibility of policies that depend upon structural solutions to increase water supplies is questionable. Nevertheless, the possibility of supplying water from east Texas to meet the needs of Houston is being seriously considered as an alternative to the construction of the controversial Wallisville Reservoir.

Better Management of Existing Supplies

The fragmented approach to water management in Texas means that existing supplies are not always allocated in such a way as to ensure the greatest possible yield during times of shortage. For instance, more than one authority may be responsible for the reservoirs on a single river, and this may limit the opportunities for coordinated releases. It has been shown that for the San Jacinto River, which supplies most of Houston's water, joint management of the three reservoirs, Houston, Conroe, and Livingston, would increase the firm annual yield by 8.3 percent. If groundwater supplies are also included in the management scheme, the amount of available water increases by 18.7 percent. Under this scenario, groundwater is only pumped when lake levels fall below a threshold value, thereby reducing the possibility of further subsidence in the area (Sheer 1985).

In Texas opportunities for better management of groundwater are even more elusive. Groundwater law is based on the "absolute ownership rule" and allows landowners to pump as much water as they wish as long as the water is not wasted. Attempts to regulate groundwater through local management districts have met with mixed success. In some cases the districts do little to regulate pumping and appear to have been created by voters in the local area in order to keep the Texas legislature from passing stronger legislation

POLICY OPTIONS
FOR ADDRESSING
THE IMPACTS OF
GLOBAL WARMING
ON TEXAS

217

that could mean direct state control. On the other hand, the Harris-Galveston Coastal Subsidence District has succeeded in controlling the withdrawal of groundwater in order to reduce the rate of subsidence.

Even though underground streams or aquifers are legally state property, just like surface streams and rivers, Texas courts have held that the question of a defined underground stream must be conclusively proved (Kaiser 1986, p. 32). This has become a particularly contentious issue in the case of the Edwards aquifer, the only source of water for the city of San Antonio, which has to compete with local irrigators for limited supplies. In April 1992, the Texas Water Commission (TWC) attempted to classify the Edwards aquifer as an underground stream so that it could regulate withdrawals. The aquifer has direct hydrological links with the San Antonio and Nueces rivers, which provide more than half of the recharge waters, and the Guadalupe River, which receives approximately 25 percent of its baseflow (more in dry years) from the aquifer at Comal and San Marcos springs. If the issue is not resolved locally, regulation of withdrawals may be mandated by the federal courts as a result of a lawsuit filed to protect endangered species dependent on flows at Comal and San Marcos springs.

Water Conservation

Water conservation will constitute a valuable first response mechanism for reducing future demand for water supplies. Although conservation is an important front-line policy for water shortages, such efforts will be insufficient in themselves to meet future water demands in the state. Expected savings through conservation are in the range of 20 percent and will, at best, slow the rate of increase in demand. Although the largest potential savings can be made in the agricultural sector, there is considerable pressure on municipalities to implement water conservation plans, particularly in areas that are using all of their existing supplies.

A number of improvements in the distribution and application of water to crops have been implemented, and an expansion of this effort could realize substantial savings. Many of the technological improvements available for delivering water to crops can save 20–30 percent of the water currently applied. They include low energy precision application sprinklers (LEPAS), surge flow irrigation systems, and

JUDITH CLARKSON
AND
JURGEN SCHMANDT

drip irrigation. Additional savings could be realized by better maintenance of water transmission systems, including lining canals to reduce seepage and limiting evaporation.

The TWDB predicts declining water use for irrigation in the next 50 years, based on the assumption that the amount of irrigated acreage will decrease. Over the last 10 years, this trend has already become apparent, particularly in the Lower Rio Grande Valley, where financial incentives have been used to encourage farmers to convert their agricultural water rights to municipal use. However, global warming predictions indicate that, in order to grow the same crops, increased irrigation will be required due to decreased soil moisture and increased evapotranspiration rates. Where water supplies are limited, farming practices will have to change.

Municipal users, including residential, commercial, and institutional customers, make up the fastest growing use sector in Texas and have significant potential for conserving water. Water utilities in Texas currently cannot account for 15–20 percent of the water they treat and distribute. Of this amount, half is lost through leaks in distribution systems. Proper auditing techniques and modern, electrical leak detection equipment could be used to reduce transmission and distribution losses.

While many industrial users have improved water use efficiency to keep costs down, additional conservation possibilities exist. Many techniques common to municipal and commercial users are applicable to industry, as well as specific process modifications. One area with a lot of potential for water conservation is the use of water for cooling. Alternatives include the use of air, saline water, or treated effluent. Conservation of steam and hot water would have the added benefit of saving energy. Statewide water savings in the industrial sector could be as high as 5.4 percent over the next 30 years.

Treated effluent discharges are predicted to be 3.8 maf by 2040. Current discharges are 2.5 maf per year, of which only about 175,000 acre-feet are reused for such purposes as industrial water supply, landscape and agricultural irrigation, direct recharge of aquifers, and aesthetic and environmental uses. The Texas Water Development Board's plans for future urban water supplies depend on reuse of approximately 560,000 acre-feet per year by 2040. Care must be taken that extensive reuse and consumption not adversely affect return flows to streams, bays, and estuaries. However, reuse could benefit downstream environments by reducing withdrawals of higher quality water from the streambed (TWDB 1990, p. 2-13).

Drought Management

In addition to planning for increases in water demand at a time when supplies may be limited, planning for years of less than average precipitation is an important component of water resource management in arid western states. The majority of western states have adopted drought management plans that are coordinated by the state in response to specific trigger conditions. Often the Palmer Drought Severity Index, which rates drought conditions on a severity rating of 1 to 5, is used. Once the index falls below 2, certain measures, often voluntary, are instituted. At this stage the main goal is to educate the public of the potential for water shortages. As drought conditions become more severe, interagency task forces are activated and specific programs implemented. As necessary, the governor will typically work with these task forces to solicit additional legislative authority and to secure financial assistance from the federal government.

Texas does not have a coordinated, statewide program to address drought conditions. Various local programs do exist, and state funds made available in 1985 for water development and planning are contingent upon the adoption of a water conservation plan, which often includes a drought contingency plan. The governor has certain powers under the Texas Disaster Act of 1975 to commandeer or utilize private property during an emergency, but the power of the governor to reallocate water during a drought has never been tested.

Other specific provisions allow the Texas Water Commission to modify permits for the temporary transfer of water to another use, provided that this change does not impair existing water rights. The TWC also has the authority to direct junior water right holders to cease diversions of water. Another statutory provision, unique to Texas and as yet untested, is the Wagstaff Act of 1931 (Texas Water Code Section 11.028). This act gives cities the right to preempt other, non-municipal water uses without canceling, taking, or paying for those water rights. Because water distribution in the Rio Grande is subject to international treaties, the Wagstaff Act does not apply to this river. If the act were invoked in other river basins, the TWC or the courts would have to intervene to apportion the water, and it is unclear how effective or fea-

JUDITH CLARKSON
AND
JURGEN SCHMANDT

sible this provision would be (Western States Water Council 1986).

If Texas had to face a drought as severe as that in the 1950's, it would not be in a position to implement a coordinated response. Responding to crises once the situation has deteriorated is never as effective as taking preventative actions. Already there have been isolated instances of conflict between water users during times of shortage, and a significant, large-scale drought would exacerbate these situations. The first step is to develop an adequate data-collecting network that could alert farmers to the possibility of water shortages before the growing season begins. If reallocation of water to municipalities became a necessity, such a program could reduce some of the potential losses to the agricultural sector. Municipal and industrial users should also be required to reduce their consumption as the situation becomes threatening, so that the burden is more equitably distributed between different sectors of society.

Market-Based Pricing of Water

Water is typically priced at a rate that reflects the cost of operating the collection and purification systems and the distribution network. It does not include all of the costs, such as capital expenditures associated with constructing reservoirs and conveyance infrastructure. This is largely because much of this expense has been subsidized by the federal government. State and local contributions to these costs are generally in the range of 5 percent.

Another method of pricing water would be to use the marginal cost. This would allow water to be priced at its replacement cost and would more closely approximate its market value. Taking into account the geographic region of the state, type of water use, and capital costs, an economic pricing system for water could be constructed. Under this system, market forces would help to distribute the resource to those who most desire it, as indicated through their willingness to pay. The marketplace pricing of water would require a fundamental cultural change and would raise controversial political questions, including the ability of poorer citizens to pay. Unfortunately, the data base required for an analysis of this topic is beyond the scope of this chapter. Needless to say, the implementation of such a system would not be easy, with user groups vigorously challenging such price hikes. Agricultural users, in particular, would be hard hit, and many crops could not be grown profitably without subsidized water supplies. The economic foundation of many rural communities could be severely undermined.

The use of economic factors as a means of redistributing current supplies is being used in the Lower Rio Grande Valley, where a market has developed for water rights. In 1991, active water rights for irrigation alone in the LRGV exceeded 1.7 maf, well above the firm yield of the system. It is only in years of above-average precipitation that farmers are able to exercise options to the full extent of their water rights. With population growth, there has been a shift from agricultural to municipal water use, and irrigators have been able to sell or lease their rights to growing municipalities. However, when water rights are converted from agricultural to municipal use, the priority of the right changes. Because of this, an adjustment in the amount of water transferred is necessary. Presently, a municipality receives a dependable 40–50 percent of water rights purchased from the irrigation districts. This conversion formula is based upon the firm annual yield of the system, so that if all the water were converted to municipal use, it would not exceed the amount of water available from the system under drought conditions (Boyd and Chitwood 1992).

The Watermaster Program

The proliferation of special and general law districts, including 14 river authorities, has lead to an uncoordinated approach to the management of water in Texas, in which overlapping jurisdictions are the norm. In contrast, the administration of water rights is highly centralized. With few exceptions, water rights disputes are handled through the central Texas Water Commission office in Austin, and this has proved to be inadequate in the past. In 1984, Texas was struck with severe drought. As river levels declined, disputes over who had rights to limited water supplies increased, and water users filed for clarification of their rights with the TWC. With limited staff resources, the TWC's central office was ill equipped to handle the flood of disputes (TWC 1990). Although these conflicts were eventually settled, the 1984 drought illustrated that any highly centralized administrative system may function as an inefficient bureaucracy. With increasing pressure on existing supplies, the frequency and severity of disputes is likely to increase in the future and a

JUDITH CLARKSON
AND
JURGEN SCHMANDT

222

repeat of the 1984 drought experience is likely, unless modifications are made to the current management structure.

With water supplies in many river basins fully appropriated, it will be important to monitor withdrawals and enforce the existing system for allocating water between users during times of shortage. The watermaster program provides for an individual with specialized knowledge of hydrology, together with an understanding of local concerns, to resolve disputes between user groups at the regional level, before they reach TWC's central office. Unlike other entities set up for regional coordination, such as river authorities, the watermaster has legal jurisdiction over all water rights holders in the division.

Currently, two divisions are administered by watermasters appointed by the TWC. The first is the Rio Grande Water Division, created in 1971 as a result of a landmark court case, in which severe water rights disputes were resolved through a court appointed watermaster. Though there was initial apprehension among water users in the Lower Rio Grande Valley, the program has worked well. With a small staff and low administrative costs, a fair and equitable management system has emerged. While water curtailments were imminent during a drought period, these were never implemented, as last-minute rainfalls alleviated the shortages. Therefore, the program has not yet met the test of administering curtailments. The South Texas Water Division, which includes the Guadalupe, Nueces, and San Antonio rivers, plus some coastal areas, was created in August 1989 under the statutory authority of the 1967 Water Rights Adjudication Act. Each division contains approximately 1,500 adjudicated water rights.

The expansion of this program statewide, together with a statewide coordinator, has been put on hold for an indefinite period, in response to opposition from regional water authorities. Over time, such a program will be needed. It would provide the framework for developing statewide water management policies with input from each of the regions. The watermaster program would also create an institutional mechanism for the development of a statewide drought management plan, and the possibility of developing policies for interbasin transfers of water. Attention could also be given to water quality issues and the effects of upstream diversions on natural users such as bays and estuaries. Ultimately, a modified version of the watermaster program may enable

POLICY OPTIONS
FOR ADDRESSING
THE IMPACTS OF
GLOBAL WARMING
ON TEXAS

223

the state to cope with increased demand and the effects of climate change. Such a program would improve upon the present fragmented management structure, by providing a regionally sensitive framework that could be centrally coordinated at the state level.

Potential Effects of Sea-Level Rise

Significant portions of the Texas Gulf Coast currently suffer from land subsidence and coastal erosion. Both subsidence and erosion subject Texas coastal land to regular flooding. The Texas coast, therefore, is a particularly useful model for studying the potential effects of global warming–induced sea-level rise. The impacts are potentially devastating for urban areas, as described in Chapter 8, and coastal ecosystems. As described in Chapter 5, increasing demand for fresh water inland and the possibility of reductions in supplies under a global warming scenario will place additional strains on the coastal environment.

A number of agencies, with overlapping and sometimes conflicting authority, share responsibility for the coastal zone. The Texas Water Commission, for example, controls waste discharges into the Gulf, while the Texas Water Development Board conducts studies on the freshwater inflow needs of the estuaries. The state owns the coastline below the high water mark and attempts to clean beaches and remove squatters through the Texas General Land Office. The Texas Parks and Wildlife Department is responsible for the management of biological resources along the coast; the Texas Railroad Commission has exclusive authority over oil and gas wells; and the Texas Health Department is responsible for certifying shellfish for human consumption. Thus, it is not surprising that an integrated approach to management of the coast has been difficult to develop.

Policy Options

Currently Texas has no comprehensive policies for the management of its coastline. There have been local efforts to mitigate some of the most dramatic impacts of shoreline erosion and storm damage, most notably the construction of a seawall on Galveston Island and the introduction of improved management practices by the Houston-Galveston

JUDITH CLARKSON
AND
JURGEN SCHMANDT

Coastal Subsidence District. In general, policies that address these problems fall into two categories. The first, shoreline engineering, consists of physical modifications to the coast to hold it in its present position. The second is adaptation. Recognizing that the coast will change, the goal is to minimize damage from sea-level rise by, for instance, limiting development in sensitive areas. Here we examine some of the structural and institutional approaches that have been implemented and review the attempts to develop a coastal zone management plan for Texas (see Schmandt et al. 1992).

Structural Responses

Of the possible approaches to shoreline engineering, beach replenishment is the most environmentally sound. This procedure consists of pumping sand, usually dredged from off shore, onto or near the beach. However, there are a number of problems with this approach, not the least of which is cost. In addition, after replenishment the beach is steeper, causing waves to strike with greater force than before and accelerating the rate of erosion. Other potential problems arise from the facts that the sand used for replenishment differs from the original beach sand, and that offshore dredge pits, which alter wave action, can have potentially negative effects.

Another method to deal specifically with erosion is to construct groins. Groins are walls built perpendicular to the coast intended to capture sand carried in longshore currents. Typically, groins have worked well and sped accretion to local areas. Unfortunately, by capturing more sand locally, they speed erosion farther along the coast. Jetties also function in the same way. Like groins, jetties are constructed perpendicular to the coast, but are several times longer. The primary purpose of jetties is to protect ship channels from silting. While very successful in ensuring safe entry and exit from harbors, they also capture as much as 50 percent of the sand supply that would otherwise go to Texas beaches.

The most dramatic example of shoreline engineering is the construction of seawalls. Constructed back from the shoreline, seawalls are intended primarily to protect inland property from storm damage. The obvious example is the Galveston seawall, constructed to prevent a repeat of the devastation caused by the 1900 hurricane. However, the cost of construction is tremendous, roughly $7 million per mile, and outside of the most developed locales, like the city of

Galveston, the cost of a seawall is greater than the value of the property it protects.

Typically, a massive seawall like that at Galveston is part of an ongoing process that began with small bulkheads intended to mitigate the effects of occasional wave impacts. Even a small bulkhead will disrupt the beach environment in several ways by (1) reflecting wave energy, causing a steeper beach slope and faster erosion; (2) increasing intensity of longshore currents, hastening removal of sand; (3) preventing the exchange of sand between dunes and the beach; (4) keeping the beach from responding naturally to storms; and (5) concentrating wave and current energy at the ends of the wall, accelerating erosion at these points. Because of these factors, increasingly massive structures become necessary as more and more pressure comes to bear. In the end, there will be no beach left, just a huge wall overlooking the wreckage of its predecessors.

Institutional Responses

There has already been some success with new types of institutional responses to coastal problems. The Harris-Galveston Coastal Subsidence District, for example, has been successful in reducing land subsidence by restricting groundwater withdrawal. Most of the areas have effectively decreased the amount of groundwater used to 10 percent of the total water demand through conversion to surface water and water conservation (Houston-Galveston Coastal Subsidence District 1990, p. 3). However, reliance on surface water for public supplies will create additional problems, if the availability of surface water decreases under global warming.

In addition to legislative requirements, there have been court decisions aimed at limiting fluid withdrawals. Historically, Texas has allowed unlimited groundwater withdrawal under the conditions of absolute ownership of the overlying land, with no liability for damage incurred by other property. The current trend is to hold pumpers responsible for any subsidence that occurs as a result of their actions. In *Coastal Industries Water Authority v. W. B. York*, the court decided that York did not lose title to his property due to inundation resulting from subsidence. In a Texas Supreme Court case in 1978, the court limited the common-law rule of absolute ownership of groundwater, by making the landowner liable if the manner of pumping is negligent or malicious (Poland 1984, p. 125).

JUDITH CLARKSON
AND
JURGEN SCHMANDT

226

National policies also affect coastal development. The National Flood Insurance Act of 1968 created the National Flood Insurance Program to provide low-cost flood insurance on the condition that the community direct new development out of the hazardous area, a condition that was not effectively enforced. The Flood Disaster Protection Act of 1973 required flood insurance with any type of financial loan that was federally insured for any property in a hazardous area prone to flooding and flood related erosion. This act also directed the Federal Emergency Management Agency to identify flood related erosion zones. The Upton-Jones Amendment encourages the demolition or relocation of structures in the hazardous areas by advancing payment. And the Coastal Barriers Resource Act limits federal investment on undeveloped coastal barriers.

Another option is to have a laissez-faire coastal policy. This would entail no actual regulation of the coast, but also no government action that might encourage development, such as government loans for construction, federal flood or disaster insurance, or publicly funded shoreline engineering. In the absence of regulation, the chief government function with regards to the coast would be to educate people about the hazards involved in coastal development. This approach could be augmented by the public acquisition of land that would allow coastal beach and wetland environments to migrate. Clearly, this approach is not suited to heavily developed areas, like Galveston and South Padre Island, but would be much more cost-effective in less developed areas.

Coastal Zone Management in Texas

The history of the coastal management in Texas has been checkered. Texas remains one of only two coastal states (the other is Georgia) with no federally approved and funded plan to manage the coastal zone. Responding to federal financial incentives through the Coastal Management Act of 1972 (amended in 1974 and 1976), attempts have been made in the past to formulate comprehensive management policies toward the coastal zone. These attempts—the Texas Coastal Management Program of 1976 and the Texas Coastal Plan of 1979—failed for a myriad of reasons: the disinterest of the state executive; the multitude of competing interests along the coast (particularly between developers and environmentalists); lack of grassroots support; the desire, prevalent in

POLICY OPTIONS
FOR ADDRESSING
THE IMPACTS OF
GLOBAL WARMING
ON TEXAS

227

Texas, for as little governmental interference as possible; the resistance to a lead "superagency"; and, as mundane as it may seem, resistance to labels such as *zone* and *management* that imply a burgeoning bureaucracy and mountains of red tape (Curley 1990). Both the General Land Office and Curley suggest that the federal economic incentives simply did not outweigh the inability of coastal concerns to identify shared goals.

Despite past failures, in 1989 the 72d Texas Legislature enacted SB 1571, which was signed into law by Governor Bill Clements on June 16, 1989. It designated the General Land Office

> as the lead agency to develop a long-term plan for the management of Texas coastal public land, in cooperation with other state agencies that have duties relating to coastal matters including the Parks and Wildlife Department, the Attorney General's Office, the Texas Water Commission, the Texas Water Development Board, the State Department of Highways and Public Transportation and the Railroad Commission of Texas.

The current efforts of the General Land Office to put together a comprehensive coastal management plan provide an opportunity to include some consideration of the likely impacts of global warming–induced sea-level rise. However, although public participants in the process identified coastal erosion and wetlands loss as areas of major concern, and these problems will be exacerbated by global warming, there have been no explicit references to global warming in any statewide coastal management policy.

It should not be construed, however, that the only possible policy responses to sea-level rise rest with the implementation of a statewide coastal management plan. A Texas coastal management plan offers a simplification of the process, including economic advantages of scale, but many responses are already possible. Indeed, given the potential threat to life, livelihood, and property, these responses should be implemented as quickly as possible. Whether future flooding and increased wave action are caused by global warming or land subsidence is immaterial. The resulting economic and social losses are the same. There must now be a concerted effort to manage, in a comprehensive fashion, the valuable resources of the coast.

JUDITH CLARKSON
AND
JURGEN SCHMANDT

228

The Potential for a Statewide Response

Texas is not a stranger to hard times and has dealt with problems similar to those associated with anticipated greenhouse effects. Cataclysmic floods and droughts between 1913 and 1915 prompted the legislature to give regional entities the authority they needed to raise funds for water development projects. The very severe drought of the 1950's elicited a more active role for the state in water planning. Today the TWDB is responsible for developing a state water plan and administering funds for regional water planning.

These problems are similar to many of the commonly anticipated consequences of global warming, as enumerated in prior chapters. It is evident that these same agencies provide a regulatory framework that could begin to deal with the additional problems of global warming. However, at present, climate change is viewed by state regulatory and planning agencies as controversial, largely as the result of widely varying estimates of sea level, temperature, and precipitation change from various researchers and scientific panels. In addition, the opinions of a number of credible skeptics do not instill confidence that climate change is a real problem. Until independent estimates of the effects of climate change begin to converge and critics modify their outlook, most state agency officials and legislators will probably ignore climate change as an issue. Direction from the executive branch or an unusual period of heat or drought could change that viewpoint.

Currently, the Texas Air Control Board has in place an extensive system for permitting and monitoring a broad range of gases emitted into the atmosphere by industry. Depending on how one chooses to interpret the definitions of *air contaminants* and *air pollution,* one could argue that the Texas Clean Air Act already provides the board with the power it needs to address the issue of greenhouse gas emissions and their relationship to global warming. The act defines air contaminants in generic terms and allows the Texas Air Control Board to specify those contaminants it will monitor and control. The act's inclusion of *gas* in its definition of air contaminants could be interpreted to include greenhouse gases, such as carbon dioxide and methane.

The Public Utility Commission has a mandate to consider conservation in its determination of rates and for authorization to construct new plants. By allowing utilities to profit from acquiring more energy efficient equipment and promot-

POLICY OPTIONS
FOR ADDRESSING
THE IMPACTS OF
GLOBAL WARMING
ON TEXAS

229

ing end-use efficiency, significant reductions in the rate of increase in electricity demand could be realized. This would have a direct impact on the production of greenhouse gases. Such an approach would be a significant step toward expanding least-cost planning methodologies that include all environmental externalities.

In 1984 the Texas Department of Water Resources was divided into two state agencies. While the TWDB was given the responsibility for state water planning, the Texas Water Commission was given primary responsibility for implementing state water law, including regulation and enforcement. The TWC has an existing watermaster program in place to deal with problems of water allocation at the regional level. If this program were expanded statewide, it would provide the framework for dealing with problems of water allocation under conditions of reduced supply. By providing the forum for resolving disputes before a critical situation arises, the potential for conflict and litigation would be reduced.

In summary, many of the essential elements of a structure to begin a serious, state-initiated program of greenhouse gas reductions are already in place. Making significant progress will require policymakers and regulators to consider the potential impacts of global warming in their current work. As we have stressed several times, the most effective approaches will have immediate, short-term benefits, such as lower electric bills and cleaner air. In the case of global warming, therefore, immediate action is possible without new legislation and massive appropriations.

However, it is important that the problem not be understated. This will not be a simple issue for regulatory agencies to add to their agenda, because greenhouse gases are more complex and not as fully understood as conventional pollutants. Nor can it be said that all the elements currently exist. Emission reductions will not be implemented without a greater recognition of the large amounts of greenhouse gases emitted in Texas and the vulnerability this creates for the state's economy, should federal regulation be mandated. In the case of coastal problems, the responsibility for their solution is widely spread among various agencies. On the other hand, the 1993 consolidation of the Texas Water Commission and the Texas Air Control Board into a single state agency provides an opportunity for a more coordinated approach to environmental protection and resource management.

JUDITH CLARKSON
AND
JURGEN SCHMANDT

References

Boyd, J., and J. Chitwood, 1992. Water Rights and Uses. Texas Water Commission, Interview by Joy Sisolak, March.

Curley, S., 1990. Texas Coastal Plan: Analysis of a Failure. *Coastal Management* 18:1–14.

Houston-Galveston Coastal Subsidence District, 1990. *Subsidence 1990.* Houston.

IPCC, 1990. *Climate Change: The IPCC Scientific Assessment.* Cambridge University Press, New York.

Kaiser, R. A., 1986. *Handbook of Texas Water Law: Problems and Needs,* Texas Water Resources Institute, College Station.

Kellogg, W., and R. Schware, 1981. *Climate Change and Society.* Westview Press, Boulder, Colo.

Poland, J. F. (ed.), 1984. *Guidebook to the Studies of Land Subsidence Due to Groundwater Withdrawal.* UNESCO Studies and Reports in Hydrology 40.

Schmandt, J., S. Hadden, and G. Ward, 1992. *Texas and Global Warming: Emissions, Surface Water Supplies and Sea Level Rise.* University of Texas at Austin.

Schmandt, J., and X. Mu, 1992. *Water and Development in the Lower Rio Grande Valley.* University of Texas at Austin.

Schmandt, J., and G. Ward, 1991. *Texas and Global Warming: Water Supply and Demand in Four Hydrological Regions.* University of Texas at Austin.

Sheer, D. P., 1985. The Importance of Operating Procedures in Determining the Yield of Water Resources Available to the San Jacinto Basin, Texas. Study for the Bureau of Reclamation, Washington, D.C.

Texas A&M University, 1988. *Executive Briefing: Sustainable Agriculture.* Texas Agricultural Experiment Station, College Station.

Texas Legislative Budget Office, 1991. Financing Government Services in Texas: The Tradeoffs, the Troubles. Austin.

Texas Water Commission (TWC), 1990. Watermaster. Austin.

Texas Water Development Board (TWDB), 1990. *Water for Texas Today and Tomorrow.* TWDB, Document No. GP-5-1, Austin.

Western States Water Council, 1986. *Western State Drought Management.* Salt Lake City.

World Commission on Environment and Development, 1987. *Our Common Future.* Oxford University Press, Oxford and New York.

Conclusions

In the preceding chapters, we have discussed possible impacts of climate change in Texas and policy responses that may be considered. In some areas—water supply and demand and agricultural production—we have made projections using specific assumptions about the future climate in Texas. In other areas we have been forced to argue intuitively, using analogy and relying on results from studies in other regions of the country and world. Admittedly, the emerging picture is incomplete, but it represents a combination of the best possible overview at the current state of the art and informed scientific judgment.

Yet, the presence of uncertainty need not immobilize us. There is enough information to craft a sound program for a rational response to climate change in Texas. Without being unnecessarily alarmist, prudent steps can be taken to reduce the risk of climate change and mitigate the potential impacts.

Texas is a large state and has a reputation for meeting challenges head-on. Sometime fairly soon, this approach will be needed to cope with emissions of greenhouse gases. As pointed out in Chapter 3, Texas produces nearly twice as much CO_2 as any other state and more than 10 percent of the U.S. total. On an international basis, Texas would rank seventh in the world in total CO_2 production, and second in the world in per capita emissions. If international or national action is taken to address the concerns of global warming, Texas will be one of the places that is most affected.

Yet is climate change a real risk? And if it is, must action be initiated now? In Chapter 1 an assessment of our understanding of the potential impacts of a steady increase in the concentration of greenhouse gases is presented. Greenhouse gases, by definition, trap heat and tend to increase the Earth's temperature. The evidence is conclusive that greenhouse gases have been increasing over the last 200 years due to human activities, so far primarily in developed countries. However, it is not easy to translate this realization into a simulation of future global climate.

Existing models of the behavior of the Earth's atmosphere show that today's climate is the result of a large natural greenhouse effect, which makes the planet 40°C (72°F) warmer than it would be otherwise. Without this effect the planet would, like Mars, be uninhabitable. A doubling of the atmospheric CO_2 concentration could increase greenhouse warming to 43°C (77.4°F). This is a small increment compared to the natural greenhouse effect. At the same time, it is at least as large as the change that has been experienced on Earth over the last 10,000 years, and more important, it is occurring at a much faster rate. The doubling of CO_2 could happen in the next 50 years, depending on energy use and population growth worldwide and how certain geophysical processes react to this anticipated increase in concentration.

Although there are some concerns about the reliability and availability of climate data, a measured record of the Earth's temperature over the last 150 years shows a worldwide increase of about 0.5°C. Climate model simulations do not match this increase exactly, but the record is well within the margin of error for these models. As the expected rate of warming increases in the next few decades, we will have a final indication of the reliability of these models. Yet this information likely will not become available until after the year 2000 (if the models are correct) and perhaps as late as 2020 (if the models overestimate the rate of greenhouse warming). By that time, it may be too late to attempt to stabilize greenhouse gas concentrations and avoid very serious changes to the Earth's climate and ecosystems.

Finally, the recent eruption of Mount Pinatubo has given us an opportunity to test some of our theories about global warming. A leading climate modeling group has made predictions about the amount of cooling that should be expected from Mount Pinatubo. Early evidence suggests that their predictions are on track, and by the time this book is published we may have a strong authentication of the power of today's climate models.

What about Texas? Can the climate of Texas really change? The Texas climate, as pointed out in Chapter 2, has wide regional and interannual variation. It is also characterized by extreme events—blizzards in north Texas, hurricanes along the coast, and droughts and floods in all regions. Texas has some of the driest as well as wettest places in the country, with mean annual precipitation varying from 8 inches in the far west to 56 inches in the east. Some of the worst droughts have been broken by heavy rains accompanied by severe flooding, the worst effects of which have been mitigated in recent years through construction of flood control structures. Rather frequent, devastating droughts have struck Texas in the past, most notably in the 1950's, and will almost certainly do so again in the future. Historically, at least three major droughts occur in a century, with a really severe drought occurring approximately every 90 years. Counting on "climate as usual," based on recent experience (typically 30 years), is not realistic, even if there is little or no global warming.

In Chapters 4 through 9, we have outlined some expected impacts of climate change in Texas. These six chapters cover a broad range of impacts and present several new or counter-intuitive findings.

In Chapter 4, a persuasive case is made that the water supplies in Texas are under serious strain. Modest changes in temperature and precipitation may lead to a reduction of 25 percent in runoff and 35 percent in flows to the coast. Freshwater supplies for coastal estuaries are *already* a concern, and competition between agricultural and municipal uses is increasing. These findings suggest that the problem will get worse—potentially much worse.

Impacts of reduced freshwater flows to coastal estuaries are examined in Chapter 5. Using several scenarios, the report finds that, in general, with higher salinity regimes resulting from reduced freshwater inflows and higher sea levels, coastal wetlands will decrease in area, while seagrass beds and wind-tidal flats will increase in area. Coastal wetlands (especially marshlands) are crucial to the Texas fishing industry and to large populations of migratory waterfowl. The Gulf Coast is a very important region for the state's economy, and the costs of adaptation to higher sea level are likely to be high. Actions taken today to mitigate some of these future costs could be a wise investment. Further analysis of the economic impacts of sea-level rise are addressed in Chapter 9.

Current concerns, as well as the potential for future sea-level rise, suggest that state policy should support and encourage coastal efforts to improve the sustainability of this ecologically and economically critical region. Coastal areas are a resource for all of Texas, and it will be necessary to provide assistance for coping with changes that are beyond the immediate control of coastal residents. Specifically, Texas could accept the philosophy of coastal zone management, which recognizes that many different, small steps are necessary to protect this region, and that these steps are best accomplished if the effort is coordinated rather than parceled out among various state and regional agencies.

Risks to terrestrial ecosystems are highlighted in Chapter 6. Although the risks to specific ecosystems cannot be predicted at this time, the uneven distribution of biotic preserves across the state places many ecosystems at real risk. Furthermore, the design of existing preserves assumes a stable climate—an assumption we no longer regard as valid. Thus, this analysis suggests that a reexamination of the system of biotic preserves in Texas is needed to identify additional needs, if Texas is to maintain its present diversity of ecosystems and habitats.

Model results presented in Chapter 7 on the agricultural impacts of climate change and CO_2 enrichment suggest that the consequences of global warming in Texas may not be very serious. Although agricultural production may go down somewhat statewide, significant declines are more likely in specific regions of the state. In general, increases in the price of agricultural products are likely to result in a marginal impact on agricultural producers, but could have an adverse impact on consumers. However, these model results do not take into account other changes that are likely to occur over the next 50 years, including increasing population pressure on land and water resources and further declines in groundwater tables. From a broader perspective, it is worth noting that significant technological advances may be necessary. With increasing competition for limited, and possibly reduced, water supplies, increased water use efficiency will assume greater importance. In addition, our dependence on a few genetically uniform varieties of food stocks will make us vulnerable to changes in climate and pests. The maintenance of genetically diverse seed stocks and the development of new, drought resistant varieties may be critical.

Urban areas, examined in Chapter 8, are not especially sensitive to climate change. Although climate change–induced water supply shortages, coastal impacts, and higher agricultural prices could influence the quality of life in urban areas, such urban areas are fairly well insulated from climatic effects. Impacts on public health, local air pollution, and urban ecosystems were also examined, but found to be fairly moderate. Thus, with the exception of coastal cities and areas with limited water supplies, climate change is unlikely to be a major concern for urban areas.

In addition to the economic impact of water shortages and agricultural price increases, climate change will affect the economy through increased energy demand and costs, particularly as a result of emission control measures. Chapter 9 examines the probable changes in the energy sector on the economy. Higher summer temperatures are likely to place significant demands on the electric utility sector, because generating capacity must be designed to meet peak demand. It is possible that generating capacity will have to be increased by 20–30 percent, while overall demand will increase by 10–15 percent. This will result in a significant rise in the unit cost of electricity.

Texas can address the impact of climate change on the energy sector unilaterally, and to a limited extent, it would seem wise to do so. Experience in California has shown that greater flexibility is available to a state that takes a leadership position in environmental protection than to states only following national directives. Because Texas is a major emitter of greenhouse gases, a national climate change policy is likely to have a major impact on the state—but that policy will be designed with the entire country in mind, not just Texas. A Texas-specific strategy, designed by Texans but meeting general national goals, would give Texas the flexibility to address this issue in its own way.

Encouraging energy efficiency, for instance, is a policy that has economic benefits, even without considering climate change. California realized substantial savings as more creative regulation encouraged utilities to find new ways to reduce energy use by demand management. The key to the success of such programs is to allow utilities to make a similar return on investment for conservation programs as for investments in new plants and equipment. Even though some of these provisions are available to Texas' utilities, they have not been aggressively pursued. Such measures would improve the economy of Texas and make it less sensitive to world energy price fluctuations.

Policies designed to reduce greenhouse gas emissions would assist efforts in Houston and El Paso to combat local air pollution, without placing these cities at a competitive disadvantage. While energy conservation, to the extent it is possible, would have the greatest benefits to the economy, another interim strategy would be increased use of natural gas, an abundant resource in Texas. For the long run, nuclear power may be an option, but significant technological advances will be necessary to overcome the current economic and waste disposal problems.

On the other hand, there are some commonly advocated steps that would not be appropriate state-level policy. Massive unilateral actions to reduce greenhouse gas emissions are not in the best interests of Texas and would not be sustainable. For instance, imposing a state-level carbon tax would place Texas at an economic disadvantage and would fail to provide sufficient global benefits—especially because large emissions sources could simply move to another state. Often suggested is an increase in motor fuel taxes that would help to reduce highway congestion and local air pollution, while also reducing greenhouse gas emissions. Although it requires a relatively large tax to have a significant impact on travel behavior, a moderate tax could provide funds for removing older gas guzzlers from the road, as well as provide an incentive for purchasing more efficient vehicles.

Chapter 10 describes some other policy options for Texas. The main focus is adaptive strategies, primarily related to management of the state's water resources. These policies will be particularly important if the predictions made in Chapter 4 become a reality. Chapter 10 describes ways in which Texas could develop water conservation and drought management programs, as well as address the problem of allocation and administration of water rights. As one specific measure, expansion of the successful watermaster program to cover all major Texas river basins would be a worthwhile step. Except in water-rich areas, some form of groundwater regulation will be needed eventually. Groundwater supplies statewide are under increasing pressure, and this seems certain to be exacerbated if climate change results in a reduction in surface water supplies. Our goal should be to manage all of our water supplies as a sustainable resource, in order to meet economic, recreational, flood prevention, and ecological needs.

This volume has covered a great many aspects of life in Texas that may be affected by global climate change. So far, there has not been a coordinated effort at either the state or the national level to address the potential magnitude and impacts of global warming. Within Texas there is almost no research directed at this problem, and no funding sources exist. In the short run, a piecemeal approach to the potential consequences of climate change may be the best we can hope for. But a more deliberate research and policy development effort must follow. We hope to lay the groundwork for this by focusing on those issues that appear to contribute to our vulnerability and describing policy options that will have immediate as well as long-term benefits, given what we know about the variability of climate in Texas and likely climatic changes in the future.

Index

Texas climate
  determining factors, 24–25, 32–33, 36–41
  growing season, 25–26, 45, 131, 153
  impacts of global warming, 33–34, 41–47
  interannual variability, 30–33, 47
  pan evaporation rates, 43–44
  Prairie Coastal, 28–30
  precipitation, 26–34, 47, 69–70
  seasonal cycles, 25–34, 44, 45, 128–129
  Southern Great Plains, 26–28
  South Texas, 32–34, 45–47
  temperature, 26–34, 39, 47
  tropical storms, 32, 35–36, 172, 183
  variability, 39–40, 70
  Western Plateau, 27–29
Texas Parks and Wildlife Department, 141, 211
Transportation, 58–61
  carbon dioxide production, 54, 59
  energy conservation, 59–60
  energy use, 59
Trinity River, 85–86, 175

Urban heat island bias, 19
Urbanization, 134

Volcanic eruptions, 20–21, 38

Water
  budgets, 73–83, 84–85
  conservation, 176, 215, 218–220
  cooling, 73
  demand, 2, 72–73, 76–77, 85–86, 151–152, 170, 175, 214–215, 219
  ground, 71, 75–78, 160, 171, 175, 176, 217–218
  intake facilities, 170–171
  interbasin transfers, 79, 176, 217
  management, 169–178, 213–224
  pricing, 221–222
  quality, 177, 182–183
  reuse, 176, 219–220
  rights, 86, 175, 222, 223
  stress, 151–152
  supply, 69–72, 152, 159, 175, 214–215, 233
  surface, 69, 77–78, 82, 160, 175
  vapor, 7, 11, 14
Watermaster, 222–224
Weather forecasting, 12
Wetlands, 96–105, 107–117, 174, 182–183, 200, 234
Wind-tidal flats, 97–98, 100–105, 108, 110–115

96

$29.95